INTERNATIONAL FINANCE AND DEVELOPMENT

edited by
JOSÉ ANTONIO OCAMPO
JAN KREGEL
STEPHANY GRIFFITH-JONES

Orient Longman

Zed Books
London and New York

TWN
Third World Network

Published in association with the United Nations

International Finance and Development was first published in 2007.

Published in association with the United Nations

Published in the Indian Subcontinent, South East Asia (except Malaysia and Singapore), West Asia, China and Africa by
ORIENT LONGMAN PRIVATE LIMITED
Registered office: 3-6-752 Himayatnagar, Hyderabad 500 029 (A.P.), India
Email: info@orientlongman.com *Website:* www.orientlongman.com
Other offices: Bangalore / Bhopal / Bhubaneshwar / Chennai / Ernakulam / Guwahati / Hyderabad / Jaipur / Kolkata / Lucknow / Mumbai / New Delhi / Patna

Published in the UK, Europe, USA, Canada and Australia by
ZED BOOKS LTD
7 Cynthia Street, London N1 9JF, UK, and
Room 400, 175 Fifth Avenue, New York, NY 10010, USA
www.zedbooks.co.uk
Distributed in the USA on behalf of Zed Books by
Palgrave Macmillan, a division of St Martin's Press, LLC
175 Fifth Avenue, New York, NY 10010, USA

Published in Malaysia and Singapore by
THIRD WORLD NETWORK
131 Jalan Macalister, 10400 Penang, Malaysia
www.twnside.org.sg

Published worldwide by the United Nations and distributed worldwide via the UN specialized network of agents.
United Nations Publications
2 United Nations Plaza, Room DC2-853, New York, NY 10017, USA
http:/unp.un.org *Email:* publications@un.org

United Nations' sales number: E.06.IV.7
ISBN: 978 81 250 3065 2 Pb (Orient Longman)
ISBN: 978 1 84277 861 6 Hb (Zed Books)
ISBN: 978 1 84277 862 3 Pb (Zed Books)

A catalogue record for this book is available from the British Library
US CIP data is available from the Library of Congress

Cover designed by Andrew Corbett, Cambridge, UK
Typeset at Tulika Print Communication Services, New Delhi, India
Printed in India by Orion Printers Private Limited, Hyderabad 500 004

Contents

Notes on Editors

José Antonio Ocampo is Under-Secretary General for Economic and Social Affairs at the United Nations since mid-2003.

Jan Kregel was Chief of the Policy Analysis and Development Branch of the Financing for Development Office in the Department of Economic and Social Affairs, United Nations, until August 2006.

Stephany Griffith-Jones is Professorial Fellow at the Institute of Development Studies, University of Sussex, Falmer, and was a visitor at the Department of Economic and Social Affairs, United Nations, in 2005.

Explanatory Notes

The following symbols have been used in the tables throughout the report:

..	Two dots indicate that data are not available or are not separately reported.
–	A dash indicates that the amount is nil or negligible.
-	A hyphen (-) indicates that the item is not applicable.
-	A minus sign (-) indicates deficit or decrease, except as indicated.
.	A full stop (.) is used to indicate decimals.
/	A slash (/) between years indicates a crop year or financial year, for example, 1990/91.
-	Use of a hyphen (-) between years, for example, 1990-1991, signifies the full period involved, including the beginning and end years.
	Reference to "dollars" ($) indicates United States dollars, unless otherwise stated.
	Reference to "tons" indicates metric tons, unless otherwise stated.
	Annual rates of growth or change, unless otherwise stated, refer to annual compound rates.
	In most cases, the growth rate forecasts for 2004 and 2005 are rounded to the nearest quarter of a percentage point.
	Details and percentages in tables do not necessarily add to totals, because of rounding.

The following abbreviations have been used:

ADR	American Depository Receipt
APEC	Asia-Pacific Economic Cooperation
ASEAN	Association of Southeast Asian Nations
BIS	Bank for International Settlements
CAC	collective action clause
CACM	Central American Common Market
CARICOM	Caribbean Community and Common Market
CCL	Contingent Credit Line (IMF)
CFF	Compensatory Financing Facility (CFF)
CGE	computable general equilibrium (model)
c.i.f.	cost, insurance and freight
CIS	Commonwealth of Independent States
CMI	Chiang Mai Initiative

COMESA	Common Market for Eastern and Southern Africa
COMTRADE	United Nations Commodity Trade Statistics Database
CPIA	Country Policy and Institutional Assessment (World Bank)
CPSS	Committee on Payment and Settlement Systems
DAC	Development Assistance Committee (OECD)
EAEC	East Asian Economic Caucus
EBRD	European Bank for Reconstruction and Development
ECA	Economic Commission for Africa
ECE	Economic Commission for Europe
ECLAC	Economic Commission for Latin America & the Caribbean
ECOWAS	Economic Community of West African States
EIB	European Investment Bank
ESCAP	Economic and Social Commission for Asia and the Pacific
EU	European Union
FATF	Financial Action Task Force on Money Laundering
FDI	foreign direct investment
FLAR	Latin American Reserve Fund
FSF	Financial Stability Forum
FTAA	Free Trade Area of the Americas
GAVI	Global Alliance for Vaccines and Immunization
GDDS	General Data Dissemination System (IMF)
GDP	gross domestic product
GNI	gross national income
GSP	Generalized System of Preferences
HIPC	heavily indebted poor countries
IAIS	International Association of Insurance Supervisors
IASB	International Accounting Standards Board
IBRD	International Bank for Reconstruction and Development
ICT	information and communication technologies
IDA	International Development Association
IFAC	International Federation of Accountants
IFC	International Finance Cooperation
IFF	International Finance Facility
IIF	Institute of International Finance
ILO	International Labour Organization
IMF	International Monetary Fund
IOSCO	International Organization of Securities Commissions
IRB	internal ratings-based
LAIA	Latin American Integration Association
LIBOR	London Interbank Offered Rate

M&A	mergers and acquisitions
MERCOSUR	Southern Common Market
MFN	most favoured nation
MIGA	Multilateral Investment Guarantee Agency
NAFTA	North American Free Trade Agreement
NBER	National Bureau of Economic Research (Cambridge, Massachsetts)
NDF	non-deliverable forwards
NPL	non-performing loan
NPV	net present value
ODA	official development assistance
OECD	Organization for Economic Cooperation and Development
PPP	purchasing power parity
PRGF	Poverty Reduction and Growth Facility (IMF)
PRSP	Poverty Reduction Strategy Paper (IMF and World Bank)
R&D	research and development
ROSC	Report on the Observance of Standards and Codes (IMF)
ROSCA	rotating savings and credit association
SADC	Southern African Development Community
SDA	Special Disbursement Account (IMF)
SDDS	Special Data Dissemination Standard (IMF)
SDR	Special Drawing Right
SDT	special and differential treatment
SEC	United States Securities and Exchange Commission
SITC	Standard International Trade Classification
SRF	Supplemental Reserve Facility (IMF)
TIM	Trade Integration Mechanism (IMF)
TNC	transnational corporation
UDEAC	Central African Customs and Economic Union
UNCTAD	United Nations Conference on Trade and Development
UN/DESA	Department of Economic and Social Affairs of the United Nations Secretariat
UNDP	United Nations Development Programme
UNFPA	United Nations Population Fund
UNU	United Nations University
URR	unremunerated reserve requirement
WIDER	World Institute for Development Economics Research (WIDER)
WIPO	World Intellectual Poverty Organization

ACKNOWLEDGEMENTS

This book presents an update to mid-2006 of selected chapters of the *World Economic and Social Survey* issued by the United Nations Department of Economic and Social Affairs in June 2005. It has been revised and updated by José Antonio Ocampo, Jan Kregel and Stephany Griffith-Jones who, together with Ian Kinniburgh, were responsible for the original edition of the *Survey*. The following also contributed to original version of these chapters: Tserenpuntsag Batbold, Leonides Buencamino, Juliet Capili, Jane d'Arista, Sergei Gorbunov, Cordelia Gow, Hazem Fahmy, Pingfan Hong, Valerian Monteiro, Kalu Odege, Masakatsu Ohyama, Ann Orr, Cristian Ossa, Maria Angela Parra, Daniel Platz, Benu Schneider, Julien Serre, Krishnan Sharma, Shari Spiegel, Lynn Lynn Thway.

Overview

The Monterrey Consensus adopted by the Heads of State and Government at the International Conference on Financing for Development in 2002 (United Nations, 2002b) provides the internationally agreed framework for international cooperation for development. In the 2005 United Nations World Summit Outcome (UN 2005c), UN Member States reaffirmed the Monterrey Consensus as the unifying framework for achieving the International Development Goals that have emerged from the UN Summits and Conferences on development of the 1990s and 2000s, including the Millennium Development Goals which lie at their heart.

The Consensus is built on the contemporary view that international cooperation for development should be viewed as a partnership between developed and developing countries. In the partnership, each developing country accepted primary responsibility for its own development—strengthening governance, combating corruption and putting in place the policies and investments to drive economic growth and employment, thereby maximizing domestic resources available to fund national development strategies. Developed countries, on their part, undertook that developing countries which adopted transparent, credible and properly crafted development strategies would receive the full support they need, in the form of increased development assistance, a more development-oriented trade system, wider and deeper debt relief and increased private financing. The major institutional stakeholders joined that Consensus and agreed to improve the coherence, coordination and cooperation in the formulation of their activities and in the implementation of international development policies, and in particular of the international financial system.

Although the mobilization of domestic resources for development and the use of international trade as an instrument of development are crucial parts of the holistic approach to financing for development adopted in Monterrey, an increasingly interdependent global economic system has given international finance increasing importance. This book thus concentrates on the role of international private capital flows, official financing, debt and the systemic dimensions of the international financial system in the complex process of financing development.

INTERNATIONAL PRIVATE CAPITAL FLOWS

Private capital flows can make a major contribution to development to the extent that they flow from capital-abundant, usually developed countries to capital-scarce developing countries and help to smooth spending throughout the business cycle in the recipient countries. However, and in contrast to this stylized view, capital, and particularly financial, flows have been highly volatile and reversible in recent decades, generating high costs for developing countries. In addition, such flows have largely bypassed the poorest countries. These features are by no means inevitable: national and international policies can be adopted to generate increased and more stable private financial flows that will be of benefit to a larger number of developing countries.

Recent history has been characterized by two waves of international financial flows to developing countries. In the 1970s, driven by the recycling of the external surpluses of the petroleum producing countries and the move towards deregulation in domestic and international financial markets, a rapid increase in bank lending to the developing world was followed by the debt crisis of the 1980s in Latin American and other parts of the developing world. In the 1990s another wave of financial flows to developing countries, led by portfolio and direct investments was interrupted by the Asian crisis in 1997 and the global liquidity crunch set off by the Russian default in mid-1998.

By 2003 improving economic conditions in developing countries, as well as higher global growth and the persistence of low interest rates introduced to counter the global slowdown in 2000-2001, brought a recovery of private capital flows to developing countries in 2003-2005. This may be seen as the beginning of a third cycle. However, the events in world equity and emerging markets of May-June 2006 could indicate that the expansionary phase of this new cycle may turn out to be the shortest of all the waves experienced by the developing world over the past four decades.

The recovery in international financial flows to developing countries of recent years differs also in one additional and important characteristic. Net transfers of financial resources from developing to developed countries continued to increase in 2005 for the eighth consecutive year, reaching over a half trillion US dollars.. This has in fact generated continuity between the downward financial phase of the second cycle mentioned above and the upward financing phase of the new cycle, which is in sharp contrast to previous historical experience. Initially these transfers were the result of capital outflows from the developing world, but they increasingly reflect the large foreign-exchange reserve accumulation taking place in many developing countries, particularly in Asia. This accumulation of reserves initially had a large component of "self-insurance" (a "war chest") against financial crises and involved a rational decision of individual countries in the face of the limited "collective insurance" provided by the international financial system against such crises. However, reserve accumulation in several countries in Asia now appears to exceed the need for self-insurance, raising questions about the balance of costs and benefits of additional accumulation, especially if such reserves are invested in low-yielding assets and in a currency, the United States dollar that is expected to continue to experience depreciation.

Different types of capital flows are subject to different degrees of volatility and different forms of flows have different implications for development. Foreign direct investment (FDI) has become the most important source of external finance in the last cycle, and has proved to be more stable that other financial flows.

Developing countries have historically adopted investment policies to maximize the benefits from FDI. In the current environment, the development impact of FDI can be bolstered through policies that promote linkages between foreign firms and the host economy, in particular to encourage exports with higher value-added and the transfer of skills, knowledge and technology. Backward production linkages between foreign and domestic firms can be promoted through better information flows. Incentives can also be provided for foreign firms to invest in employee training. Successful clusters attract foreign investment; their success depends on the existence of an enabling investment climate, skilled labour and infrastructure. To increase the contribution of FDI in extractive industries to the development of the host country, initiatives on transparency-related codes of conduct (for example, the Extractive Industries Transparency Initiative) should be supported and the feasibility of their application to other sectors examined.

Trade financing is essential to facilitating international trade and is particularly important for poorer countries, given their limited access to other forms of financial flows. In this regard, the role of export credit agencies and multilateral development banks could be enhanced if they acted in a more counter-cyclical manner by providing guarantees and trade credit loans to countries after crises in order to avert a trade credit "squeeze" and to facilitate export-led recoveries.

Bank lending and portfolio flows tend to be volatile and pro-cyclical. In addition, international banks have retrenched cross-border lending since 1997 and have shifted towards lending through their domestic subsidiaries. Portfolio debt flows, though volatile, can be a valuable source of external financing to both the public sector and large private firms in the developing world.

There has been a global explosion in the development of financial derivatives since 1990. Derivatives can be very efficient in pricing and adequately distributing risks among market agents, but they can also facilitate speculation and increase macroeconomic volatility. Even in developed countries, regulators find it difficult to monitor and regulate derivatives and it is even more difficult to do so in offshore markets. The introduction of well-designed regulations might nonetheless minimize risk.

To counter boom-bust cycles in international capital flows, market institutions and instruments can be designed to encourage more stable flows. Introducing explicit counter-cyclical elements in the risk evaluations of the multilateral development banks and export credit agencies for guarantees for lending to developing countries would be valuable. This could help catalyse long-term private credit, especially for infrastructure, during periods of declining capital flows. Multilateral development banks could also play a bigger role in guaranteeing developing-country bonds in periods of capital drought.

Commodity-linked bonds and gross domestic product (GDP)-linked bonds can be designed to reduce the likelihood of debt crises and defaults, by smoothing debt-service payments through the business cycle. Industrialized countries should establish the example of issuing such bonds in order to help establish precedents for their issuance by developing countries. Similarly, bonds issued in the borrower's local currency reduce currency mismatches. The creation and marketing of investment funds holding a diversified portfolio of such emerging market local currency debt could provide, because of diversification, risk-adjusted rates of return that are attractive to foreign investors.

Capital-account regulations can provide room for counter-cyclical macroeconomic policies and improve external debt profiles of developing countries. When these regulations are well implemented, such benefits outweigh any costs. Both price-based and quantity-based regulations can be useful. Permanent regulatory regimes that are tightened or loosened during the cycle are superior to ad hoc interventions. Capital-account regulations facilitate sensible counter-cyclical macroeconomic policies, but they are not a substitute for them.

The right regulatory regime for banks is essential for financial stability. It is widely recognized today that financial liberalization should be accompanied by strong prudential regulation and supervision of domestic financial systems. However, the focus on microeconomic regulations aimed at avoiding excessive risk taking and encouraging risk diversification has not fully taken into account the vulnerability of financial agents to boom-bust cycles, macroeconomic policy variables and the interdependence of financial institutions when faced with similar shocks. Indeed, in the face of common shocks, the market-based risk instruments commonly used to evaluate microeconomic risks may actually make financial systems more, rather than less, volatile. It is therefore increasingly important that *macroprudential* elements be incorporated into financial regulation, both in developed and in developing countries. More specifically, this implies analyzing more explicitly the interdependence of market agents, and introducing counter-cyclical elements into financial regulation, particularly forward-looking provisions against future loan losses, to compensate for the tendency of banks to be pro-cyclical in their lending.

The New Basel Capital Accord (Basel II) has positive features, but there is a risk that it will increase the pro-cyclicality of bank lending, both domestically and internationally. Furthermore, it is likely to reduce international lending to developing countries and increase the cost of borrowing by developing countries. It would measure risk more precisely, and would therefore be technically correct, if the benefits of the diversification of lending by international banks to developing countries were explicitly incorporated into the Accord; this would also be economically desirable, as it would avoid an excessive reduction of bank lending to developing countries and reduce its pro-cyclicality.

Low-income countries are at a disadvantage in attracting capital flows and so special national and international efforts are needed to increase private flows to these countries. Improved information flows for potential investors are essential in this regard. Programmes are also required to support the development of market instruments to mitigate risks (for example, markets in exchange-rate futures) and the broader use by low-income countries of bilateral and multilateral instruments to deal with risk mitigation for private investments (insurance and guarantee schemes). Donors should also consider providing targeted funding with additional resources to multilateral agencies (such as the Multilateral Investment Guarantee Agency, MIGA, and the political risk insurance facilities being opened up in regional banks) and bilateral agencies to cover political and other non-commercial risk at a lower cost in these countries. New facilities could also be set up in the form of separate funds owned by international financial institutions to address both the entry cost and the post-entry risk barriers for investors.

Official Development Financing

Official assistance continues to play a crucial role in supplementing the resources of developing countries, particularly the poorest among them. However, from a peak of over 0.5 per cent of developed-country gross national income (GNI) in the 1960s, official development assistance (ODA) had declined until it reached a historic low of 0.21 per cent as Heads of State and Government were approving the United Nations Millennium Declaration. To counter this tendency, the Monterrey Consensus sought to reaffirm the 0.7 per cent target. This motivated many developed countries to announce increased ODA contributions and many pledged to meet fixed target dates for reaching the 0.7 per cent goal. As a result, the decline in the share of ODA in developed-country GNI was reversed and it rose to 0.33 per cent in 2005. Despite this positive trend, the current and projected levels of ODA for the period from 2006 to 2010 still fall far short of the various estimates of the support deemed necessary for the developing countries to attain the Millennium Development Goals by 2015. Furthermore, when corrected for price and exchange-rate changes, the recent reversal of the decline in aid flows has barely brought assistance back to its real levels in 1990.

In order to secure the increased ODA required, the Secretary-General of the United Nations has urged all developed countries to establish fixed timetables for reaching the 0.7 per cent target by 2015 at the latest, with an intermediate target of roughly doubling aid to 0.5 per cent of the GNI of the developed countries in 2009. Currently only Denmark, Luxembourg, the Netherlands, Norway and Sweden meet or exceed the 0.7 per cent target. In 2005, the 15 pre-enlargement member States of the European Union (EU) set a target date of 2015 for reaching the 0.7 per cent goal, with an intermediate target of 0.51 per cent of GNI by 2010. Those countries that joined EU after 2002 have agreed to strive to achieve a ratio of 0.17 per cent of their GNI by 2010 and 0.33 per cent by 2015.

Not only has ODA to increase substantially in order for the developing countries to achieve the Millennium Development Goals, it is also essential that more ODA be directed to the poorest developing countries. With the adoption of the Programme of Action for the Least Developed Countries for the 1990s, developed countries agreed that, within their 0.7 per cent overall ODA target, they would provide at least 0.15-0.20 per cent of their GNI to assist these countries. Nevertheless, aggregate ODA flows to the least developed countries have declined to about half that ratio during the 1990s. There has also been a reversal in this trend since Monterrey: ODA to the least developed countries has increased sharply and nine developed countries

(Belgium, Denmark, France, Ireland, Luxembourg, Netherlands, Norway, Portugal, and Sweden) met the target in 2004.

While the decline in total ODA has been reversed, its composition appears to make its contribution to meeting the Millennium Development Goals less efficient. Over the 1990s, the shares of debt relief, emergency aid and technical assistance in total aid flows have increased substantially. While these flows have important objectives, emergency aid is not designed to assist long-term development and debt relief does not generally provide additional resources to debtor countries. Technical cooperation, in turn, can provide a variety of benefits for development, but its direct financial impact is small. Consequently, despite the recent recovery in donor contributions, ODA has been a declining source of budgetary resources for the developing countries to support the achievement of the Millennium Development Goals.

Donors have been increasingly concerned with the effectiveness of their aid in meeting the international development objectives. The Rome High-level Forum on Harmonization focusing on joint progress towards enhanced aid effectiveness held in 2003 elaborated a plan of action to harmonize aid policies, procedures and practices of donors with those of their developing-country partners. Participants at the second High-level Forum held in 2005 committed to a practical blueprint through which to provide aid in more streamlined ways and to improve accountability by monitoring the blueprint's implementation. They defined five major principles of aid effectiveness: (a) ownership of development strategies by partner countries; (b) alignment of donor support to those strategies; (c) harmonization of donor actions; (d) managing for results; and (e) mutual accountability of donors and partners. Full implementation of these principles, based on a clear set of targets (most of which have already been agreed), is essential to increasing the quality of aid flows.

An important implication of the evolving new approach to aid, both in terms of its contribution to the Millennium Development Goals, as well as the full application of the principles of ownership and alignment, is that ODA should be increasingly channeled through the budgets of recipient countries. This means, in turn, that the proportion of aid so channeled should become a specific target of international assistance.

In addition to official government financing, developing countries receive loans from the World Bank and regional and subregional development banks. The multilateral development banks will continue to play a fundamental role in several areas. First, they need to channel funds to low-income countries, where their role is central. With regard to middle-income countries, they will continue to play a particularly important role, not only as lenders under better financial conditions than those offered by the private markets, but as a counter-cyclical balance to fluctuations in private capital markets, giving developing countries access to long-term borrowing during times of crisis. As crises hurt the poor, the counter-cyclical character of multilateral development banks financing is consistent with their role in poverty reduction.

The multilateral development banks also perform a vast array of financial tasks, encompassing, inter alia, the traditional "value added" of multilateral financing, lending-related technical assistance; knowledge generation and brokering; and the provision of global and regional public goods, including, in the case of most regional and subregional development banks, support to regional integration processes. In addition, new functions of multilateral development banks have grown in recent years, for example, the provision of guarantees issued for the support to public-private partnerships in infrastructure. They could also be used more actively to guarantee bond issues by countries that have experienced financial crises, as well as initial bond issues by developing (especially poor) countries entering private capital markets. They could also play a more prominent role in trade financing during crises, and in the promotion of local currency bond markets in developing countries, and as "market makers" for commodity- and GDP-linked bonds. Recent discussions have also emphasized the need for multilateral development banks to embrace intellectual diversity and to avoid the hegemony of a single view of economic development. There have also been calls to reduce the financial and non-financial costs of doing business with the multilateral development banks by clarifying policies, simplifying procedures, streamlining internal processes and reducing conditionality in lending operations.

The revealed success of several regional and subregional development banks clearly indicates that this is a promising area of cooperation among developing countries. These are successful financial institutions that have earned good credit ratings without capital from industrialized countries. Furthermore, a different approach to conditionality makes them attractive to borrowing countries. This should become a priority for South-South cooperation.

A number of countries have followed up on the call in the Monterrey Consensus to investigate alternative mechanisms to supplement official assistance, as attested by, for example, the group of independent experts formed at the request of the President of France; the initiative to combat hunger and poverty launched in January 2004 by the presidents of Brazil, Chile and France, with the support of the Secretary-General, and later endorsed also by the Governments of Spain, Germany and Algeria; and the meeting of more than 100 world leaders convened by the President of

Brazil and held at the United Nations in September 2004. The conclusions of a special study led by the United Nations University/World Institute for Development Economics Research had also been presented to the General Assembly in September 2004. In April 2005, the Development Committee and the International Monetary and Financial Committee (IMFC) reviewed proposals to complement increased aid flows with innovative mechanisms.

An International Finance Facility (IFF) was initially proposed by the United Kingdom of Great Britain and Northern Ireland in 2003 and the Secretary General has called upon the international community to launch it in 2005. Since the Facility builds on commitments to reach the 0.7 per cent ODA target no later than 2015, it constitutes a complement to traditional commitments. Its particular function is to enable the front-loading of aid flows through issues of bonds guaranteed by participating Governments, allowing aid commitments to be spent before they are budgeted.

A pilot finance facility (IFFIm) has been launched that will provide resources to support the work of Global Alliance for Vaccines and Immunization (GAVI Fund, formerly Vaccine Fund). Among the most advanced projects is a "solidarity contribution" on air travel tickets to be introduced by establishing or raising existing airport taxes and charges. Three countries (Chile, France, and the United Kingdom) have made rapid progress toward implementing an air ticket contribution in 2006.

Among other additional sources of innovative financing for development mechanisms studied in the various reports were: several nationally applied but internationally coordinated taxes (environmental, on international financial transactions, on aviation fuel or ticket prices, and on arms sales); allocation of special drawing rights (SDRs) for development purposes; mobilizing emigrant remittances for development; and private donations. Most of the technical reports concluded that financial transactions taxes and environmental taxes might provide the largest amounts of additional resources in the long term. However, realizing the potential of such sources would normally require the full agreement of, and compliance by, most countries and this might not be easy—or possible—to achieve. Therefore, it might be necessary to concentrate first on the sources that can be mobilized on a regional or other non-universal basis, while consensus is developed on the others. All reports stressed that the proposals should be seen as strictly additional and complementary to existing ODA commitments and targets.

External Debt

External finance is meant to supplement and support developing counties' domestic resource mobilization. However, since the nineteenth century, developing countries have repeatedly experienced periodic increases in debt-service burdens that led to slower growth or recession, resulting, in many cases, in rescheduling and renegotiations. As debt service currently absorbs a large proportion of external official aid and private lending, the Monterrey Consensus recognized that the elimination of excessive debt burdens would make available a major source of additional finance for development. Debt reduction may thus support the introduction of policies that promote mobilization of domestic resources as well as free domestic resources from debt service so that they can be used to achieve the Millennium Development Goals. But alleviating debt overhang is only part of the solution for, as emphasized in the Consensus, debt must be maintained at sustainable levels if it is going to be effective in complementing domestic mobilization of resources for development.

While progress has been made in reducing the impediment of unsustainable debt burdens for developing countries, much more needs to be done. In contrast to the debt burdens of developing countries in general, those of the poorest developing countries continued to increase through the first half of the 1990s. To respond to this problem, the Heavily Indebted Poor Countries (HIPC) Initiative was launched in 1996, enhanced in 1999 and recently extended by two years to allow those countries that are eligible to fulfill the criteria so as to actually benefit from debt relief under the Initiative. To date, 29 HIPCs have received debt relief, with 19 countries having reached completion point and 10 countries at decision point. Due to expire at the end of 2004, the Initiative has been extended for two years. Staffs of IDA and the IMF have identified 11 additional countries that meet the income and indebtedness criteria at end-2004, which could be considered for debt relief under the Initiative before it is terminated (Central African Republic, Comoros, Côte d'Ivoire, Eritrea, Haiti, Kyrgyz Republic, Liberia, Nepal, Somalia, Sudan, and Togo). Although Bhutan, Lao PDR, and Sri Lanka meet the eligibility criteria, they have indicated that they do not wish to be considered.

Despite its success in increasing social spending for some countries, the commitments on social spending by some countries have exceeded the savings on debt service, leading to accumulation of additional indebtedness. It is now realized that several of the assumptions on which HIPC programmes had been based were over-optimistic, in terms of the evolution of GDP, the level of exports and the evolution of commodity prices, among other variables.

Also, most of the debt reduction that took place in the HIPC countries took the form of writing off bilateral debts already in arrears, thus freeing up a smaller amount of real resources for poverty reduction spending than had been originally foreseen.

Due to the problems identified in the HIPC Initiative in terms of generating sustainable debt burdens for the poor countries, in September the shareholders of the IMF and the World Bank Group agreed on the Multilateral Debt Relief Initiative (MDRI) to cancel an estimated $55 billion in debt owed by HIPC completion point countries to IMF, IDA and the African Development Fund (AfDF). Similar relief should be available to existing HIPC countries upon reaching completion point. The relief was intended to be in addition to official assistance available to other low-income countries and was to preserve the lending capacity of the multilateral financial institutions. For relief on IDA and AfDF loans, the G-8 pledged to cover the full cost to offset dollar for dollar the foregone principal and interest repayments of the debt cancelled for the duration of the cancelled loans. Compensation from donors for costs of providing this relief will take place via an additional contribution to the current replenishment. The IMF, on the other hand, will meet the costs of debt relief from its own resources.

For many heavily indebted non-HIPC and middle-income countries, debt sustainability will require significantly more debt reduction than has yet been proposed in these initiatives. Although these countries have not yet been included in the discussion on additional debt relief, new mechanisms have been proposed, such as the Paris Club "Evian approach", that seek to give more latitude in dealing with debt overhang in these countries. This new approach has already been tried in a number of countries and has been successfully applied to the relief of Iraq's debt.

Even after agreement on fuller debt relief, long-term sustainability of debt depends very much on the growth and export prospects of debtor countries. Debt sustainability should be part of the overall development strategy of a country, which treats debt, trade and finance in a coherent framework. Development partners could also contribute to finding durable solutions to developing countries' debt problems if debtor countries were adequately supported in enhancing their export capacity. It is also important to strengthen developing countries' capacity on debt management, which should be an integral part of the institutional and policy framework, and should be consistent with the broad macroeconomic and sectoral policies of a country.

Although the evidence is persuasive that the recent debt initiatives have unlocked resources that are critical for the achievement of the Millennium

Development Goals in the poorest countries, they still fall far short of what is needed. To move forward, the 2005 report of the United Nations Secretary-General entitled "In Larger Freedom: towards development, security and human rights for all" proposed that debt sustainability be redefined as the level of debt that allows a country to achieve the Millennium Development Goals and reach 2015 without an increase in its debt ratios. This implies placing development objectives at the centre of debt sustainability; in particular, the capacity to repay debt must take into account national priorities of human development and poverty reduction, as well as determine a level of debt that does not hinder future growth. It is expected that for most HIPC countries, this will require exclusively grant-based finance and 100 per cent debt cancellation.

Finally, it is important to recognize the contribution that efficient and equitable burden-sharing between debtors and creditors can bring to alleviating unsustainable debt burdens. Given the large number of financial crises in the 1990s, a debate began on the creation of a mechanism to provide for orderly international debt resolution based on existing private sector bankruptcy legislation applied at the national level. It is important that the explorations of debt workout mechanisms, including voluntary codes as well as international mediation or arbitration mechanisms, continue with the full support of all stakeholders. With only two exceptions, sovereign bonds issued under New York law since May 2003 included collective action clauses (CACs) and are now considered the market standard for emerging market sovereign bonds. The outstanding stock of sovereign bonds with CACs is now nearly 60 per cent. While there has not been an observed increase in the cost of the bonds issued with CACs their ability to facilitate debt restructuring remains untested.

SYSTEMIC ISSUES

The systemic agenda addressed by the Monterrey Consensus covers two broad groups of issues. The first relates to the structural features of the international monetary and financial system, and the possible vulnerabilities that they generate for the world economy or for developing countries in particular. The second relates to the institutional design of the current international financial system. It is urgent that the international community address these issues, and take measures to help overcome the challenges they present.

The importance of the first of these issues has been highlighted by growing concerns about global macroeconomic imbalances. Currently the global economy is characterized by large and increasing imbalances across regions. These imbalances have become larger and lasted longer than in the 1980s. The risks associated with various ways in which the imbalances might be adjusted will have direct implications for world economic growth. Problems would be accentuated if sharp adjustment in exchange rates was accompanied by falls in the prices of bonds and stocks. There is growing agreement that the measures that need to be taken include restraining of aggregate demand in deficit countries and more expansionary policies in the surplus countries to stimulate their aggregate demand. However, progress in their implementation is very limited, at a time when urgent and decisive action is required.

Even if the imbalances were sustainable, or could be adjusted in a smooth manner, their large magnitude and skewed distribution suggest a less than efficient and less than equitable allocation of global resources between developed and developing countries. This also counters basic economic logic which suggests that, in the longer term, the industrialized countries should be running current-account surpluses and lending to, and investing in, the developing world, not the reverse.

There is a clear need for greater international cooperation and coordination to ensure a smooth global rebalancing that does not lead to a slowdown of global growth, nor to problems in financial markets. IMF should play a far more central role in ensuring consistency and coherence of macroeconomic policies of major economies. Indeed, IMF is the only international forum where developing countries can express their views on the macroeconomic imbalances of the industrialized economies. The recent decision by IMF to engage in multilateral surveillance should include increased attention to the system as a whole; this implies a more central role for IMF in the management of the world economy.

The global financial system has undergone profound changes over the past several decades. Though they have important positive effects, these changes may pose new and often yet unknown potential increases in systemic risk. Factors such as increased concentration in the financial industry, which has led to the formation of a small number of large financial conglomerates, and expansion of loosely regulated or unregulated activities (such as derivatives) and institutions (such as hedge funds) have transformed and possibly increased risk. Opaqueness of risk transfer is also problematic. Consequently, there are fears that increased opportunities for risk transfer may imply that risk ends up in parts of the financial system where supervision and disclosure are weakest.

Many developing countries have made significant domestic progress in reducing their vulnerability to crisis, including improvements in financial regulation, use of more flexible exchange rates and higher levels of reserves. However, they continue to be vulnerable to external shocks, caused by changes in commodity prices, rises in developed countries' interest rates, and capital flow volatility, as well as natural disasters.

There is therefore a need to further enhance IMF facilities to help ensure that external shocks do not impose excessive costs on developing-country and global growth, and that gives them room to adopt counter-cyclical macroeconomic policies. For both middle-income and low-income countries, this includes the need for facilities that allow countries to effectively weather temporary terms-of-trade shocks. To deal with capital account volatility and contagion, it also includes a contingency financing that would allow countries with good fundamentals to have access to fairly automatic access to IMF support.

In response, the IMF has created an Exogenous Shocks Facility (ESF) to provide policy support and financial assistance to low-income countries facing exogenous shocks. It is available to countries eligible for the Poverty Reduction and Growth Facility but that do not have a program in place. Financing terms are equivalent to a PRGF arrangement and more concessional than under other IMF emergency lending facilities. At the April 2006 meeting of the IMFC, support was also given to further examination of a proposal to create a new instrument to provide high access contingent financing for countries that have strong macroeconomic policies, sustainable debt, and transparent reporting but remain vulnerable to shocks.

In the 1990s, IMF conditionality expanded to include structural reforms, which resulted in increases in the number of performance criteria. The adoption by the IMF Executive Board of guidelines for streamlining conditionality was therefore a welcome development; however, progress in their implementation has been slow and uneven. Furthermore, IMF has agreed that domestic ownership of macroeconomic policies is the main obstacle to effective programme implementation. In broader terms, the conditionality attached to all forms of international financial cooperation should be streamlined and made consistent with the principle of ownership of macroeconomic and development policies by recipient countries. Ownership would also be promoted by an effective discussion of the virtues of alternative policies.

The more active use of SDRs would also improve the functioning of the international monetary system. Recent proposals in this regard follow two different models. The first calls for SDRs to be issued temporarily during episodes of financial stress, and destroyed once financial conditions normalize. This would develop a counter-cyclical element in world liquidity management, helping to finance additional IMF programmes during crises, without generating permanent increases in global liquidity. The second would use permanent allocations to generate a more even distribution of seigniorage powers at the global level. Allocations to industrialized countries could be used to finance international development cooperation. The additional global liquidity created would, in any case, be small. For example, the most recent allocation of SDRs approved in 1997, but not yet ratified, of SDR 21 billion, represents less than 0.5 per cent of the money supply (M2) of the United States and an even smaller proportion of the world's total money supply.

A valuable complement to the role that IMF plays at the global level can be provided by regional reserve funds, as evidenced by the recent decision of the IMFC to seek ways to support their creation. Such funds can offer a first line of defence, particularly as large currency crises have been regional in nature, and provide a framework for macroeconomic policy dialogue and coordination. Positive experiences in this regard include the Latin American Reserve Fund, active for some time in the Andean region, and the more recent Chiang Mai Initiative of the Association of Southeast Asian Nations (ASEAN), China, Japan and the Republic of Korea. Looking into the future, an organizational structure might be conceived where a dense network of complementary multilateral and regional institutions could be established in the international monetary field, to provide complementary financing, as well as possible macroeconomic surveillance. This system would be akin to that of the multilateral development banks or, in the monetary area, to the European Central Bank and the federal structure of the United States Federal Reserve System.

Democracy is becoming an increasingly important aim of nations and of the international community. Developing countries have significantly increased their share in the world economy. As a consequence, a clear mandate was given in the Monterrey Consensus to improve the voice of developing countries in international economic decision-making and norm-setting institutions. This would not just increase these institutions' legitimacy, but also make them more effective. Unfortunately, progress on increasing voice and participation of developing countries has been slow. Discussions on ways to improve voice and participation of developing countries in the Bretton Woods institutions have already started, and it is important that the political will be present to take and implement decisions in this regard. However, the Consensus goes beyond the Bretton Woods institutions and highlights the need to extend the discussion of voice and participation to other policymaking and standard-setting bodies, including informal and ad hoc groups. In several of these institutions, no formal participation of developing countries exists today. It is therefore time to initiate discussions regarding these institutions.

Chapter I
International Private Capital Flows

Standard economic theory argues that efficient international financial markets should allocate capital to those areas in which it can produce the highest returns. As a result, private international capital flows can maximize global growth when they flow from capital-abundant industrialized countries to capital-scarce developing countries. They can also improve growth performance by smoothing spending throughout the business cycle in capital-recipient countries.

However, reality tends to contradict both aspects of this standard view. Since 1997 developing countries have made increasingly large transfers of resources to developed countries. In addition, private capital flows to developing countries have been concentrated in a small group of large middle-income countries, generally bypassing low-income and small countries. Further, private capital flows to developing countries have been highly volatile and reversible. Rather than smoothing domestic expenditure, private capital flows seem to have contributed to making it more volatile. In many cases they have produced costly currency and financial crises that have reversed development gains.

These features of international capital flows are by no means inevitable. An appropriate domestic and international environment can improve the capacity of developing countries to benefit from private capital flows. The present chapter analyses both characteristics of private capital flows to developing countries and the policy options that would improve their development impact. It looks first at the main features of those flows, followed by a deeper analysis of different categories of private flows (foreign direct investment (FDI), and financial flows, including bank credit and portfolio flows) and of the impact of derivatives. It then considers policy options to counter the observed pro-cyclicality of private flows, the expected effects of the new framework for banking regulation (Basel II) on developing countries, and measures to encourage private flows to poorer and smaller developing economies.

MAIN FEATURES OF PRIVATE FLOWS TO DEVELOPING COUNTRIES

The volatility and reversibility of capital flows to emerging market economies and the marginalization of many of the poorer and smaller developing economies with respect to financial markets are rooted in the combination of financial market failures and basic asymmetries in the world economy (Ocampo, 2003b).

Instability appears to be inherent in the functioning of financial markets (Keynes, 1936; Minsky, 1982). Indeed, boom-bust patterns in financial markets have occurred for centuries (Kindleberger, 1978). The basic reason for the existence of these patterns is that finance deals with future outcomes that cannot be forecast with certainty; therefore, opinions and expectations about the future rather than factual information dominate financial market decisions. This is compounded by asymmetries of information that characterize financial markets (Stiglitz, 2001). Owing to the non-existence or large asymmetries in the dissemination of information, financial agents rely to a large extent on the actions of other market agents, leading to interdependence in their behaviour manifested in contagion and herding. At the macroeconomic level, the contagion of opinions and expectations about future macroeconomic conditions tends to generate alternating phases of euphoria and panic. At a microeconomic level, it can result in either permanent or cyclical rationing of lending to market agents that are perceived by the market as risky borrowers.

Herding and volatility are accentuated by some features of the functioning of markets. The increasing use of similar market-sensitive risk management statistical techniques (Persaud, 2000) and the dominance of investment managers aiming for very short-term profits, and evaluated and paid at very short term intervals (Griffith-Jones, 1998; Williamson, 2003), seem to have increased the frequency and depth of boom-bust cycles. For example, the downgrade of a sovereign borrower by a credit rating agency, or other unexpected information, may lead investors to sell the country's bonds as well as bonds of other borrowers considered to have a highly correlated behaviour. The decline in bond prices may be reinforced by other factors, such as margin calls associated with derivative contracts linked to bond prices or other asset prices. This will create demands for bank lending to liquidate positions, just as banks may be cutting back lending due to the increased uncertainty over asset values. Through these and other mechanisms, contagion spreads both across countries and across different flows.

Different types of capital flows are subject, however, to different volatility patterns. In particular, the higher volatility of short-term capital (Rodrik and

Velasco, 1999), compared to other forms of capital flows such as FDI indicates that reliance on such financing is more risky. The instability of different types of capital flows to developing countries will be explored in detail in the following sections of this chapter.

The basic asymmetries that characterize global financial markets are largely (though not exclusively) due to differences between industrialized and developing countries (Ocampo and Martin, 2003). Such asymmetries are caused by three basic differences: (a) the incapacity of most developing countries to issue liabilities denominated in their own currencies, a phenomenon that has come to be referred to as "original sin" (Eichengreen, Hausman and Panizza, 2003; Hausman and Panizza, 2003, Eichengreen and Hausman, 2005)[1] (b) differences in the degrees of domestic financial and capital market development, which lead to an undersupply of long-term financial instruments in developing countries; and (c) the small size of developing countries' domestic financial markets vis-à-vis the magnitude of the speculative pressures they may face (Mead and Schwenninger, 2000).

Taking the first two phenomena together, they imply that domestic financial markets in the developing world are significantly more "incomplete" than those in the industrialized world and therefore that some financial intermediation must necessarily be conducted through international markets. As a result, developing countries are plagued by variable combinations of currency and maturity mismatches in the balance sheets of economic agents. Naturally, such risks tend to become less important as financial development deepens.

Owing to these asymmetries, boom-bust cycles of capital flows have been particularly damaging for developing countries, where they both directly increase macroeconomic instability and reduce the room for manoeuvre to adopt counter-cyclical macroeconomic policies, and indeed generate strong biases towards adopting pro-cyclical macroeconomic policies (Kaminsky and others, 2004; Stiglitz and others, 2006). Furthermore, there is now overwhelming evidence that pro-cyclical financial markets and pro-cyclical macroeconomic policies do not encourage growth and, on the contrary, have increased growth volatility in those developing countries that have integrated to a larger extent into international financial markets (Prasad and others, 2003).

The costs of financial volatility in terms of reduced economic growth are high, as high volatility can generate cumulative effects on capital accumulation (Easterly, 2001). Indeed, major reversals of private flows have led to many costly financial crises that have reduced output and consumption well below what they would have been if those crises had not occurred. Eichengreen (2004b) estimated that income of developing countries has been 25 per cent lower during the last quarter-century than it would have been in the absence of such crises; the average annual cost of the crises being just over $100 billion. Griffith-Jones and Gottschalk (2006) have estimated a somewhat higher annual average cost of crises of $150 billion in terms of lost gross domestic product (GDP) in the period 1995-2002.

Capital flow reversals involve very intense short-term cyclical movements of spreads and the interruption or rationing of financing. These phenomena were observed during the 1997-1998 Asian crisis and were even more pronounced during the 1998 Russian crisis. However and perhaps more importantly, they also involve *medium-term* fluctuations, as the experience of the past three decades indicates. During those decades, the developing world experienced two such medium-term cycles that left strong imprints on the growth rates of many countries: a boom of external financing (mostly in the form of syndicated bank loans) in the 1970s, followed by a debt crisis in a large part of the developing world in the 1980s, and a new boom in the early 1990s (now mostly portfolio flows), followed by a sharp reduction in net flows since the Tequila and then the Asian and Russian crises. The withdrawal of funds since the Asian crisis had initially reflected investors' perception of increasing risk of investing in developing countries, as a result of financial turmoil and crises. This was further reinforced by the collapse of the technology and telecommunications investment boom in 2000 and the subsequent global economic slowdown.

A rapid recovery in the US produced by low interest rates and expansionary fiscal policy brought higher global growth and improved economic conditions in developing countries. The accompanying expansion in global liquidity produced a recovery of private capital flows to developing countries since 2003 that may be seen as the beginning of a new lending cycle (table I.1). The fact that recovery in private flows took place in the presence of the continued increase in net resource transfers from developing to developed countries is a characteristic that distinguishes the current cycle from previous experience.

The short periods of increased yield spreads on emerging market bonds in 2004, 2005 and in May 2006, in response to uncertainty concerning the pace of the return of interest rates to normal levels (particularly the United States of America and Japan), underscored the possible vulnerability of financial flows to increasing interest rates and the possible reversal of the new upward phase of this financing cycle. If the current moderation in flows were to become more pronounced, this cycle would be shorter than the previous two, calling into question even its denomination as a "medium-term cycle".

More importantly, net transfers of financial resources[2] from developing countries have not recovered and, on the contrary, continued to deteriorate in

2005 for the eighth year in a row, reaching an estimated $527 billion (see table I.2). Periods of negative net transfers of financial resources from developing countries (especially from Latin America) have been frequent throughout history; indeed, Kregel (2004) provides evidence that suggests that negative net transfers have been the rule rather than the exception in this region.

From 1999 to 2002, these large, increasing net transfers of financial resources were explained by the combination of relatively low net private financial flows and accumulation of very large foreign-exchange reserves. However, net transfers continued to increase despite the sharp recovery in private flows in 2003 and 2004. Data for 2005 suggest a moderation in this increasing trend in private flows.

The most significant aspect of this large increase in net outflows from developing countries in recent years has been the growth in official reserves, particularly in Asia (table I.1). The initial justification for the accumulation of reserves was the need to provide "self-insurance" against financial instability (or, as it is often said , to provide "bullet-proofing" or a "war chest" against financial crises), a rational decision of individual countries in the face of the limited "collective insurance" provided by the international financial system (see chap. IV). However, reserve accumulation in Asia has now clearly exceeded the need in several countries for self-insurance, raising increasing questions about the balance of costs and benefits of additional accumulation. Some estimates suggest that interest rates in countries such as China, Malaysia and Thailand were sufficiently low that costs were negligible or even provided net earnings, while for countries such as India and Korea costs could be as high as a half per cent of GDP (Genberg, McCauley, Park and Persaud, 2005). The recent increases in US interest rates will further reduce the costs of excess reserves. However, this would be reversed by any depreciation of the United States dollar, but most Asian countries have resisted large exchange rate adjustments.

Divergence in regional trends in private financial flows has also resulted in changes in regional distribution of these flows since the 1990s. The most striking aspect of such developments is the significant increase in the concentration of flows to Eastern and Southern Asia, in particular, to China, at the expense of Latin America. Private financial flows to Eastern and Southern Asia recovered at the end of the 1990s and peaked in 2004. In contrast, after a period of financial turmoil and crises private financial flows to Latin America declined sharply in 1999 and have remained far below their 1997 peak, although 2005 saw a modest recovery (see table I.1).

As private flows start to recover, an important question for policymakers in developing countries is not only whether they will be sufficient to finance

Table I.1.
NET FINANCIAL FLOWS TO DEVELOPING ECONOMIES AND ECONOMIES IN TRANSITION, 1995-2005

	1995	1996	1997	1998	1999	2000	2001	2002	2003	2004	2005
Developing countries											
Net private capital flows	135.0	202.7	172.6	41.0	63.8	71.7	43.4	41.5	102.4	171.6	165.2
Net direct investment	82.4	100.6	130.8	134.7	150.3	141.1	153.8	119.6	136.7	138.5	174.3
Net portfolio investment[a]	31.0	81.7	40.3	29.6	71.4	25.4	-74.4	-81.4	-6.8	9.5	22.4
Other net investment[b]	21.6	20.4	1.4	-123.4	-157.9	-94.7	-36.0	3.2	-27.5	23.5	-31.5
Net official flows	24.4	-14.1	10.9	48.4	29.5	-38.5	9.1	21.3	-51.5	-72.9	-120.3
Total net flows	159.4	188.5	183.5	89.4	93.3	33.2	52.6	62.7	50.9	98.7	45.0
Change in reserves	-82.5	-96.7	-96.5	-33.1	-88.9	-101.7	-108.0	-164.3	-311.5	-445.9	-481.9
Africa											
Net private capital flows	5.3	0.3	10.1	8.1	7.6	1.7	12.0	8.4	6.0	12.2	30.5
Net direct investment	2.2	3.9	8.0	6.9	8.9	10.4	25.1	16.2	18.0	18.9	26.5
Net portfolio investment[a]	3.5	3.5	8.1	3.8	8.9	-2.0	-8.8	-0.8	-0.9	4.5	3.6
Other net investment[b]	-0.5	-7.1	-6.1	-2.6	-10.2	-6.8	-4.3	-7.1	-11.0	-11.2	0.5
Net official flows	4.3	-0.4	-3.4	8.7	7.0	2.7	-4.0	3.7	3.1	1.1	-7.4
Total net flows	9.5	-0.1	6.6	16.8	14.6	4.3	8.0	12.0	9.1	13.3	23.1
Change in reserves	-5.1	-8.8	-12.2	2.5	-0.9	-16.2	-10.3	-5.6	-15.1	-39.0	-60.3
Eastern and Southern Asia											
Net private capital flows	98.6	115.9	48.4	-54.3	-0.4	4.3	21.1	23.9	68.2	126.3	55.3
Net direct investment	51.5	53.6	57.3	57.1	71.4	59.7	53.9	51.9	70.3	61.7	73.7
Net portfolio investment[a]	22.9	32.0	6.8	8.8	56.9	20.2	-51.2	-58.8	4.4	3.8	-31.1
Other net investment[b]	24.2	30.3	-15.8	-120.2	-128.8	-75.7	18.4	30.8	-6.5	60.7	12.6
Net official flows	-4.6	-15.9	14.1	19.7	1.9	-11.7	-11.7	4.6	-17.5	2.1	5.5
Total net flows	94.0	100.0	62.5	-34.6	1.5	-7.4	9.4	28.5	50.7	128.3	60.8
Change in reserves	-45.1	-49.5	-31.6	-51.6	-90.1	-60.3	-94.6	-152.3	-230.2	-348.4	-296.8

Table I.1 (cont'd)

	1995	1996	1997	1998	1999	2000	2001	2002	2003	2004	2005
West Asia											
Net private capital flows	10.0	12.6	13.4	16.1	11.9	15.8	-12.9	11.3	12.7	27.1	54.3
Net direct investment	4.0	3.6	7.8	9.2	4.1	1.3	8.1	6.4	13.3	9.8	23.0
Net portfolio investment[a]	-0.3	0.7	-5.8	-8.6	4.3	4.5	-6.9	-6.9	-1.9	15.1	22.3
Other net investment[b]	6.3	8.4	11.3	15.4	3.5	10.0	-14.1	11.7	1.3	2.2	9.0
Net official flows	8.3	3.6	-0.6	5.8	14.1	-24.3	-1.4	-5.5	-43.1	-69.0	-93.2
Total net flows	18.3	16.3	12.8	21.9	26.1	-8.4	-14.3	5.8	-30.5	-42.0	-38.9
Change in reserves	-7.1	-18.2	-22.6	7.6	-5.8	-22.4	-4.9	-4.2	-30.8	-34.2	-93.3
Latin America and the Caribbean											
Net private capital flows	21.1	73.9	100.8	71.2	44.7	49.9	23.1	-2.1	15.5	6.0	25.2
Net direct investment	24.7	39.6	57.6	61.5	65.9	69.6	66.8	45.0	35.1	48.1	51.2
Net portfolio investment[a]	4.9	45.5	31.2	25.6	1.3	2.6	-7.6	-14.9	-8.4	-13.9	27.6
Other net investment[b]	-8.5	-11.2	11.9	-15.9	-22.5	-22.3	-36.1	-32.2	-11.2	-28.1	-53.6
Net official flows	16.5	-1.5	0.8	14.2	6.4	-5.2	26.3	18.5	6.1	-7.1	-25.2
Total net flows	37.5	72.3	101.5	85.3	51.1	44.8	49.5	16.4	21.6	-1.0	0.0
Change in reserves	-25.3	-20.2	-30.1	8.4	7.9	-2.8	1.9	-2.2	-35.5	-24.3	-31.6
Economies in transition											
Net private capital flows	5.5	-0.3	50.1	2.0	-9.0	-21.4	12.7	23.6	27.2	21.3	40.5
Net direct investment	3.8	5.8	8.1	9.2	8.0	6.0	9.1	8.8	11.6	22.8	16.1
Net portfolio investment[a]	-2.5	5.8	48.4	7.6	-0.7	-9.3	0.4	0.2	0.9	5.3	0.6
Other net investment[b]	4.4	-11.5	-6.4	-15.1	-16.4	-18.3	2.9	14.4	14.7	-6.6	23.8
Net official flows	1.7	-4.3	-0.6	1.8	-1.9	-6.3	-5.6	-10.7	-8.2	-7.6	-15.4
Total net flows	7.4	-4.2	49.5	3.6	-11.0	-27.9	6.8	12.7	19.0	13.9	25.1
Change in reserves	-6.9	5.2	-5.8	12.8	-7.4	-23.2	-16.5	-18.8	-35.2	-65.2	-83.0

Source: International Monetary Fund (IMF), *World Economic Outlook Database*, April 2006.

a Including portfolio debt and equity investment.
b Including short- and long-term bank lending, and possibly including some official flows to data limitations.

Table I.2.
NET TRANSFER OF FINANCIAL RESOURCES TO DEVELOPING ECONOMIES AND ECONOMIES IN TRANSITION, 1995-2005
(Billions of dollars)

	1995	1996	1997	1998	1999	2000	2001	2002	2003	2004	2005
Developing economies	49.4	26.5	-0.1	-34.0	-123.0	-187.9	-153.7	-202.2	-294.6	-367.8	-526.9
Africa	6.0	-5.5	-4.7	15.6	4.1	-27.7	-16.8	-6.7	-21.2	-34.5	-57.8
Sub-Saharan (excluding Nigeria and South Africa)	7.6	5.4	7.5	12.1	8.9	2.9	7.0	5.3	6.8	4.5	5.1
Eastern and Southern Asia	22.5	18.8	-32.7	-128.4	-143.0	-124.8	-117.2	-146.5	-172.5	-186.2	-243.0
Western Asia	22.6	12.7	14.0	34.1	5.5	-34.3	-23.8	-17.4	-40.9	-69.1	-132.7
Latin America	-1.7	0.6	23.3	44.7	10.3	-1.1	4.2	-31.7	-60.1	-78.0	-93.4
Economies in transition	-2.5	-6.1	2.9	3.6	-23.7	-49.4	-28.7	-24.8	-32.8	-53.5	-80.1
Memorandum item:											
Heavily indebted poor countries (HIPCs)	6.8	7.2	7.5	9.0	10.1	8.3	8.3	10.4	9.6	10.1	11.8
Least developed countries	12.0	10.4	9.3	12.6	11.1	5.6	9.0	6.6	8.1	5.9	7.1

Source: UN/DESA, based on International Monetary Fund (IMF), *World Economic Outlook*, April 2006, and IMF, *Balance of Payments Statistics.*

development, but whether they will be more stable than in the past, reducing the need for self-insurance through reserve accumulation, and even reversing the negative net transfer of resources that has characterized the world economy since the Asian crisis.

In this regard, the increasing share of more stable FDI in total private flows is important. However, as we will see below, not all components of FDI are equally stable. Furthermore, multinational companies, especially those producing for domestic markets, increasingly hedge their short-term foreign-exchange risks, particularly when devaluations seem likely. This can lead to major temporary outflows of capital and significant pressure on exchange rates (Ffrench-Davis and Griffith-Jones, 2003; Persaud, 2003). More generally, the increasing use of financial engineering and of derivatives (as well as the growing scale and complexity of derivatives discussed below) seems to make the hypothesis of a hierarchy of volatility, whereby some categories of flows are more stable than others, less clear-cut.

Another potentially positive effect is the greater interest shown by institutional investors (such as life insurers) in investing in emerging countries (European Central Bank, 2005). However, the large rise in "carry trades" involving developing country markets —that is borrowing at low interest rates in developed countries to finance holdings of higher yielding emerging market instruments—makes those flows vulnerable to narrowing interest rate differentials. Furthermore, the large fall in emerging markets' bond spreads (while naturally positive in itself for borrowing countries) has raised concerns that this may reflect a shift in the investor base towards "crossover" investors, i.e. investors who traditional invest in other safer asset markets, but who are attracted by higher yields, which can increase the vulnerability of developing countries, especially those with large external financing, to changes in United States interest rates.

Finally, there are two structural trends that may add stability. The first is the recent increase in the issue of local currency bonds in developing country and international financial markets; the second is the increasing importance of international banks lending from their local branches in local currency with funding from domestic liabilities. This makes countries less vulnerable to crises, although it also implies that foreign banks are contributing little, if any, foreign savings.

There are thus mixed signs in respect of whether the new inflows will be more stable than in the past. Therefore, policy efforts must be made, both in source and in recipient countries, to encourage more stable flows and discourage large flows that are potentially more reversible.

FOREIGN DIRECT INVESTMENT

Trends and composition of foreign direct investment

Net FDI flows to developing countries and economies in transition grew rapidly in the 1990s, peaking in 2001. During the Asian financial crisis and subsequent financial crises in emerging market countries, FDI was the most resilient and became the consistently largest component of net private capital flow to these countries. The different modalities of FDI, greenfield investment and cross-border mergers and acquisitions (M&A) have different effects on the domestic economy, in terms of both net financial contribution and linkages with the host economy.

Liberalization of FDI through legislative and regulatory changes in a growing number of countries since the 1990s has attracted higher levels of FDI. Extensive privatization, particularly in Latin American and Central and Eastern European countries, and acquisitions by international investors of distressed financial and non-financial institutions after the Asian crisis were major sources of the surge in FDI in the 1990s. In turn, the opportunities provided by low production costs and its growing domestic market have been the major sources of attraction towards China, the major recipient of FDI in the developing world.

The decline in US equity prices, the exhaustion of State assets available for privatization and mergers and acquisitions, joined by macroeconomic volatility in some developing countries, resulted in a brief decline in FDI in 2002-2003. However, this was followed by a broad-based recovery in FDI flows across developing regions and economies in transition owing to improvement in a combination of cyclical, institutional and structural factors.

Although FDI inflows to developing countries have been more resilient than flows from other sources, they are concentrated in a small number of mainly middle-income countries. The top 10 developing-country recipients of FDI accounted for almost three-fourths of total FDI flow to developing countries in 2003. This is true even if estimates are adjusted by the size of the economy. The World Bank estimates that the ratio of FDI to GDP in the top 10 recipient countries was more than twice that in low-income countries in 2003 (World Bank, 2004a, p. 79).

FDI inflows to least developed countries have increased, nevertheless, from the late 1990s, albeit from low levels, raising the least developed countries' share in total FDI in developing countries from approximately 2 per cent in 1995 to 5 per cent in 2003 (World Bank, 2005a). In particular, the least developed countries with large natural resource sectors have attracted growing amounts of FDI. There has also been some diversification of investment into the agricultural, brewing and light manufacturing sectors in some African least developed countries (United Nations Conference on Trade and Development, 2004a; Bhinda and others, 1999). In any case, FDI flows to least developed countries are smaller than official development assistance (ODA) in all but a few countries (United Nations Conference on Trade and Development, 2004a).

The growth in FDI flows has been accompanied by significant changes in its composition. The most important trend has been the rapid growth of investment in services since the 1990s. This process has been associated both with the expansion of transnational corporations into developing countries' service sectors, facilitated in many cases by privatization and the opening of domestic markets (for example, in financial activities, telecommunications and, to a lesser extent, public utilities) and, more recently, with the rapid growth of offshoring of services by transnational corporations. The share of services in the stock of inward FDI in developing countries increased from 47 per cent in 1990 to 55 per cent in 2002. At the same time, the share of manufacturing in FDI stock declined from 46 to 38 per cent. The small share of the primary sector remained unchanged at 7 per cent. FDI in services has grown at the expense of FDI in manufacturing in all developing regions except Africa. Until the 1990s, FDI in services was primarily in finance and trade, having accounted for over 70 per cent of total inward FDI stock in services by 1990. Since the 1990s, the share of FDI stock in other services, namely, business services, telecommunications and utilities, has increased, while that of finance and trade has declined (United Nations Conference on Trade and Development, 2004a, pp. 29-31 and 99).

The effect of service sector FDI on competition in the host country has varied among countries. Agosin and Mayer (2000) suggest that when FDI shifted towards services as the result of privatization in Latin America in the 1990s, there was a crowding out of domestic firms. In general, anti-competitive behaviour by transnational corporations can lead to more negative consequences in cases where domestic competition law is weak. Also, the impact of FDI on competitiveness has varied by country. In the case of large scale FDI in commercial banks in Latin America, the banking sector has not become more competitive (Economic Commission for Latin America and the Caribbean, 2005, p. 113), while the result of FDI liberalization in financial services in Thailand has been more positive (Asian Development Bank, 2004, p. 231). Similarly, in Eastern European countries, after multinational banks acquired a large market share, domestic bank lending to local enterprises increased, complementing multinational bank lending (Weller, 2001).

FDI in offshoring of services, involving relocation of lower value added corporate functions, including computer programming, customer service and chip design, has been increasing in a number of developing countries. This type of FDI has a relatively large spillover effect particularly through improvement of information and communication technologies (ICT) infrastructure and capacity-building in human capital, as in the case of the offshoring of software development in India (United Nations Conference on Trade and Development, 2004a, pp. 169-170). However, because of its relatively high-skill and ICT infrastructure requirements, FDI in offshoring is limited to a small number of countries.

An interesting long-term change in the pattern of FDI has also been the increase in South-South FDI flows. By the end of the 1990s, more than one third of total FDI inflows to developing countries were from other developing countries. This trend has meant the provision of access to more sources of FDI for developing countries, particularly small low-income countries (Akyut and Ratha, 2004). Offsetting this benefit is the possibility that investment flows from developing source countries are more volatile than those from developed source countries, undermining the stability of FDI flows (Levy-Yeyati and others, 2003). Cases in point are the sharp decline in FDI from Asian countries impacted by the 1997 financial crisis and the decline in FDI from Latin American countries in financial crisis in 2000-2002. Any differences in investment and financial strategies between developing-country and developed-country transnational corporations with regard to earnings reinvestment and intercompany loans can also have an impact on the stability of FDI flows.

How stable is FDI?

Total FDI flows to developing countries and economies in transition as a group have been resilient overall during and after economic crises. However, this overall trend masks significant variation in performance by region and country. Since the late 1990s, FDI in non-crisis countries has remained stable, but investment flows to crisis countries have declined (International Monetary Fund, 2004b, pp. 132-133). Further, the different components of FDI flows can differ significantly in their stability in economic crises.

Equity capital flows, which reflect primarily the strategic investment decision by transnational corporations, are the most stable of the three components of FDI. They are also the largest component, having constituted more than two-thirds of total FDI flows in the period 1990-2002. The size of this component varies by the sector of investment (World Bank, 2004a, pp. 86-87). Initial equity capital flows are extremely large in FDI in many infrastructure industries but smaller in investment in financial institutions and even more so in other service industries such as corporate services. Furthermore, under the conditions of significantly increased risk that existed in 2001-2002 in Latin America, new investment was postponed.

Earnings from foreign operations that are not repatriated and inter-company loans, the other two components of FDI flows, tend to be more volatile. On the one hand, these two categories of investment are sources of recurrent financing for investment in foreign affiliates after the initial equity investment. On the other hand, transnational corporations can adjust the flow of these two components to make short-term changes in their exposure to the financial risks in the host country (Working Group of the Capital Markets Consultative Group, 2003, pp. 25-28).

The share of non-repatriated earnings in total earnings has averaged about 40 per cent since the 1990s but has ranged from 35 to 65 per cent in different industries (World Bank, 2004a, pp. 82-84; United Nations Conference on Trade and Development, 2004a, p. 126). This category of FDI tends to be pro-cyclical with regard to host countries' economic conditions, as transnational corporations increase earnings repatriation and therefore reduce reinvestment to reduce their exposure to deteriorating local economic conditions, potentially exacerbating the situation. During and after the Asian financial crisis and the 2001-2002 Argentine crisis, for example, there was a significant increase in repatriation of earnings (World Bank, 2004a, pp. 88 and 90).

Inflows of intercompany loans may be almost as volatile and pro-cyclical as international debt flows. Transnational corporations call loans to foreign affiliates when financial risk in the host country rises, as happened in Brazil during the 2002 crisis. The negative trend in total FDI flows to Indonesia in the aftermath of the Asian crisis was the result of the large repayment of inter-company loans, outweighing steady capital equity inflow (World Bank, 2004a, pp. 87-88). Also, parent companies can reduce inter-company loans as a means of financing for foreign affiliates so as to reduce currency risk in anticipation of the depreciation of the currency of the host country. They may also avoid international capital markets when obtaining extra-corporate financing and turn to the local credit market of the host country, thereby reducing the inflow of capital to the host country at a time when it is most needed. The composition of overall FDI flows can therefore have a significant effect on the stability of net financial flow to developing countries (Kregel, 1996, pp. 59-61).

These two FDI components are also affected by the financial condition of the parent company, which is in turn affected by conditions of the economy of the source country and the global economy. Earnings repatriation and/or inter-company loan repayments are increased when financial resources are needed to improve the overall balance sheet of the parent company (United Nations Conference on Trade and Development, 2004a, p. 127).

In addition to the other features discussed above, adjustments in earnings repatriation and inter-company loans vary among companies in different sectors. Transnational corporations with investment in production of tradables are less quick to make these adjustments, as they are buffered by earnings in foreign exchange. With currency devaluation, the attractiveness of foreign investment in the tradable sectors is also enhanced. This was reflected in the resilience of non-repatriated earnings and inter-company loans flows to Mexico, the Republic of Korea, Thailand and Turkey after currency devaluations following financial crises in the 1990s (World Bank, 2003; Lipsey, 2001). In contrast, investors in non-tradable goods and services lack the foreign-exchange earnings and face a higher currency risk. The decline in FDI in Brazil and Argentina in 2002-2003, for example, illustrated this sensitivity of FDI in infrastructure and financial services. These sectoral differences suggest that a shift in FDI away from infrastructure and financial services and towards tradable services can have a stabilizing effect on FDI flows.

Particular benefits of FDI

In addition to its relatively higher resilience as a source of capital flow to developing countries, FDI is regarded as a potential catalyst for raising productivity in developing host countries through the transfer of technology and managerial know-how, and for facilitating access to international markets. The general conclusion from empirical studies points to net benefits for host countries but the benefits are markedly uneven, both among and within countries (Economic Commission for Latin American and the Caribbean, 2005; Asian Development Bank, 2004, pp. 213-269; United Nations Conference on Trade and Development, 2003a, pp. 142-144; Basu and Srinivasan, 2002; Hanson, 2001). Potential negative effects include limited domestic linkages, exacerbating trade deficits, limiting competition and the excessive share of the investment risk assumed by the host country. Additionally, there is strong debate on the magnitude of, and lags in, the materialization of positive effects as well as on the mechanisms by which they are transmitted to the host economy.

There is general agreement that an enabling investment climate in the host country is a necessary condition for encouraging both domestic and foreign investment. In addition, the levels of human resource development and entrepreneurial capacity of the host country are significant factors in the location decisions of investors as well as in the transfer of technology and know-how and the linkages of local firms to international production networks and markets. Besides improving the investment climate and strengthening domestic capacity, developing countries have also put in place fiscal and other incentives to compete for FDI. Evidence suggests, however, that these incentives are relatively minor factors in location decisions of transnational corporations (Asian Development Bank, 2004, p. 260). They thus undermine the fiscal base of developing countries without yielding the desired results.

Developing countries have also historically implemented investment policies to promote the desired benefits and minimize the negative effects of FDI. While there has been a move away from investment policies in the last decade, and the effectiveness of investment policies has been varied, it may be desirable to reinstate the use of investment policies, particularly to promote linkages between foreign firms and the host economy. Moreover, individual countries should have the policy space within which to customize specific interventions that are consistent with their development objectives and concerns with respect to FDI (Asian Development Bank, 2004, p. 262; Economic Commission for Latin America and the Caribbean, 2005).[3] Indeed, according to some analysts, the success of Asian countries was achieved by the Governments' commitment to assessing the results of their FDI policies on an ongoing basis to determine whether they were producing the expected benefits (Economic Commission for Latin America and the Caribbean, 2004, p. 70).

Transnational corporations can play an important role in providing access to markets, thereby helping to build competitive export capacity in host countries. Intra-firm trade offers access to firm-specific technology and being part of the production network of transnational corporations can provide foreign affiliates with established brand names that have access to international markets. These benefits vary depending, in particular, on the export versus domestic market orientation of transnational corporations in specific countries. Transnational corporations played an important role in building competitive export sectors and expanding exports in China, Mexico and a number of countries in South-East Asia, Central America and Eastern Europe. In other countries, for example, Brazil, Argentina and African countries, these benefits did not materialize. In Brazil, the fact that transnational corporations imported capital goods and focused on selling to the domestic market in the 1990s had a negative effect on the current-account balance; similar results were observed in Argentina (United Nations Conference on Trade and Development, 2003a, p. 143).

The decline in developing country tariffs following the Uruguay Round, combined with the reduced transportation and communications costs have allowed transnational corporations to develop integrated international production networks to take advantage of the comparative cost advantages of different countries. This has caused a redistribution of the benefits of FDI for different recipient countries in these geographically differentiated production chains. Some will benefit from larger export markets for their higher-technology products, while others will specialize in low domestic value added exports such as assembly activities. In turn, when transnational corporations invest only in order to sell to the domestic market of the recipient country, they may aggravate balance-of-payments pressures. Furthermore, mergers and acquisitions may actually result in the replacement of domestic suppliers by the international production chain of the new parent firm, thus leading initially to reduced domestic linkages. While it is possible that over time, transnational corporations will increase local inputs by transferring technologies to local suppliers so as to take advantage of geographical proximity and cost-effectiveness, this process is not necessarily rapid or smooth, and active linkage policies, including programmes aimed at accelerating technology transfers from transnational corporations to domestic firms, may be required .

Perhaps of greater importance than the transfer of production technologies is the transfer of the managerial and organizational practices employed by transnationals. Diffusion from foreign affiliates to the host country takes place more generally through competition with local firms, linkage with local suppliers, labour mobility from foreign affiliates to domestic firms, and geographical proximity between foreign and local firms. The transfer of technology and its efficient application depend on both transnational corporations' corporate policies and the level of development in the host country, as manifested in local skills and capabilities and capacities of local affiliates to absorb technology transfer (United Nations Conference on Trade and Development, 2000, p. 175).

In this regard, there is a significant difference between greenfield investment and mergers and acquisitions. Greenfield investment is more likely to involve technology transfer through introduction of imported new capital goods at inception (United Nations Conference on Trade and Development, 2000, p. 176). On the other hand, mergers and acquisitions are more likely to transfer technology and managerial capabilities to already existing local firms, targeting those with the capacity to be integrated into their production network. However, despite the different methods of technology transfer of these two forms of FDI, it is still unclear which exerts the stronger impact on technological upgrading of affiliates over time.

Research and development (R&D)-related FDI has a relatively large impact on upgrading technology and knowledge capacity in host countries, but it has been growing in only a limited number of countries. Since the 1990s, FDI in R&D has shifted from mainly developing products for local markets to reducing the cost of R&D in industrialized countries. This is part of a global trend toward offshoring R&D enabled by advanced ICT as well as the emergence of increasing demand for scientific expertise on a global scale (United Nations Conference on Trade and Development, 2005). A number of middle-income economies place priority on FDI in R&D as a means of moving up the technology ladder and have offered fiscal incentives to encourage it (World Bank, 2005a, p. 173). Asian countries, mainly Taiwan, China and India, have been successful in attracting FDI in R&D because of their abundant supply of engineers and scientists available at relatively low wages, while Latin American countries have been relatively unsuccessful in attracting this form of FDI. This is primarily the result of the repatriation of high-skilled Asian nationals with entrepreneurial experience gained from education and work in high technology firms in the United States.

The backward production linkages between foreign affiliates and domestic firms can be a channel for diffusing skills, knowledge and technology from foreign affiliates to local firms. On a large scale, such transfers can in turn lead to spillovers for the rest of the host economy (United Nations Conference on Trade and Development, 2001b, pp. 129-133). However, not all linkages are equally beneficial. For instance, suppliers of relatively simple, standardized low-technology products and services may be highly vulnerable to market fluctuations and their linkages with foreign companies are unlikely to involve much transfer of knowledge. Where there is the requisite level of skill among domestic suppliers, transnational corporations have established supplier development programmes in host countries (Poland, Costa Rica, Brazil, Malaysia, Viet Nam and India) and often provided financing, training, technology transfer and information (United Nations Conference on Trade and Development, 2001b, p. 160).

The objective of host countries should therefore be to promote linkages where they are beneficial. As linkage promotion policies are often a function of country circumstances, they need to be adapted accordingly. The focus appears to be on policies designed to address market failures at different levels in the linkage formation process. In this respect, measures to provide information for both buyers and suppliers about linkage opportunities and to bring domestic suppliers and foreign affiliates together in the key areas of information, technology, training and finance are important. Broader measures to strengthen the quality of local entrepreneurship are also vital in inducing foreign affiliates to form beneficial linkages. A few countries (the Republic of Korea, Singapore and Thailand) have introduced financial incentives for firms, including foreign affiliates, to invest in employee training (United Nations Conference on Trade and Development, 2001b, pp. 163-193).

Another way in which FDI can be linked to the domestic economy is via clusters, or industrial districts, defined as "geographically proximate groups of interconnected companies, suppliers, service providers, and associated institutions in a particular field, linked by commonalities and complementarities" (World Economic Forum, 2004, p. 23). Examples are the software industry in India and the shoemaking industry in Italy. Such concentrations of resources and capabilities can attract FDI that responds to agglomeration economies. Foreign investors can also add to the strength and dynamism of clusters when they join them by attracting new skills and capital and thereby transmitting benefits to the domestic economy. A virtuous cycle thus builds up and generates the dynamic agglomeration economies, for example, financial services in Singapore and software in Bangalore, India (United Nations Conference on Trade and Development, 2001b, p. xix).

The success of clusters depends on an enabling investment climate and especially the competitiveness of domestic enterprises and the available pool of skilled labour. Given these imposing requirements, the development of dynamic clusters that are able to attract and develop a symbiotic relationship with transnational corporations may be more feasible for those developing countries that have the requisite enabling infrastructure and environment.

FINANCIAL FLOWS

Bank credit

Trade finance, tied to international trade transactions, has important implications for development. It is provided by banks, non-financial firms, official export agencies, multilateral development banks, private insurers and specialized firms, and is indirectly supported by insurance, guarantees and lending with accounts receivable as collateral. This type of financing rose sharply in the 1990s up until the Asian crisis. Also, the average spread on trade finance declined significantly from more than 700 basis points in the mid-1980s to 150 before the Asian crisis and on average was 28 basis points lower than spreads on bank loans over the period 1996-2002 (World Bank, 2004a, pp. 127-130).

Trade finance is particularly important for less creditworthy and poorer countries' access to international loans, as traded goods serve as collateral. Many low-income developing countries, which lack other forms of access to commercial banks, still can borrow for trade finance. In almost every year since 1980, the share of trade finance commitments in total bank lending has been higher for non-investment grade or unrated developing countries than rated ones.

Security arrangements linked to traded goods and government policies directed at promoting exports should make trade finance more resilient during crises, and help countries grow out of crises by exporting. However, the opposite pattern has been common during recent crises, as evidenced by the experience of Indonesia, Malaysia and Thailand during the 1997-1998 Asian crisis and by that of Brazil and Argentina in later years. The contraction in trade finance was sharper than justified by fundamentals and risks involved, and ended up exacerbating the crises. After the Asian crisis, more than 80 per cent of domestic firms and 20 per cent of foreign-owned firms showed a drop in trade credit. However, credit from suppliers and customers was more resilient compared with bank credit.

In recent years trade finance has recovered, driven by the expansion of developing countries' trade, but its stability in the future cannot be taken for granted. Governments can facilitate trade finance by providing legal standing for electronic documents and for the assignment of receivables. A more effective approach to alleviating the problem of a collapse of trade finance during crises could be built around multilateral development banks' trade finance facilities, complemented by actions by official export credit agencies. The multilateral development banks have indeed used their trade finance facilities to support emerging markets during recent crises, but they could play a more prominent role. For instance, they could act as "insurer of record" on behalf of an emerging market borrower, providing transfer and convertibility risk mitigation through their preferred creditor status. The risks incurred could be covered by reinsurance with private sector insurers.

Trade financing from export credit agencies, including guarantees, insurance and Government-backed loans, has so far declined relative to the activity of private insurance companies, which accounted for nearly half of new commitments by international credit and investment insurers by 2002. The new commitments by private insurers are heavily skewed towards short-term export credit. However, export credit agencies could explore ways in which to play a more counter-cyclical role, especially in the recovery stage, immediately after crises. This could include rolling over or expanding short-term credit lines and facilitating medium- and long-term financing. Export credit agencies might also give consideration to allowing a special exception to normal credit-risk practices in crisis situations. Formal international rules, such as the World Trade Organization rules on subsidies or the relevant Organization for Economic Cooperation and Development (OECD) guidelines, could be modified to remove the disincentives to counter-cyclical operations of export credit agencies.

Other bank lending to developing countries experienced a similar large upswing in the 1990s until the Asian crisis. Bank lending had been assumed to be more stable than capital market financing; however, recent history has shown that the dominance of short-term loans makes it easy for banks to rapidly retrench. About one-third of international bank lending is short-term and this proportion had risen in the first half of the 1990s. Net international bank lending to developing countries collapsed with the East Asian crisis, and was negative from 1998 to 2002. A sharp retrenchment followed the Asian and Russian crises which had a negative impact on global liquidity. This reflected not only reduced willingness to lend, but also a weaker desire for loans by borrowers. However, the improved economic climate led to positive net bank lending since 2003.

In addition, the maturity of bank loans has increased since the Asian crisis. According to World Bank data, the ratio of short-term to total international bank lending fell from 54 per cent in 1996 to 46.5 per cent in 2000 for all developing countries, with a particularly sharp decline in East Asia and the Pacific. Emerging market banks now have a more balanced external position vis-à-vis banks reporting to the Bank for International Settlements than in 1997-1998 and official reserve coverage of the banking system's net liability positions has increased (International Monetary Fund, 2004a, p. 36).

There has been a general retrenchment of banks from cross-border lending since 1997 and a large scale shift towards lending via domestic subsidiaries, which grew on average by 29.4 per cent annually between 1996 and 2002 (see table I.3). North American and Japanese banks have sharply reduced their cross-border lending to developing countries, while European banks have increased their exposure and now account for nearly two-thirds of such lending. Important structural changes also occurred in regional patterns of borrowing. International claims on East Asia and the Pacific declined sharply, although there have been some recent signs of revival. Claims on Latin American countries expanded between 1997 and 2000, but have since stalled. Lending to "emerging Europe" performed better, entirely accounted for by European lenders. In turn, emerging Europe and Latin America have experienced the fastest growth of lending by domestic subsidiaries of foreign banks. Also, as a result of greater lending by European banks, lending to the

Table I.3.
BANK LENDING IN EMERGING MARKETS, 1993-1996

	Billions of dollars	Percentage	Billions of dollars	Percentage
	Total lending	Average annual growth	Total lending	Average annual growth
	1996	1993-1996	2002	1997-2002
East Asia				
Domestic banks	769.5	18.1	876.1	2.4
Local subsidiaries of foreign banks	29.8	15.4	84.9	21.2
Cross-border	282.2	29.0	130.3	-11.6
Latin America				
Domestic banks	563.7	17.3	484.8	-2.7
Local subsidiaries of foreign banks	58.5	28.6	241.7	31.2
Cross-border	199.9	6.2	166.1	-2.8
Eastern Europe				
Domestic banks	242.5	9.4	252.8	0.8
Local subsidiaries of foreign banks	9.6	80.5	96.3	48.5
Cross-border	74.7	1.6	70.4	-0.6
All Emerging Markets				
Domestic banks	1,575.7	12.7	1,613.7	0.4
Local subsidiaries of foreign banks	97.8	24.4	422.8	29.4
Cross-border	556.7	14.5	366.9	-6.5

Source: IMF, 2004b, p. 128.

Middle East, Northern Africa, South Asia and sub-Saharan Africa has edged up compared with that of 1997. In contrast, the presence of developing country banking institutions in London and New York has contracted since 1996.

Although foreign entry could increase efficiency through competition and modernization, it could also result in the crowding out of domestic banks and vulnerable customers as foreign banks concentrate on the most remunerative and low-risk activities. Empirical studies indicate that the competitive pressures exerted by foreign banks vary by country (Clarke and others, 2001b, p. 17), and that domestic banks displaced by foreign competition might seek new market niches, for example, through providing credit to small and medium-sized enterprises (Bonin and Abel, 2000). One survey in 38 developing and transition countries found that foreign bank penetration improves firms' access to credit, although it benefits large enterprises more than small ones (Clarke and others, 2001a, pp. 20-21).

There is legitimate concern in developing countries that foreign banks may curtail their lending more than local banks in times of crisis owing to their more sophisticated risk management systems. The sharp drop in lending by foreign banks following recent emerging market crises confirms this fear. For instance, the real supply of credit fell sharply in Mexico after the 1994 crisis, dropping from 35 to 10 per cent of GDP by 2001. Although this was basically a reflection of a deep domestic financial crisis, the rapid penetration of foreign banks during those years did not in any way counteract the process. Also, after the Argentine crisis, restrictions on support to ailing subsidiaries severely limited funds supplied by parent companies (Economic Commission for Latin America and the Caribbean, 2003, pp. 140-142).

Foreign banks are also more sensitive to shocks originating in advanced economies. Excessive exposure to banks from a single country increases such risks. There is concern that Latin American banking sectors have become vulnerable to economic fluctuations in Spain owing to the dominance of Spanish banks (Clarke and others, 2001b, p. 18).

Portfolio flows

Net portfolio flows tend to be pro-cyclical as well as volatile. Net portfolio investment flows had surged in the early 1990s and at their peak surpassed the level of FDI, but this was followed by a collapse during the series of crises that started in East Asia in 1997. The rapid growth of bond financing was matched during the boom by the increase of foreign purchases of developing-country stocks, however both declined thereafter. In the case of stocks, the initial surge was linked to the privatization processes; later, as foreign investors resorted to direct investment to acquire control of privatized companies, portfolio equity flows declined.

From 1997, the level of portfolio debt flows, measured by net issuance of debt in the international market had begun a major downturn, reaching a trough in 2001. In 2003-2005, there was a broad-based rebound: net issuance levels reached a new peak of $96 billion in 2005, more than twice the annual average in 1999-2003. (Bank for International Settlements, 2005, p. 36, 2006, p. 34). In spite of persistent large reversals, net portfolio debt flows became the major source of debt financing for emerging market countries, particularly in Latin America. Indeed, fixed income financing conditions in emerging markets were exceptionally resilient up to May 2006 to rising international interest rates and markedly increased volatility in equity markets.

While there has been an overall decline in net portfolio debt flows to developing countries since the Asian financial crisis, the pattern differs significantly between crisis and non-crisis countries (International Monetary Fund, 2004b, p. 133). Since 1998, there have been large net portfolio debt outflows from Asian crisis countries. Similarly, in 2000-2002, countries in financial crisis or turmoil, such as Argentina, Brazil and Turkey, experienced sharp declines in net portfolio debt flows. On the contrary, flows to other countries increased.

Countries' sudden loss of access to primary markets for international bonds is demonstrated by the very low level of issuance activity. The across-the-board market closure following the Russian crisis in 1998 was an extreme case, while in 2002 loss of access was limited to a small number of countries. The riskiest borrowers were most likely to lose access to financing. Borrowers with lower credit ratings regained access after lower-risk borrowers when markets reopened (World Bank, 2004a, pp. 50-51). When developing countries do not totally lose market access, they are often subject to sharp increases in risk premiums, which are also characterized by significant cross-correlation among issuers (contagion effects). The pro-cyclical downgrades of credit rating agencies often exacerbate both lack of access to the bond market and the spreads at which such bonds can be issued.

Market access can depend on investor reaction not only to events specific to emerging market countries, but also to conditions in global financial markets. While the former were dominant in the late 1990s, the latter appear to be exerting an increasing effect on emerging market bond market closure and reopening in recent years (International Monetary Fund, 2004b, p. 66). This was illustrated by the market closure in 2002. In the subsequent rally in emerging bond markets, financial conditions had a positive effect on emerging markets, an experience similar to that of the early 1990s. Low international interest rates and increased investor search for yield was reflected in an increase in the appetite for risk. However, the negative impact of international factors on the emerging bond markets was underscored again when expectations of larger-than-anticipated United States interest rate increases were raised in April 2004 and early 2005, resulting in abrupt and sharp reversals in the tightening of yield spreads of emerging market bonds. Although emerging market countries were able to weather the heightened volatility, these developments raise questions about the sustainability of the favourable external financing environment for developing countries. The continued tightening of US interest rates and an increased risk of inflation from rising commodity prices, in particular petroleum, has brought increased volatility to asset prices in emerging bond markets.

Recent developments in bond markets have also affected the composition of debt flows. The upgrading of credit ratings of a number of developing countries, including the increased number of investment grade emerging market bonds, has broadened the investor base. The increase in "crossover" investors, including institutional investors, who invest in emerging market debt as a supplement to their traditional portfolio of mature market debt, has also made a larger source of funds available. However, crossover investors can generate greater volatility, as their decisions are more sensitive to the returns of other investments in their portfolios. Also, to the extent that international banks have historically had a more diversified portfolio than other investors, increased bond issues by developing countries are not a substitute for the reduction of cross-border bank lending, and may lead to a concentration of capital flows in those countries that are regarded by the market as low-risk borrowers, at the cost of a further marginalization of high-risk borrowers (Bank for International Settlements, 2003, pp. 51-52).

There has also been a rapid development of domestic bond markets in many emerging market economies since the late 1990s aimed at mobilizing domestic saving, reducing dependency on external financing and lowering currency mismatch (see below). These domestic capital markets have attracted increasing financing from domestic as well as foreign investors, but they are not immune to volatility in interest rates. A case in point was the sharp rise in local currency bond spreads in Brazil and Turkey when emerging market bond yield spreads spiked in April and May 2004 (International Monetary Fund, 2004b, p. 23). Also, the stress on Asian local currency bond markets (China, the Republic of Korea and Thailand) in 2003 emanated from the sell-off in United States Treasury bonds (Bank for International Settlements, 2004a, pp. 74-75). These experiences raise some questions about the effectiveness of local capital markets as a complete buffer against the volatility of external portfolio debt financing.

Net portfolio equity flows have experienced a cycle similar to that of bond financing, but their relative magnitudes differ. They declined sharply between 1997 and 2002 after reaching a peak in the early 1990s but have remained a small source of external financing for emerging market economies, even after the rebound in 2003-2004. The strength of the recovery was concentrated in Asia, with a high level of issuance by China and India.

Volatility in emerging market portfolio equity flows since the late 1990s can be attributed to a sudden loss of access to primary markets, as in the case of portfolio debt flows. In addition, synchronization with mature markets makes emerging market stocks more susceptible to international developments as evidenced by the ramifications of the bursting of the so-called "dot.com" bubble in 2000.

An underlying factor in a long-term decline of portfolio equity flows was the lower risk-adjusted return on emerging market stocks compared with return on portfolio debt investment in the 1990s, making the latter the preferable investment (World Bank, 2003, pp. 100-101). Underdeveloped stock markets, lack of minority shareholder protection, and limited disclosure requirements contribute to the higher risk of emerging market stocks for international investors. Also, higher volatility of returns to emerging market equities relative to bonds in an environment of macroeconomic instability reflects the seniority of debt over equity in bankruptcy proceedings. In addition, as investors seek to exert more control over the operations of enterprises and to protect their own interests, they have shifted from portfolio equity investment to FDI.

Recent liberalization of ownership and other restrictions in emerging markets has helped strengthen portfolio equity flows. This has been particularly evident in China and India where economic liberalization and prospects for sustained strong economic growth have boosted portfolio equity flows. China has succeeded in raising large amounts of foreign capital for its most successful State-owned enterprises through the listing of shares in the major international stock exchanges, although this limited fund-raising capacity for smaller domestic enterprises (Euromoney, 2004, pp. 92-99).

Impact of derivatives

The 1990s saw an explosion in the global derivatives market that was further enhanced in the first half of the 2000s. Financial derivatives became an important factor in the growth of cross-border capital flows, including emerging markets. In Mexico, for example, banks used derivatives to leverage their currency and interest rate exposure. When pressure on the exchange rate began to build, these positions contributed to the 1994 Mexican crisis. Bank lending and portfolio flows, especially to Asian developing countries, were increasingly intermediated through structured derivative instruments.

The growth in derivative products is in large part due to their ability to unbundle and isolate risks. Floating exchange rates gave a major impulse to this growth by generating demand by investors to hedge against changes in exchange rates. Derivatives can redistribute risk away from those who do not want it to those theoretically better able to manage it. Derivatives can also provide a tool for pricing different risks, thus increasing market efficiency. They give investors the ability to hedge specific risks and gain access to others, creating opportunities for portfolio diversification.

At the same time, however, derivative products increase leverage in markets, provide tools for short-term speculation and can increase macroeconomic volatility. Because derivatives are often complex, non-transparent and poorly regulated, they can also be used for tax avoidance, manipulation and fraud. Thus, the use of derivatives has added to systemic risk and macroeconomic volatility, especially for developing countries.

Standard derivative contracts used to hedge risk, such as forwards, futures and options, are quite well known. While foreign-currency forwards are traded over the counter (OTC), many basic futures and options contracts are standardized and traded in organized and regulated markets. Futures and forward contracts illustrate how derivatives can transfer risk. When counterparties with offsetting long and short positions in the same asset can be brought together to agree on a price for the future exchange of the asset through a futures contract, then risk for both has been eliminated. However, in the absence of perfectly offsetting risks, derivative contracts increasingly simply transfer risk from one agent to another. In the absence of an agent with an offsetting risk position, the counterparty to the contract will be whoever is willing to take on the risk of providing a guarantee of the contracted price on the stipulated date. These agents are interested in derivative contracts primarily to speculate on future price movements, rather than to hedge risk.

Forward contracts in foreign exchange constitute the most liquid derivative instrument traded in emerging markets. In these contracts, counterparties agree to buy one currency and sell the other on a specified date at an agreed upon price. Originally used for hedging purposes, forward foreign-exchange contracts have increasingly been used for currency speculation. For example, in the early 2000s speculators used forwards as the main tool for betting on an appreciation of the Chinese renminbi. Forward contracts also offer implicit access to the interest rates of the currency being bought, funded by the currency being sold. In what is called the "carry trade", investors use currency forwards to invest in high short-term local interest rates in developing countries, funded by lower United States dollar, yen or euro rates. Forwards also give speculators the ability to short the local currency.

Forward contracts highlight several important characteristics of derivatives and their potentially very problematic impact on developing countries. First, they add leverage to the markets, exacerbating problems of short-term capital flows and hot money. Derivative products that allow investors to leverage currency risk have increased volatility in exchange markets and exacerbated boom-bust cycles in developing countries. For example, open currency and interest rate positions in Asia in the mid-1990s grew to excessive proportions relative to domestic GDP and were a major factor in the Asian crisis (International Monetary Fund, 2002a). This was especially pronounced in Indonesia where, prior to the crisis, otherwise viable companies had been speculating on the exchange rate through foreign-exchange forwards and swaps. When pressure on the currency built, foreigners sold their local currency positions and these companies were forced to buy dollars to cover their dollar shorts, causing increasing losses and the currency to fall further. As a result many became insolvent and were forced into bankruptcy when the currency devalued.

The forward foreign-exchange market also demonstrates the difficulty of regulating derivatives. As a response to the crisis, Asian central banks attempted to use capital controls to restrict currency speculation, however, the global nature of derivatives, combined with their lack of transparency, made it harder to enforce capital-account regulations. The result has been the growth of offshore markets designed to circumvent domestic restrictions. For example, tightening of controls since the Asian crisis has led to new growth of such markets, and Asian non-deliverable forwards markets now make up over 70 per cent of all global non-deliverable forwards markets (Ma, Ho and McCauley, 2004).

Other derivative products unbundle risks even more. For example, contracts can be written that limit exposure to convertibility risk, local settlement risk, etc. The result of these packages is a change in the credit-risk characteristics of the bond whereby risks are shifted to different individuals. Investors can use these products to gain access to their desired emerging market exposure, and borrowers can use them to reduce the cost of funding. However, because of their complexity, they can also be used to hide risks from regulators and, sometimes, even from the investors themselves. In addition, like forwards, they can also increase systemic risk and macroeconomic volatility. In a number of countries where severe restrictions in the cash market prevail, these derivative products allow investors to go around such restrictions (Chew, 1996, p. 49).

Structured products have been the basis for the growing market in credit default swaps, which are currently the most popular form of credit derivatives. Under the terms of the credit default swap, the counterparty buying protection against a credit event makes a periodic payment to the seller. She is paid by the seller if the credit event occurs. Credit default swaps provide protection only against agreed upon credit events, such as bankruptcy, a change in credit ratings, a debt moratorium or a debt restructuring. The most liquid credit default swaps contracts are on sovereign external debt.

While the credit default swaps market provides an efficient tool for pricing credit risk it also opens the way to abuses, and can be particularly difficult to monitor and regulate since, like the non-deliverable forwards market, the credit default swaps market is not domestic. Most trades experience no geographical limitations. Furthermore, credit default swaps can mask the true ownership structure of a country's debt. This becomes an issue if a country goes into default. All bondholders have equal rights to negotiate a settlement; but there can be bondholders who also have a short position through swaps, and might negotiate against other bondholders' interests.

The increasing use of credit derivatives has reduced transparency and increased the difficulty in assessing the final return on an investment. Many of the contracts used include embedded options and leverage that increase the risk of the position often beyond the investors' knowledge.

In theory, derivatives can be used to decouple risks, giving investors the opportunity to diversify their portfolios. At the same time, they should lead to additional sources of financing for borrowers, and help develop local capital markets. Furthermore, new instruments can limit risks through diversification.

However, derivatives can also destabilize markets and have contributed to boom-and-bust cycles in emerging markets. The way in which particular swap contracts and credit derivatives combine currency risk and market price risks explains why these markets tend to move in sympathy, creating contagion that can produce unexpected declines and excessive instability in both currency and asset markets during crises. Also, the characteristics of the derivative contracts suggest that they are often motivated by factors not directly related to the allocation of funds to their highest global returns. Rather, they are linked to attempts to circumvent particular prudential regulations and provide banks with fee and commission income, rather than to profit from assessing relative risk-adjusted returns (Kregel, 1998).

Yet, derivatives in developing countries appear set to continue to grow. Recent figures indicate a recovery of cross-border bank lending. In particular, inflows into China have increased substantially, driven by an anticipated appreciation of the Chinese currency. These flows have been encouraged by China's decision to adopt more liberal rules on Derivatives Business of Financial Institutions in March 2004, which allow foreign banks to expand their derivatives activities with Chinese companies. The new rules permit over-the-counter derivatives trades for any commercially reasonable purpose, not just for hedging purposes, as previously required. In August of 2005 the People's Bank of China (PBOC) issued new regulations allowing banks to offer renminbi (RMB) cross-currency swaps for the first time. The regulations make it possible for more banks, including foreign banks, to get approval to offer RMB forwards. This represents the first action taken by the PBOC to liberalize the RMB derivatives market since the publication of the derivatives guidelines by the Chinese banking regulator, the China Banking Regulatory Commission (CBRC), in 2004. Both domestic and foreign banks could qualify to offer RMB forwards and swaps.

One lesson to be derived from the history of derivatives in the 1990s is that short-term instruments linked to currencies and money markets can be particularly destabilizing. The experience of Malaysia, however, shows how well-designed regulations and controls can effectively restrict this market, and can even be used to cut off the development of an offshore market. Derivatives tied to longer-term instruments are perhaps less risky, and some risks can be potentially minimized through well-designed regulations (Dodd, 2005). When opening their markets in order to obtain the benefits that derivatives can offer, policymakers need to focus on new regulatory structures so as to minimize not only risk to the investor but above all systemic risk, and undesired potential macroeconomic effects.

MEASURES TO COUNTER PRO-CYCLICALITY OF PRIVATE CAPITAL FLOWS

To counter the pro-cyclical pattern that characterizes private capital flows, several options are available to developing countries. We consider in the present section two alternatives: (a) designing mechanisms to encourage more stable private flows (counter-cyclical guarantees) or that distribute better the risk faced by developing countries throughout the business cycle (indexed bonds and bonds denominated in the currency of developing countries); (b) introducing prudential capital account regulations; and (c) adopting counter-cyclical prudential regulations for the domestic financial system. We also consider the likely effect of the New Basel Capital Accord (Basel II) on the cyclical patterns of capital flows to developing countries. The pro-cyclical pattern of private capital flows gives a compensatory role also to official financing; this issue will be considered in chapters II and IV, in relation to official development financing and to emergency (balance of payments) financing, respectively.

Counter-cyclical financing instruments

One way of addressing the problems created by the inherent tendency of private flows to be pro-cyclical is for public institutions to issue guarantees that have counter-cyclical elements (Griffith-Jones and Fuzzo de Lima, 2005).

In this regard, multilateral development banks and export credit agencies could introduce explicit counter-cyclical elements in the risk evaluations they make for issuing guarantees for lending to developing countries. This would imply that when banks or other lenders lowered their exposure to a country, multilateral development banks or export credit agencies would increase their level of guarantees, if they considered that the country's long-term fundamentals were basically sound. When private banks' willingness to lend increased, multilateral development banks or export credit agencies could reduce their exposure. This implies that the models used to assess risks should utilize measures of risk focused on long-term fundamentals and would therefore be less affected by the short-term fluctuations that tend to influence markets.

Alternatively, there could be special stand-alone guarantee mechanisms for long-term private credit that had a strong explicit counter-cyclical element. This could be activated in periods of sharp decline in capital flows and its aim would be to try to increase long-term private credit flows, especially to finance infrastructure. Multilateral development banks could also play a more active role in issuing guarantees for developing country bonds issued in private capital markets during periods of limited risk appetite.

The introduction of counter-cyclical elements in guarantees would become more meaningful if the number of guarantees issued by multilateral and regional development banks expanded to offset the decline in guarantees issued by some export credit agencies. As we will see in chapter II, existing problems—such as excessive restrictiveness of criteria and approval processes for granting and other related costs—would need to be addressed, and the resources of the international financial institutions should also be better leveraged in providing guarantees.

Commodity-linked bonds can also play a useful role in reducing developing countries' cyclical vulnerabilities. Examples of commodity-indexed bonds include oil-backed bonds, such as Petrobonds first issued by the Government of Mexico (Atta-Mensah, 2004). In such instruments, the coupon or principal payments to the buyer are linked to the price of a referenced commodity. By issuing this type of bond, the developing country can shift some of the risk of a fall in commodity prices to its bond investors. However, commodity-linked bonds can be expensive, owing to the greater complexity of these instruments, in comparison with conventional bonds (Dodd, 2004).

There have also been proposals to introduce GDP-indexed bonds. The coupon payments on these bonds would vary with the growth rate of the debtor's economy, being higher in years of rapid growth of GDP (measured in an international currency) and lower in years of below-trend growth. It has been argued that such instruments would improve the cushioning of emerging market borrowers against adverse shocks by making debt payments more contingent on the borrower's ability to pay. GDP-indexed bonds would therefore restrict the range of variation of the debt-to-GDP ratio and hence reduce the likelihood of debt crises and defaults. At the same time, they also reduce the likelihood of pro-cyclical fiscal policy responses to adverse shocks.

This instrument would allow countries to insure against a broader set of risks than would commodity-linked bonds, and thus is likely to be more useful for those developing countries that have fairly diversified production and exports and therefore do not have a natural commodity price to link to bond payments (Council of Economic Advisers, 2004; Goldstein, 2005, Griffith-Jones and Sharma, 2006). However, the introduction of GDP-indexed bonds may encounter some obstacles, such as concerns about the quality of GDP data in some developing countries. Their introduction would thus need to be preceded by efforts to improve the quality of macroeconomic information.

It has been suggested that the advanced industrialized countries should issue these instruments first. This would have a demonstration effect and make it easier for developing countries to join in (Shiller, 2005). The precedent of introducing collective action clauses into bonds, undertaken first by developed countries which were later followed by developing countries, would seem to indicate that such demonstration effects can be very effective in introducing innovations in financial instruments.

Another alternative for better managing the risks faced by developing countries throughout the business cycle consists in the introduction of local currency-denominated bonds. These bonds offer, in particular, a cure against the currency mismatches that characterize the debt structure of developing countries. At the domestic level, the development of domestic capital markets, especially bond markets, also creates a more stable source of local funding for both the public and private sectors, thereby mitigating the funding difficulties created by sudden stops in cross-border capital flows (some limitations of these instruments, particularly the relative incapacity to isolate domestic markets from external market shocks, were discussed above). Progress has also been made in developing domestic capital markets in developing countries.

In addition to proposals for institutional measures to develop local capital markets, there have also been innovative proposals to make local currency investments more attractive to international investors. Spiegel and Dodd (2004) have suggested raising capital in international markets by forming diversified portfolios of emerging market local currency debt issued by sovereign Governments. These portfolios of local currency government debt securities (LCD portfolios) would employ risk management techniques of diversification to generate risk-adjusted returns that competed favourably with other major capital market security indices. Based on data starting in 1994, the authors show that a portfolio of emerging market local currency debt can earn risk-adjusted rates of return that compete with those of major securities indices in international capital markets. The insight offered by portfolio theory is that a portfolio consisting of different securities whose returns are sufficiently independent (especially if they are negatively correlated) can yield risk-adjusted rates of returns superior to those of the individual securities. Thus, the volatility of the whole is less than the sum of its parts. The proposed LCD portfolio would consist of local currency government debt instruments from many different developing countries, so as to have a return and variance that were competitive in international capital markets.

However, the authors admit that there are some challenges that need to be overcome. The first is the disappointing history of local currency funds in the mid- to late 1990s which has led investors to be wary of this asset class. This relates to funds that took large concentrated bets in a few countries, and thus did not maintain a diversified portfolio. As local currency bond markets have continued to develop, there is now a greater possibility of benefiting from portfolio diversification. The second is that Governments may not respond to the interest of foreign investors in local debt by easing regulations and transactions costs involved with investing in these markets. This may be due to the fact that foreign financing may be more attractive, since it is often cheaper than domestic financing. Some countries may also fear the impact that surges and reversals of short-term hot money could have on small domestic capital markets. In this light, regulations can be viewed as a means of restricting capital flows. Given the legitimacy of these concerns, the challenge is to construct the portfolio in such a way as to allow policymakers the option to continue to selectively use capital-account regulations to limit short-term inflows. According to Spiegel and Dodd, this can indeed be done and they cite the example of Hungary where foreigners were given permission to buy into long-term closed-end funds even when they were not allowed to access the local bond market directly. As suggested in chapter II, multilateral development banks could play an active role in the development of domestic bond markets.

Prudential capital account regulations

In the previous section, we suggested a set of financial instruments that could be used in international financial markets to either smooth out private flows to developing countries or manage better the risks they generate. However, there are also important policy measures that can be taken nationally to either smooth private flows or manage such risks, particularly prudential regulations on the capital account and counter-cyclical prudential regulations.

The accumulation of risks that developing countries face during capital-account booms depends not only on the magnitude of private and public sector debts but also on maturity and currency mismatches on the balance sheets of financial and non-financial agents. Thus, capital-account regulations potentially have a dual role: as a macroeconomic policy tool with which to provide some room for counter-cyclical monetary policies that smooth out debt ratios and spending; and as a "liability policy" designed to improve private sector external debt profiles (Ocampo, 2003a).

Viewed as a macroeconomic policy tool, capital-account regulations aim at the direct source of boom-bust cycles: unstable capital flows. If successful, they provide some room to "lean against the wind" during periods of financial euphoria through the adoption of a contractionary monetary policy and/or reduced appreciation pressures. If effective, they also reduce or eliminate the quasi-fiscal costs of sterilized foreign-exchange accumulation. During crises, they provide breathing space for expansionary monetary policies. In both cases, capital-account regulations improve the authorities' ability to mix additional degrees of monetary independence with a more active exchange-rate policy.

In their role as a liability policy, capital-account regulations recognize the fact that the market rewards sound external debt profiles (Rodrik and Velasco, 1999). This reflects the fact that, during times of uncertainty, the market responds to gross (and not merely net) financing requirements, which means that the rollover of short-term liabilities is not financially neutral. Under these circumstances, a maturity profile that leans towards longer-term obligations will reduce domestic liquidity risks. An essential component of economic policy management during booms should thus be measures to improve the maturity structures of external and domestic liabilities.

Overall, the experiences with capital-account regulations in the 1990s were useful for improving debt profiles, giving Governments more latitude in pursuing stabilizing macroeconomic policies, and insulating countries from some of the vagaries of capital markets. There is much evidence that, if well implemented, the benefits far outweigh the costs (Stiglitz and others, 2006; Epstein and others, 2003; Ocampo and Palma, 2005).

A key question for countries considering capital market interventions is what form the interventions should take. They can be either price-based (unremunerated reserve requirements or taxes) or quantity-based (administrative restrictions on certain forms of borrowing). Aside from price- and quantity-based interventions in capital markets, other domestic prudential regulations can also be used to affect both the ability to borrow abroad and the associated returns. They include limits on banks' short-term foreign borrowing; regulations that force banks to match their foreign currency liabilities and assets; and regulations that restrict them from lending in foreign currencies to firms that do not have equivalent revenues in those currencies, or impose higher capital adequacy requirements or loan-loss provisions for short-term lending in foreign currency and lending that involves a currency mismatch. Authorities can also apply adverse tax or bankruptcy treatment to foreign-denominated borrowing. These interventions are not mutually exclusive, and thus Governments can use a mix of instruments to manage the risks associated to foreign borrowing.

The basic advantages of price-based instruments are their simplicity and their focus on averting the build-up of macroeconomic disequilibria and, ultimately, preventing crises. A highly significant innovation in this sphere during the 1990s was the establishment in Chile and Colombia of an unremunerated reserve requirement for capital inflows. Since the unremunerated reserve requirement could be substituted by a payment to the central bank of its implicit costs, it also operated as a tax on capital inflows. It created a simple, non-discretionary and preventive (prudential) price-based incentive that penalized short-term foreign currency liabilities more heavily.

The effectiveness of reserve requirements has been the subject of debate (for review of different positions, see Ocampo, 2003a). It is noteworthy that institutions such as the International Monetary Fund and the Bank for International Settlements have increasingly concluded that these controls were effective in important aspects. There is broad agreement that they were effective in reducing short-term debt flows and thus in improving or maintaining good external debt profiles. There is greater controversy about their effectiveness as a macroeconomic policy tool. Nonetheless, given solid evidence on the sensitivity of capital flows to interest rate spreads in both countries, it can be asserted that reserve requirements influenced the volume of capital flows at given interest rates or (an aspect on which there is broader agreement) helped countries maintain higher domestic interest rates during periods of euphoria in international financial markets. Therefore, in terms of some, and probably most, of their main objectives, the Chilean and Colombian experiences were broadly successful. They clearly helped lengthen maturities and increased space for increasing interest rates, thereby contributing to macroeconomic equilibrium.

On the other hand, traditional foreign-exchange market interventions and quantity-based capital-account regulations might be preferable when the policy objective is to reduce domestic macroeconomic sensitivity to international capital flows. These traditional controls in essence segment the domestic and foreign-exchange markets, basically by limiting the capacity of domestic firms and residents to borrow in foreign currency (except in the cases of some specific transactions such as trade financing and long-term investment) and limiting the capacity of foreign residents to hold some types of domestic financial assets or liabilities.

Indeed, simple quantitative restrictions of this sort are also preventive in character and can be easier to administer than price-based controls, but an administrative capability must be in place in order for these regulations to work and to prevent the corruption that could be generated by the discretionary decisions that might be involved in their use. Some of them can also be mixed with price-based regulations or with other domestic prudential regulations mentioned in the beginning of this section. Thus, during the 1990s, Chile established a minimum stay period for foreign capital (one year) and was responsible for the direct approval of issuance of American Depository Receipts (ADRs), and Colombia maintained direct regulations on the inflows and composition of the portfolios of foreign investment funds operating in the country.

The experience of the Asian countries that maintained quantity-based restrictions throughout the 1990s suggests that those restrictions might indeed also be particularly effective in preventing crises. China, India, Taiwan Province of China and Viet Nam offer successful examples in this regard. Despite the slow and cautious liberalization that has taken place in several of these economies since the early 1990s, the use of such traditional regulations has helped them prevent contagion from the East Asian crisis (see, for example, in relation to India, Reddy, 2001; Rajaraman, 2001; and in relation to Taiwan Province of China, Agosin, 2000).

Malaysia offers one of the most interesting examples of effective use of quantitative regulations during the 1990s. In January 1994, it had introduced outright restrictions on short-term inflows and prohibited non-residents from buying a wide range of short-term securities. These other measures proved highly effective in reversing the booming capital inflows of the previous years (Palma, 2002). In September 1998, Malaysia established quantity-based restrictions on outflows, which basically aimed at guaranteeing that the local currency would be used only in domestic transactions, and thus at eliminating offshore trading of the currency.[4] In February 1999, these regulations were replaced by an exit levy (that is to say, a price-based regulation), which was gradually reduced in later years. Kaplan and Rodrik (2001) show that the Malaysian regulations successfully closed the offshore ringgit market and reversed financial market pressure, and gave the government space within which to enact expansionary monetary and fiscal policies that contributed to the speedy recovery of economic activity.

Although quantity-based restrictions can be effective if authorities wish to limit capital outflows during crises, crisis-driven quantitative controls generate serious credibility issues and may be ineffective in the absence of a strong administrative capacity. This implies that a tradition of regulation may be necessary, and that the tightening or loosening of permanent regulatory regimes through the cycle may be superior to the alternation of different (even opposite) capital-account regimes. In broader terms, this means that it is essential to maintain the autonomy needed to impose capital-account regulations, and thus the freedom to reimpose controls, if necessary (United Nations, 2001a; Reddy, 2001; Ocampo, 2002). This is indeed a corollary of the incomplete nature of international financial governance, particularly of the absence of a lender-of-last-resort at the global level.

It should be emphasized, in any case, that capital-account regulations should always be seen as an instrument that provides an additional degree of freedom to the authorities with respect to their adopting sensible counter-cyclical macroeconomic policies, but never as a substitute for those policies.

Counter-cyclical prudential regulation

The impact of financial crises on financial institutions is the result of both excessive risk-taking during booms—as reflected, in particular, in the rapid increase in lending—and the maturity and currency mismatches that characterize balance sheets in developing countries. Inadequate risk analysis by financial agents and weak prudential regulation and supervision of domestic financial systems exacerbate these problems. Since the Asian crisis, the principle that the development of adequate prudential regulation and supervision should precede financial liberalization has been generally accepted. Nonetheless, experience shows that even well-regulated financial systems in industrial countries are subject to periodic episodes of euphoria in which risks are underestimated. The recent crisis in Argentina is a specific case in which a system of prudential regulations considered to be one of the best in the developing world—and working within the framework of a financial sector characterized by the large-scale presence of multinational banks—clearly failed to avert the effects of major macroeconomic shocks on the domestic financial system.

One of the major problems in ensuring financial stability seems to be the focus of prudential regulation on microeconomic risks, while the traditional tendency to underestimate risks has a clear *macroeconomic* origin. The basic problem in this regard is the inability of individual financial intermediaries to internalize the collective risks assumed during boom periods. In terms of the terminology used in portfolio risk management, whereas microeconomic risk management can reduce non-systematic risks (those that depend on individual characteristics of each borrower) through diversification, they cannot reduce systematic risks (those associated with common factors that market agents face, such as economic policy and the business cycle).

Furthermore, traditional regulatory tools, including both original Basel Accord and the Revised Basel II Framework, have a pro-cyclical bias (see BIS, 2001,ch. VII; Borio, Furfine and Lowe, 2001). The basic problem in this regard is the highly pro-cyclical nature of a system in which loan-loss provisions are tied to loan delinquency or to short-term expectations of future loan losses. Under this system, the precautionary signals may be ineffective in hampering excessive risk-taking during booms, when expectations of loan losses are low. On the other hand, the sharp increase in loan delinquency during crises reduces financial institutions' capital and, hence, their lending capacity, possibly triggering a "credit squeeze"; this reinforces the downswing in economic activity and asset prices and, thus, the quality of the portfolios of financial intermediaries. Since credit ratings are also pro-cyclical, basing risk on such ratings, as proposed by Basel II, is also a pro-cyclical practice.

Given the central role that all of these processes play in the business cycles of developing countries, the crucial issue is to introduce a countercyclical element into prudential regulation and supervision (Ocampo, 2003a). In this regard, one important approach is the Spanish system of forward-looking provisions, introduced in July 2000 and reformed in January 2005 to make it compliant with international accounting standards. According to this system, provisions are made when loans are disbursed based on the expected ("latent") losses during a full business cycle (Fernández de Lis, Martinez and Saurina, 2001). This system bases provisioning on criteria traditionally used by the insurance industry (where provisions are made when the insurance policy is issued), rather than by the banking industry (where they are made when loans become due).

Under this system, provisions build up during economic expansions and are drawn upon during downturns. They are accumulated in a fund, together with special provisions (traditional provisions for non-performing assets or for borrowers under stress) and recoveries of non-performing assets. The fund can be used to cover loan losses, thus in effect entirely substituting for special provisions if resources are available in adequate amounts. Although the accumulation and drawing down of the fund has a countercyclical dynamic, this only reflects the cyclical pattern of bank lending. Thus, the system is, strictly speaking, "cycle-neutral", rather than countercyclical, but it is certainly superior to the traditional pro-cyclical provisioning for loan losses.

Such a system could be complemented by strictly countercyclical prudential provisions, which can be decreed by the regulatory authority for the financial system as a whole or for some sectors or economic agents, or by the supervisory authority for special financial institutions on the basis of the excessive growth of credit (relative to some benchmark), the bias in lending to sectors characterized by systematic risks and the growth of foreign-currency denominated loans to non-tradable sectors.

A system of provisions would be superior to the manipulation of capital adequacy ratios to manage the effects of business cycles. Capital adequacy requirements should be reserved for ensuring long-term solvency; no convincing case exists for capital adequacy requirements to be countercyclical.

Ensuring a more precise measurement of risk in bank portfolios should also be incorporated in international accounting standards. Indeed, existing standards give no room for concepts such as the "latent risks" in bank portfolios, on which the Spanish system is based. However, the principle of "fair value" that is at the centre of international accounting standards is violated in the evaluation of bank portfolios during both booms and crises, leading to an overestimation of their value during periods of euphoria and underestimation during phases of excessive pessimism. What is essential in this regard is to recognize that, although individual assets cannot be evaluated as to their "latent risks", this is possible for portfolios, based on appropriate statistical evaluation of average risk. The principle of transparency, which is also essential to appropriate accounting standards, should obviously be respected. The advantage of the Spanish system is precisely the transparency of the provisioning system used. For the same reasons, fiscal authorities should be urged to accept as an appropriate cost the provisions made in such transparent manner.

In developing countries these provisions should be supplemented by more specific regulations aimed at controlling currency and maturity mismatches (including those associated with derivative operations), and at avoiding the overvaluation of collateral generated by asset price bubbles. The strict prohibition of currency mismatches in the portfolios of financial intermediaries is the best rule in the first of these cases, but authorities should also closely monitor the currency risk of non-financial firms operating in non-tradable sectors, which may eventually become credit risks for banks. Regulations can be used to establish higher provisions and/or risk weighting for these operations, or a strict prohibition on lending in foreign currencies to non-financial firms without revenues in those currencies.

Moreover, many regulatory practices aimed at correcting risky practices on the part of financial intermediaries shift the underlying risks to non-financial agents, rather than eliminate them. This may generate indirect credit risks. Thus, for example, lower risk ratings for short-term credit and strong liquidity requirements reduce direct banking risks, but they also reinforce the short-term bias in lending. Maturity mismatches are thus transferred to non-financial agents and may result in reduced fixed capital investment. Also, prudential regulations forbidding banks from holding currency mismatches in their portfolios may encourage non-financial agents to borrow directly from abroad. The risks assumed by corporations operating in non-tradable sectors will eventually be translated into the credit risk of domestic financial institutions that are also their creditors. In all these cases, therefore, the reduced direct vulnerability of the domestic financial sector will have, as a corollary, the maturity and currency mismatches of non-financial agents. This is why prudential capital account regulations aimed at avoiding inadequate maturity structure of borrowing in external markets by all domestic agents, and at avoiding currency mismatches in the portfolios of those agents operating in non-tradable sectors, may be the best available option (Ocampo, 2003a).

The evaluation of the vulnerability of domestic financial system and the development of strong regulatory and supervisory frameworks have become essential elements of the financial sector assessments undertaken jointly by the IMF and the World Bank in recent years. It is essential that the macroeconomic dimensions of prudential regulation and supervision be routinely incorporated in such assessments and advice. They should be also mainstreamed into Basel banking, and into international accounting, standards. And, as long as there is no international lender of last resort, international rules should continue to provide room for the use of capital account regulation by developing countries. This implies, in turn, that capital account convertibility should not be incorporated into the Articles of Agreement of the IMF.

Basel II and developing countries

The right regulatory and supervisory regime is essential for maintaining domestic financial stability. In a globalized economy, some common standards of regulation and supervision may be also essential to guarantee global financial stability and to avoid regulatory arbitrage by international banks and other financial agents. This has been the major motivation behind the principles adopted by the Basel Committee on Banking Supervision in recent decades. The second generation of these standards (Basel II), agreed to in June 2004 and updated in November 2005, takes a further step in aligning regulatory capital with the risks in banks lending, and in adapting regulations to the complexities of risk management in the contemporary world. Also, the standardized approach contains several positive features from the perspective of developing countries, such as the reduction of the excessive incentive to short-term lending, which existed in Basel I.

However, when judged from the perspective of some of the main market failures that should be addressed by banking regulation, the new regime has a number of problems: it is complex where it should be simple; it is implicitly pro-cyclical when it should be explicitly counter-cyclical; and although it is supposed to align regulatory capital more accurately to the risks that banks face, in the case of lending to developing countries it ignores the proved benefits of diversification.

There are thus fears that the implementation of Basel II will create the risk of a sharp reduction in bank lending to developing countries and of an increase in the cost of a significant part of the remaining lending, particularly in the case of low-rated borrowing countries, which also have limited or costly access to international bond markets. This is contrary to the stated objective of G-10 Governments, which is to encourage private flows to developing countries, and use them as an engine for stimulating and funding growth. An equal cause for concern is the danger that Basel II will accentuate the pro-cyclicality of bank lending, which is damaging for all economies, but particularly so for fragile developing ones, which are more vulnerable to strong cyclical fluctuations of financing.

Indeed, the proposed internal ratings-based (IRB) approach of Basel II overestimates the risk of international bank lending to developing countries, primarily because it does not appropriately reflect the clear benefits of international diversification. One consequence of the adoption of this approach by internationally active banks would be that capital requirements for higher-rated borrowers will fall, while those for lower-rated borrowers will rise. This is likely to lead to an excessive increase in regulatory capital requirements and, to the extent that regulatory capital requirements feed through into the pricing of loans, will cause the pricing of loans to lower-rated borrowers—those concentrated in developing countries and particularly the lower-rated borrowing countries—to rise significantly. It has been argued that this is acceptable, since it merely reflects a more accurate assessment of the risks. However, there is a great deal of evidence that by failing to take account of the benefits of international diversification at the portfolio level, capital requirements for loans to developing countries will be significantly higher than is justified on the basis of the actual risks attached to this lending (see, for example, Griffith-Jones, Segoviano and Spratt, 2004).

Therefore, one clear way in which Basel II could be improved so as to reduce the negative and technically inappropriate effects on developing countries would be to formally recognize the benefits of diversification in the internal-ratings based approach. One of the major benefits of investing in developing and emerging economies is their relatively low correlation with mature markets. This hypothesis has been tested empirically using a wide variety of financial, market and macro variables (Griffith-Jones, Segoviano and Spratt, 2003). Every statistical test performed, regardless of variable, time period or frequency, showed that the correlation between developed markets only was higher, in every case, than that between developed and developing markets. Different simulations that compared estimated unexpected losses of portfolios that were diversified across both developed and developing countries with the losses of portfolios in developed countries only, show that the former were from 19 to 23 per cent lower.

The evidence clearly supports the hypothesis that a bank's loan portfolio that was diversified between developed and developing-country borrowers would benefit in terms of lower overall portfolio risk relative to one that focused exclusively on lending to developed countries. Therefore, if risks are measured precisely, this should be reflected in lower capital requirements. Indeed, the Chair of the Basel Committee on Banking Supervision, Jaime Caruana, acknowledged in July 2004, in his speech to the Annual Conference of Latin American Regulators (ASBA), held in Mexico City, that "geographical diversification effects clearly occur" (Caruana, 2004). Others have commented on failure of the New Basel Capital Accord (Basel II) to take account of diversification effects as being its major flaw. For example, the Governor of the Mexican Central Bank suggested in July 2004 that "any postponement of incorporating the benefits of diversification runs the risk of discouraging large international banks from maintaining and expanding their loans to emerging markets". He also expressed his serious concern about the negative effects that the new Accord could have on volatility of capital flows to emerging economies (Ortiz, 2004). These concerns have also been expressed by several senior private bankers.

An additional positive effect of taking account of the benefits of diversification is that this makes capital requirements far less pro-cyclical than they otherwise would be. Indeed, if the benefits of diversification are incorporated, simulations show that the variance over time of capital requirements will be significantly smaller than if these benefits are not incorporated. Therefore, introducing the benefits of geographical diversification significantly decreases, though it does not eliminate, the higher pro-cyclicality that the internal-ratings based approach implies. This difference may well be significant enough to prevent a "credit crunch".

This lower pro-cyclicality of capital over time of an internal-ratings based approach that incorporates the benefits of diversification (the Full Credit Risk Model (ICRM)) compared with an internal-ratings based approach that does not incorporate those benefits can be seen in figure I.1. However, even if the benefits of diversification are incorporated, the internal-ratings based approach will still be more pro-cyclical than the standardized approach, which is closer to the principles of the first Basel Capital Accord (Basel I) (see, again figure I.1). Therefore, as well as introducing the benefits of diversification, it seems desirable to introduce counter-cyclical measures (for example, counter-cyclical provisioning against losses) at the same time as Basel II is actually implemented in 2007.

Introducing the benefits of diversification soon would therefore: (a) clearly lead to a more precise measurement of risk, the main aim of Basel II; (b) appropriately reduce the excessive and inappropriate increase in cost of lending to developing countries, caused by the current lack of precision in measuring risk; and (c) diminish pro-cyclicality in the capital requirement, which will imply incentives for both greater stability in bank lending and greater stability of the whole banking system. Such changes should be introduced before countries reach the implementation stage.

Figure I.1.
CAPITAL REQUIREMENTS FOR USA
USING THREE REGULATORY REGIMES

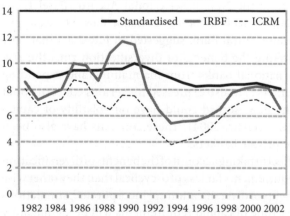

Source: Simulations based on a data set of Moody's available for United States banks for the period 1982-2003 (Griffith-Jones, Segoviano and Spratt, 2004)

Some of the problems in the New Basel Capital Accord may be linked to the fact that developing countries are not at all represented in the Basel Committee on Banking Supervision (see chap. IV for a discussion of the urgent need for developing countries to participate in the Basel Committee).

A GREATER CHALLENGE: ENCOURAGING PRIVATE FLOWS TO LOWER-INCOME DEVELOPING COUNTRIES

One of the pervasive features of poor countries is a low per capita income associated with sub-standard consumption levels and the vulnerability of a large part of their population. The human asset index for these countries, which measures nutrition, education and health status, is significantly below the average of developing countries (United Nations, 2003a). Table I.4 lists 57 low-income developing countries for which information is available. The concentration of countries in the lower left bottom of the table indicates not only that these countries are poor but that their population—and hence their economic size—is generally quite small.[5] In fact, of the 57 countries, 63 per cent have a gross national income (GNI) below US$ 3.25 billion. Most of these countries are in Africa.

By and large, the factors that determine private flows—FDI and financial flows—to this group are the same as in middle-income developing countries. Economic size is also an important determinant in FDI and private financial flows. Not only does economic size allow firms to take advantage of economies of scale in production for the domestic market but large markets tend to ease the domestic supply of inputs: available labour with diverse skills and intermediate goods and services, particularly services with large non-tradable components that cannot therefore be imported from abroad.

The countries in this group tend to face greater challenges in attracting foreign resources to spur long-term growth. A number of them are post-conflict countries, in many of them the natural resources base is scanty, they are generally more vulnerable to changing climate conditions and fluctuations in primary commodity prices,[6] their skilled labour is scarce and their infrastructure is limited. Very few of them have experienced sustained growth for a significant number of years. Their credit-rating indicators signal a comparatively high risk (World Bank, 2004d). In fact, they receive a very small share of private financial flows going to developing countries and only 5 per cent of FDI, most of which goes to a few oil-exporting countries.[7]

The above suggests that increasing private flows to these countries requires special efforts at the national and the international level, particularly when the

Table I.4.
DISTRIBUTION OF LEAST DEVELOPED COUNTRIES AND OTHER LOW
INCOME COUNTRIES BY POPULATION AND ECONOMIC SIZE, 2002[a]

Population				
Up to 40 Million		Ethiopia Nepal Uganda	Myanmar Afghanistan	Bangladesh Nigeria
			Democratic People's Republic of Korea Kenya Tanzania	
Up to 20 Million	Burkina Faso Malawi Mali Niger	Cambodia Madagascar Mozambique Zambia	Angola Côte d'Ivoire Sudan Yemen	
Up to 10 Million	Benin Burundi Chad Lao PDR Rwanda Somalia Tajikistan	Democratic Republic of the Congo Guinea Haiti Senegal		
Up to 5 Million	Central African Republic Congo Eritrea Liberia Mauritania Mongolia Sierra Leone Togo			
Up to 2.5 Million	Bhutan Cape Verde Comoros Djibouti Equatorial Guinea Guinea-Bissau Kiribati Lesotho Maldives Samoa Sao Tome and Principe Solomon Islands The Gambia Timor-Leste Tuvalu Vanuatu			
GNI billion U.S. dollars	**Up to 3.25**	**Up to 7.50**	**Up to 15.00**	

Source: United Nations DESA

a   It includes all least developed countries and those countries whose per capita gross national income (GNI) measured in dollars at current exchange rates was below 735 US dollars in 2002 except those countries whose per capita GNI measured in purchasing power parity was above 2.5 times that figure and those whose Human Asset Index was above 70.

type of flows needed help spur long-term development. Policies that enhance the domestic environment are necessary. It will take time before substantial flows materialize—unless there is a significant potential in exploitation of natural resources, particularly oil. In the meantime, international financial cooperation—official flows and technical assistance—can facilitate the transformations required.

In each country, it is the national development strategy that should define the type of external flows to be encouraged as well as the sectors where such flows could be channelled. One key aspect of FDI is the impact on the rest of the economy: diverse types of FDI can have very different externalities and their diffusion to the rest of the economy can be large or virtually nil (see above). ODA-financed programmes can be catalytic in encouraging private flows. Renewed, more targeted work of the International Finance Corporation of the World Bank and similar organs of the regional and subregional development banks could lead to the mobilization of additional private resources from sources in developed and developing countries.

Since the Asian crisis, two issues—although not new—have focused the attention of many private players: risk mitigation and improved information flows for potential investors (United Nations, 2004d). In poor countries, market instruments to mitigate risks (for example, exchange-rate futures markets) are often unavailable. The various bilateral and multilateral instruments that have been developed to deal with risk mitigation for private investments in developing countries (insurance and guarantee schemes) rarely benefit the countries in the group considered here, since most schemes adhere to rather strict commercially-based criteria. It would be useful to undertake an evaluation of existing schemes, in particular their actual impact on different groups of target countries.[8]

Donors could also consider providing targeted funding with additional resources to multilateral agencies (such as the Multilateral Investment Guarantee Agency (MIGA) and the political risk insurance facilities being opened up in regional banks) and bilateral agencies to cover political and other non-commercial risk at a lower cost in these countries.[9] Also, a new facility could be set up in the form of a separate fund owned by international financial institutions specifically for these countries to address both the entry cost and post-entry risk barriers for investors. This fund would assist private investments by offering domestic currency loans, and quasi-equity investment capital and guarantees—and by retailing a simplified form of MIGA cover for political risk. Another avenue is to create more effective regional risk cover capacity by an effective decentralization of MIGA operations or by creating regional multilateral political risk insurance agencies affiliated with the regional development banks (United Nations Conference on Trade and Development, 2003b, p. 162).

In the case of infrastructure projects, which increasingly include operations by the initial investor once the investment project is complete, exchange rate and regulatory risks are perceived by foreign investors as among the most important. Several modalities have been developed or proposed to deal with these risks, some of which are applicable to these countries, for example the establishment of credit enhancement arrangements by donors and multilateral development institutions for mobilizing available domestic funding to reduce currency risk. More generally, foreign assistance could help in deepening the domestic financial sector. Its further development would facilitate risk management.

In a rapidly changing world economy and with institutional adaptations occurring in many countries, investment opportunities and risks are not always evident for foreign investors. Often, access to credible and transparent information—including on the intricacies of the foreign investment law and bilateral investment treaties and the progress achieved in macroeconomic management and structural policies—is lacking. Reliable, relevant information on country business environments and opportunities is key to private investments decisions. It might also mitigate risks. Government has a role to play in providing such information. One avenue that has proved useful is public/private collaboration to increase the quality and quantity of information. Yet, most of the countries in this group need special assistance— multilateral and bilateral, including from other developing countries—in this regard. Open web-based information portals have become a highly cost-effective vehicle for the dissemination of information.

One important source of information for prospective investors is the perceptions of within-country domestic and foreign entrepreneurs regarding the investment climate. Work in this area has expanded considerably through private firms, business associations such as the World Economic Forum, and international institutions, particularly the World Bank. Most of this work is focused in middle-income developing countries. Special efforts will be required to expand this kind of information to the countries considered here.

Additionally, as seen in table I.4, the large majority of these countries are small. Thus, special attention should be paid in the national development strategy to the links between investment, in particular foreign investment, and exports. No small-sized economy has been able to grow on a sustained basis without a dynamic export sector. For all small-sized economies, economies of scale are a fundamental consideration if a reasonable degree of efficiency is to be achieved. The minimum size of operations needed for the production of many goods or services with a reasonable degree of efficiency can be large.

Developed countries' preferences for least developed countries have opened important investment opportunities. Regional integration among countries can also spur exports and attract foreign investments. The Southern African Development Community (SADC) has facilitated larger FDI flows from the comparatively larger economies (for example, South Africa) to less developed members. Regional integration can also give impulse to regional stock markets and joint infrastructure projects, which might attract additional private external flows (Economic Commission for Africa, 2004, pp. 141-142).

NOTES

1   The literature also indicates that, in the case of developing countries that have been able to issue such liabilities, they are largely used as coverage by foreign investors in those countries. This implies that, even in those countries, there is no net demand by foreign residents for assets denominated in the domestic currency.

2   The net financial transfer of resources statistic adds receipts of foreign investment income and financial inflows from abroad, but subtracts payments of foreign investment income and financial outflows, including increases in foreign reserve holdings. The net financial transfer of a country is thus the financial counterpart of the balance of trade in goods and services. A trade surplus is generated when the total value of domestic production exceeds domestic consumption and investment, with the excess invested abroad instead of being used domestically, and vice versa for a trade deficit.

3   It should be recalled in this regard that domestic contents and export requirements were used widely in the past for this purpose, but were severely limited by the World Trade Organization rules on trade-related investment measures.

4   The use of the ringgit was restricted to domestic transactions by residents. It became illegal to hold ringgit deposits abroad, and all such deposits held by nationals had to be repatriated. Trade transactions had to be settled in foreign currency. Ringgit deposits in the domestic financial system held by non-residents were not convertible into foreign currency for one year.

5   One fourth of these countries have a population below 2.5 million and half of them below 5 million.

6   Their economic vulnerability index is well above the average of developing countries (see United Nations, 2003a).

7   Most of the comparatively small amount of FDI in these 57 countries goes to only 5 oil producers: Angola, Chad, Equatorial Guinea, Nigeria and the Sudan.

8   As of recently, some donor countries (for example, Norway and the United States) have refocused their efforts to reach lower-income countries.

9   Many of these countries are parties to the Cotonou Agreement which offers support for investment and private sector development including a reinsurance scheme to cover FDI. Also, some of these countries can benefit from the activities of the Inter-Arab Investment Guarantee Corporation which offers an intraregional insurance scheme.

Chapter II
Official Development Financing

The architects of the post-war international economic system recognized the need for official financing to counteract the insufficiency of private capital flows and, since the 1960s, there was an increasing perception of the need to support developing countries, an issue that became embedded in the politics of decolonization and the cold war. The surge of private financial flows to developing countries beginning in the 1970s and the end of the cold war generated in some circles the view that the era of official development financing had passed. However, the vagaries of private capital flows during the 1980s and, again, since the 1997 Asian crisis, in addition to the increasing marginalization of the poorest countries from the world economy, have led to a renewed focus on the critical role of official development finance. The International Conference on Financing for Development was a landmark in this process. The present chapter explores the issues involved. It looks first at official development assistance (ODA), then at the multilateral development banks and South-South cooperation, and lastly at an array of alternatives grouped under the heading of "innovative sources of financing".

OFFICIAL DEVELOPMENT ASSISTANCE

The origins and weakening of the commitment to ODA

The transfer of resources from developed to developing countries has been at the centre of policies to promote development since the 1950s. In its resolution 400 (V) of 20 November 1950, the United Nations General Assembly had noted that the domestic financial resources of the underdeveloped countries, together with the international flow of capital for investment, had not been sufficient to assure the desired rate of economic development, and that the accelerated economic development of underdeveloped countries required a more effective and sustained mobilization of domestic savings and an expanded and more stable flow of foreign capital investment. Two years later, the General Assembly, in its resolution 520 A (VI) of 12 January 1952, called on the Economic and Social Council to draw up plans for a special capital fund to provide grants-in-aid and low-interest long-term loans to underdeveloped countries; and its resolution 823 (IX) of 11 December 1954 requested the International Bank for Reconstruction and Development (IBRD) to proceed with the creation of the International Finance Corporation (IFC).

To generate additional aid to that provided within the United Nations system and its specialized agencies, in 1958, the World Council of Churches proposed that developed countries dedicate 1 per cent of their gross domestic product (GDP) as aid for developing countries in the form of grants and concessional loans. This figure was incorporated in the objectives of the First United Nations Development Decade and reconfirmed at the first session of the United Nations Conference on Trade and Development (UNCTAD), held in Geneva in 1964. UNCTAD at its second session, held in New Delhi in 1968, set a target of three quarters of 1 per cent of external flows for ODA. Analysis of the external financial flows required to meet the Second United Nations Development Decade growth goal of at least 6 per cent per annum by the head of the Committee for Development Planning produced an estimate of 1 per cent of developed-country GDP. Since it was expected that private flows could provide only about 0.3 per cent, it was understood that the remaining sums would have to be met by official flows (Emmerij, Jolly and Weiss, 2001, pp. 55-57).

Already at its eighteenth session in 1963, the General Assembly had noted the slow progress in meeting this objective and by the twenty-first session in 1966 noted with concern the trend towards an increased outflow of capital from developing countries (Assembly resolution 2169 (XXI) of 6 December 1966) and noted with deep concern the fact that, with a few exceptions, the transfer of external resources to the developing countries had not only failed to reach the minimum target of 1 per cent net of individual national income of the developed countries but that the trend since 1961 had been one of continuous decline (Assembly resolution 2170 (XXI) of 6 December 1966). In the mid-term assessment of the Second United Nations Development Decade, the Assembly noted that the performance of countries members of the Development Assistance Committee of the Organization for Economic Cooperation and Development (OECD/DAC) in meeting the ODA target had been even less satisfactory as a whole. The ratio of ODA to their combined gross national product (GNP) had declined from 0.53 per cent during the early 1960s to about 0.39 per cent during the period 1966-1969 and to 0.32 per cent during the period 1970-1973. The poor performance of most of the developed market economy countries with regard to the target of 0.7 per cent of gross national income (GNI) for ODA was due, inter alia, to a lack of political will to reach that target by the middle of the decade (Assembly resolution 3517 (XXX) of 15 December 1975, annex, para. 26).

Concern that external flows to developing countries would decline further in a system of flexible exchange rates led to a recommendation in 1974 by the Committee of Twenty on reform of the international monetary and financial system to propose the creation of a Joint Ministerial Committee of the Boards of Governors of the IBRD and the International Monetary Fund on the Transfer of Real Resources to Developing Countries to study and recommend measures on the broad question of the transfer of real resources to developing countries, which the Committee agreed should be given encouragement.[1] The expectation of a decline in aid was confirmed as ODA for 1982-1983 had averaged 0.35 per cent but further fell to a historic low of 0.21 per cent of developed-country GNI at the beginning of the new millennium.

The resurgence of ODA

As a result of this historic declining trend, the Monterrey Consensus of the International Conference on Financing for Development (United Nations, 2002b, annex) sought to restore the central role of ODA, in particular in supporting the poorest countries, and thus reaffirmed the 0.7 per cent target. During and after the Monterrey Conference, many member countries of the OECD/DAC raised their ODA contributions, and many pledged to meet fixed target dates for reaching the 0.7 per cent goal.

As a result of the Monterrey commitments, the decline in the share of ODA in developed-country GNI was reversed, rising to 0.25 per cent in 2003 and 0.26 per cent in 2004. Preliminary estimates for 2005 show an increase to $106.5 billion representing 0.33 per cent of DAC donors GNI. However, this figure includes over $20 billion of one-time items such as debt relief to Iraq and Nigeria, and Tsunami emergency relief. However, if all current commitments are met by the target date ODA is projected to reach $130 billion in 2010. In 2002 and 2003 over half of the increase in nominal ODA was destined for sub-Saharan Africa (OECD, 2006). Half of the committed increase of aid up to 2010 is also expected to be channeled to that continent.

Despite the positive trend since 2002, the current and projected levels of ODA for 2006-2010 still fall far short of the various estimates (United Nations, 2004b; UN Millennium Project, 2005; Commission for Africa, 2005) of about $150 billion deemed necessary for the developing countries to attain the Millennium Development Goals (World Bank and International Monetary Fund, 2005). Furthermore, as can be seen from figure II.1, when corrected

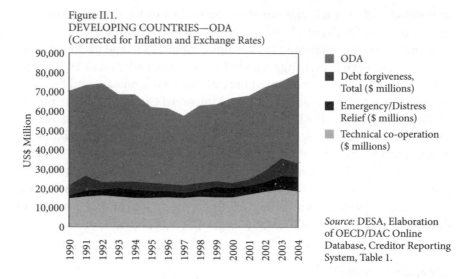

Figure II.1.
DEVELOPING COUNTRIES—ODA
(Corrected for Inflation and Exchange Rates)

Legend:
- ODA
- Debt forgiveness, Total ($ millions)
- Emergency/Distress Relief ($ millions)
- Technical co-operation ($ millions)

Source: DESA, Elaboration of OECD/DAC Online Database, Creditor Reporting System, Table 1.

for price and exchange-rate changes, the recent reversal of the decline in aid flows has barely brought real assistance back to the levels of 1990.

The European Union (EU) and its member States continue to be the largest source of aid, providing more than half of total ODA. Denmark, Luxembourg, the Netherlands, Norway and Sweden already meet or exceed the 0.7 per cent target of their national incomes dedicated to official assistance. In mid-2005, all member States of EU undertook to achieve or maintain the 0.7 per cent ODA/GNI target by 2015 and some have set earlier target dates. Those member States which joined EU after 2002 will strive to increase or maintain an ODA/GNI ratio of 0.33 per cent. The Secretary-General of the United Nations has urged that other developed countries establish fixed timetables for achieving the 0.7 per cent target of GNI for ODA by 2015 at the latest.

ODA and the Millennium Development Goals

As noted above, the original objective of the United Nations' official assistance target was to generate increased external resources in the form of grants and concessional loans to be used to supplement domestic resources so that countries could finance the aggregate growth targets in the United Nations Development Decades. Although developing countries succeeded in meeting the modest growth objectives of the First and Second United Nations Development Decades, in the 1980s growth performance in many developing countries weakened and ODA declined.

The United Nations Millennium Declaration (United Nations, 2000) marked a sharp change in approach to the United Nations' development goals from those subscribed to in the four United Nations Development Decades. The increasing evidence that the growth and aid targets were not being met, and the continued increase in disparity in the distribution of the benefits of growth in a globalizing international economic system, led to the specification of much more precise targets represented by the Millennium Development Goals. The idea was to set measurable targets that would provide visible improvements in the living conditions of the poorest within a precise time frame.

As the UN Millennium Project report (UN Millennium Project, 2005) makes clear, meeting the Millennium Development Goals will require specific amounts of funding over specific time periods. The composition of ODA must thus be adapted to provide the finance for the specific expenditures needed to achieve the Millennium Development Goals. Figure II.1 shows that over the 1990s, the shares of debt relief, emergency aid and technical assistance in total aid flows were increasing. While these flows have important objectives, emergency aid is not designed to assist long-term development, and debt relief does not generally provide fresh money to debtor countries. Technical cooperation, in turn, provides a variety of inputs towards development results but its impact in closing financial gaps is hard to gauge.[2] Consequently, despite the recent recovery in recorded donor contributions, ODA has been a declining source of budgetary resources for the developing countries, limiting their efforts to pursue the Millennium Development Goals. The call to increase ODA must thus be qualified to refer to increased resources available to fund government budget allocations for programmes designed to support the Millennium Development Goals.

Moreover, not only does ODA have to increase substantially in order for the developing countries to have a better chance of achieving the Millennium Development Goals, it is essential that ODA be directed to the poorest and least developed among the developing countries. With the adoption of the Programme of Action for the Least Developed Countries for the 1990s by the Second United Nations Conference on the Least Developed Countries in Paris in September 1990 (United Nations, 1991), developed countries had agreed that, within their 0.7 per cent overall ODA target, they would provide at least 0.15-0.20 per cent of their GNI to assist the least developed countries. A few individual donors met this target but aggregate ODA flows to the least developed countries declined to about half the target during the 1990s. The reversal in trend since Monterrey has been more positive: ODA to least developed countries has increased sharply in recent years. However, a careful look at the composition indicates that the amount of aid, measured in real terms, for least developed countries in 2004 after exclusion of the emergency, debt relief and reconstruction components, was lower in real terms than the figure for 1990 (see figure II.2). While it was assumed by many that debt relief granted under the HIPC initiative would be additional to official assistance flows, the amount of aid received by these countries in real terms, excluding debt relief and emergency assistance has declined by nearly fifty per cent during the life of the programme. (see figure II.3).

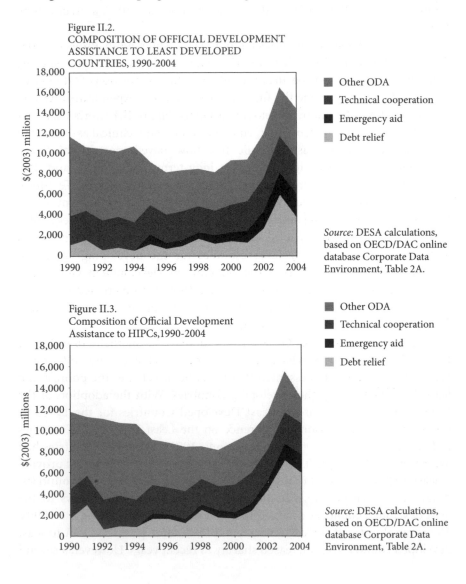

Figure II.2.
COMPOSITION OF OFFICIAL DEVELOPMENT ASSISTANCE TO LEAST DEVELOPED COUNTRIES, 1990-2004

■ Other ODA
■ Technical cooperation
■ Emergency aid
▨ Debt relief

Source: DESA calculations, based on OECD/DAC online database Corporate Data Environment, Table 2A.

Figure II.3.
Composition of Official Development Assistance to HIPCs,1990-2004

■ Other ODA
■ Technical cooperation
■ Emergency aid
▨ Debt relief

Source: DESA calculations, based on OECD/DAC online database Corporate Data Environment, Table 2A.

Volatility and conditionality of aid flows

There are a number of other factors that must be considered in order to determine the real impact of aid in achieving the Millennium Development Goals. Since meeting the Millennium Development Goals will require sustained investment, the predictability of aid flows over time is a precondition for their effective use. However, aid flows tend to rise and fall with economic cycles in donor countries, with policy assessments of the recipient countries, and with a shift in donor policies. This uncertainty has a negative impact on public investment and thus on growth, as well as on the conduct of monetary and fiscal policy. Empirical work suggests that the volatility of aid flows exceeds that of other macroeconomic variables, such as GDP or fiscal revenue. Aid is significantly more volatile than fiscal revenue, and on average tends to be procyclical (Gemmell and McGillivray, 1998). When aid falls, it leads to costly fiscal adjustments in the form of increased taxation and spending cuts that reinforce the cyclical impact of declining aid flows (Pallage and Robe, 2001; Bulír and Hamann, 2003; 2005). In this respect, the volatility of aid flows has a similar impact to volatility of commodity prices in countries that are dependent upon the exports of a single commodity. Indeed, countries receiving aid flows seem to be no better off than emerging market economies receiving private flows for, as shown in table II.1, the volatility of both types of flows as measured by their standard deviation relative to the mean value is very similar.

Surges in donor flows can also cause macroeconomic problems. In small countries these problems are compounded by low absorptive capacity and the presence of a small and often underdeveloped financial sector. Deeper financial markets in aid-recipient countries have been shown to be associated with more efficient management of aid flows, and to enhance the impact of ODA on growth. They have a positive direct impact on private investment in recipient countries, and diminish negative indirect effects resulting from the impact of ODA on domestic prices, interest rates and the exchange rate (Nkusu and Sayek, 2004). Surges in donor flows may produce exchange-rate appreciation and, if sustained over a length of time, the kind of overvaluation phenomenon known as the "Dutch disease". Attempts to sterilize the monetary effects of foreign exchange inflows can be costly. Increased donor flows may be accompanied by negative private flows or excess reserve accumulation. As a result, the beneficial impact of the aid inflows on growth and poverty reduction may be offset or even reversed.

The observed volatility of ODA flows results from more than the year-on-year variability created by donor government budget cycles. There is often a

Table II.1.
VOLATILITY OF FINANCIAL FLOWS AND BILATERAL
DAC ODA, TOP 10 RECIPIENTS, 1999-2003

Top 10 emerging market countries (Weighted GDP volume)	Financial flows (Standard deviation/mean)
Brazil	0.35
China	0.77
Hong Kong, SAR[a]	0.34
Korea, Republic of	0.08
Malaysia	0.11
Mexico	0.18
Poland	0.24
Singapore	0.41
Thailand	0.42
Turkey	0.52
Average	0.34
Top 10 net bilateral DAC ODA receipients[b]	Net bilateral ODA (Standard deviation/mean)
Bangladesh	0.12
China	0.35
Egypt	0.22
India	0.32
Indonesia	0.28
Mozambique	0.46
Pakistan	0.43
Serbia and Montenegro	0.55
United Republic of Tanzania	0.11
Viet Nam	0.27
Average	0.31

Sources: DESA calculations on OECD/DAC database; and World Bank, *Global Development Finance 2005* (Washington, D.C., 2005).

a   Special Administrative Region of China.
b   Excluding the Democratic Republic of the Congo.

large gap between budgeted aid commitments and their actual disbursement in the recipient country. Figure II.4 shows the divergence between commitments and disbursements for programme and project aid.[3] Further, the actual disbursement of aid, as distinct from its budgetary commitment, tends to be concentrated in periods of high domestic revenue and output. Not only are ODA flows more volatile than either fiscal revenue or GDP, but their relative volatility increases with the degree of aid dependency. It has

Figure II.4.
COMMITMENTS AND DISBURSEMENTS OF
PROGRAMME AND PROJECT AID, 1995-2004

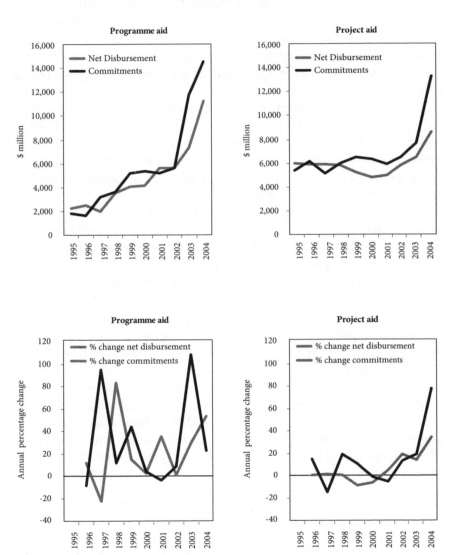

Source: DESA calculations, based on OECD/DAC online database, table 1.

also been found that countries that suffer from high revenue volatility are also countries with higher aid volatility, suggesting that aid tends to enhance budgetary and overall economic instability (Bulír and Hamann, 2001). Donors have to consider how to reduce these patterns to enable recipient countries to plan their fiscal arrangements in the context of a longer-term fiscal policy framework. The erratic behaviour of both budgeted flows and aid disbursement needs to be stabilized if aid is to finance a sustained path of growth and poverty reduction.

Aid conditionality is another source of volatility. This is due not only to the types of specific conditions required by donors, but also to the frequent requirement that aid recipients have the seal of approval of successful performance in an ongoing International Monetary Fund (IMF) programme. When performance falls short of requirements, the negative impact is intensified by the withdrawal of aid flows by donors.

The now conventional view is that conditionality is an ineffective or at least an inefficient means to attain objectives that donors wish to attach to financial support of partner countries. So long as there is no true "ownership" of the policies involved by partner countries—that is to say, so long as they are not backed by strong domestic support—they are unlikely to be sustained. This is primarily the result of the fact that ownership is essential to the institution-building that is now generally recognized as the key to successful development policies. Some authors (Morrissey, 2001) have suggested that donors should support policy processes rather than impose specific policy conditions.

Following this view, some donors have announced radical shifts away from aid conditionality. One of the most significant is the new policy on conditionality was launched by the United Kingdom in early March 2005 that will eliminate aid conditional on specific policies, including in sensitive areas like privatization and trade liberalization. Conditionality is to be limited to fiduciary concerns only and to ensuring that aid is not diverted for purposes other than those intended.

Selectivity of aid flows

Official aid from bilateral donors has tended to be concentrated in a relatively small number of countries. Figure II.5 shows that, since the 1980s, the top 20 countries have received more than half of net bilateral aid and that fewer than 50 per cent of aid recipients have received 90 per cent of all aid from DAC donors.[4] This suggests that variations in aid allocations are in large part the result of donor selection of aid recipients.

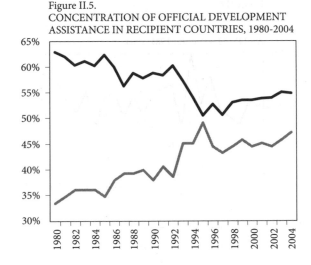

Figure II.5.
CONCENTRATION OF OFFICIAL DEVELOPMENT
ASSISTANCE IN RECIPIENT COUNTRIES, 1980-2004

Share of top 20 recipients in bilateral, net aid flows

Proportion of recipient countries accounting for 90 per cent of aid

Source: DESA calculations based on data from OECD/ DAC on geographical distribution of financial flows to Part I countries (excluding the Democratic Republic of the Congo for 2003).

The evidence of a concentration of aid in a few countries suggests herding behaviour on the part of donors. Donor selectivity would thus compound the impact of volatility. This similarity in country selection by donors may result from the idea that aid efficiency is highest in those countries that have made the most positive reform efforts (see below). As a result, aid flows tend to be concentrated in those countries that are viewed by donors as the most successful. Although selectivity has always been present, its impact seems to have increased since the late 1990s. This is partly due to the signalling mechanism set in motion through the processes associated with the Poverty Reduction Strategy Papers (PRSP) and the Heavily Indebted Poor Countries (HIPC) Initiative.

Herding behaviour among donors can also be detected by means of a measure (denoted LSV) devised by Lakonishok, Shleifer and Vishny (1992) and based on the divergence of actual changes in ODA relative to average behaviour. If all donors follow the average behaviour, the difference between actual and average behaviour is zero, indicating an absence of herding behaviour. A value of LSV greater than 0.1 indicates significant herding. Figure II.6 analyses the behaviour of 10 large and 13 small donor countries and confirms the existence of herding, especially with respect to the behaviour of small donors, with an average of collective deviation of close to 13 per cent.

Bigger and smaller donors tend to move together both when they increase and when they decrease aid. Overall, historical evidence suggests that a developing country may expect to experience a reduction in net nominal bilateral ODA volumes with a probability of about 25 per cent in any given year (see figure II.7).

Figure II.6.
COLLECTIVE DEVIATION OF FLOWS OF
OFFICIAL DEVELOPMENT ASSISTANCE
AMONG DONORS, 1981-2004

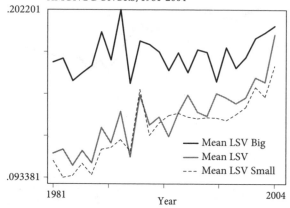

— Mean LSV Big
— Mean LSV
--- Mean LSV Small

Source: DESA calculations based on data from OECD/DAC on geographical distribution of financial flows to Part I countries (excluding the Democratic Republic of the Congo for 2003).

Figure II.7.
PROPORTION OF COUNTRIES EXPERIENCING
A DECLINE IN BILATERAL AID VOLUME,
BY DONOR GROUPING, 1981-2004

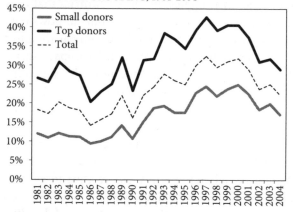

— Small donors
— Top donors
--- Total

Source: DESA calculations based on data from OECD/DAC on geographical distribution of financial flows to Part I countries (excluding the Democratic Republic of the Congo for 2003).

Although the factors that cause co-movement in bilateral selectivity of countries are different compared with the factors that cause herding in private capital markets, the ensuing macroeconomic instability is similar. While many of the discussions on the effectiveness of aid have tended to concentrate on the effects of governance and the domestic policy environment in the recipient countries, the economic costs due to problems in the supply side and limitations to the financial intermediation of donor funds are not insignificant.

Aid effectiveness

The specification of official assistance targets to support the International Development Strategies for the United Nations Development Decades assumed that increased aid would contribute to increasing growth in developing countries. Since the adoption of the United Nations Millennium Declaration, it has been argued that increased aid would allow countries to achieve the Millennium Development Goals. Nonetheless, sustaining the Millennium Development Goals will require a sustained increase in growth. However, the experience with official assistance in promoting economic growth in developing countries is, at best, mixed. The World Bank (1998) is forthright in recognizing that "if foreign aid has at times been a spectacular success ... (it) has also been, at times, an unmitigated failure". This sentence encapsulates the evidence that aid has often had weak effects on growth and poverty reduction.[5] A growing understanding of the factors that constrain the effectiveness of aid has helped identify problems in respect of both the supply of donor funds and the limitations in recipient countries.[6] The challenge for the official donor community, as well as policymakers in developing countries, has thus been to recognize the weaknesses of the earlier approaches in aid delivery and to work towards new frameworks to enhance aid effectiveness.

There are two dominant views on the factors that hinder aid effectiveness in promoting growth and reducing poverty. The first, and more dominant view, is that aid works only when government policies are effective: a more selective allocation of aid to "good policy-high poverty" countries will thus lead to a stronger impact on poverty reductions at the global level. The second view argues that aid effectiveness is not only conditional on domestic policy effectiveness. More selective allocation may generate other problems, including "aid orphans" and deepening crises in countries regarded by the donor community as "aid pariahs".

The first view is based on an influential body of evidence generated by research at the World Bank (e.g. 1998) indicating that policies matter for aid effectiveness. The implications for aid policy are straightforward: allocate more aid to a country with "good" policies. This message has turned out to be fairly influential and recent empirical work (Collier and Dollar, 1999, 2001; Burnside and Dollar, 1997, 2000) appears to support this view. Using the "Country Policy and Institutional Assessment" (CPIA) measure to rank good policy countries, these studies estimate that the impact of growth on poverty reduction across countries is higher for countries with better CPIA scores. If aid allocations between countries are directed to countries where the correlation is highest, this will maximize the number of people lifted out of poverty. The studies suggest that targeting more aid towards countries with high rates of poverty that pursue good policies could double the number of people lifted out of poverty, this being as much as could be achieved by tripling present aid budgets at their current country allocations. The World Bank research has also revealed that the pattern of the actual aid allocations—particularly bilateral aid—has been highly inefficient, being only weakly targeted to poor countries and even more weakly directed to well-managed countries.

Other studies have reached different conclusions. Some of them question the definition and assessment of "good policies" implicit in the CPIA ratings.[7] Some (Beynon, 2003) provide alternative policy interpretations of the World Bank studies,[8] while others (Hansen and Tarp, 2000; and Beynon, 2003) challenge the results on methodological and econometric grounds, in terms, for example, of sensitivity to model specification. They suggest that since aid assists countries in adjusting to external shocks, this may explain why some studies show no significant impact of aid on growth. Another difficulty in measuring the efficiency of aid flows is caused by the fact that aid flows include debt relief and, as suggested above, do not measure the real contribution of financial resources to supporting growth. Furthermore, bilateral flows are often used to clear arrears with multilateral lenders. An analysis that looks at the composition of aid and focuses on assistance that, plausibly, could stimulate growth, including budget and balance-of-payments support, investments in infrastructure, and aid for productive sectors such as agriculture and industry, finds a positive, causal relationship between this type of aid and economic growth (with diminishing returns) over a four-year period. The impact is large: at least two to three times larger than the impact found in studies that consider only aggregate aid. Even at a conservatively high discount rate, a $1 increase in short-impact aid raises output (and income) by $1.64 in present value in a typical country (Clemens, Radelet and Bhavnani, 2004).

Any econometric exercise that measures aid effectiveness should thus be based on data of aid flows that are net of debt relief and aid flows utilized for clearance of arrears. Alternative research suggests that the impact on growth is positive irrespective of the policy environment (Morrissey, 2001) while still other research suggests that a range of other variables are significant such as economic vulnerability (Chauvet and Guillaumont, 2002), external shocks (Collier and Dehn, 2002), recovery from conflict (Collier and Hoeffler, 2002) and geographical factors (Dalgaard and others 2001). Despite these findings, the emphasis on good governance and institutional change continues to dominate the discussion.

Donor efforts to increase aid effectiveness

Developed-country donors have been increasingly concerned with the impact of their aid. Initiatives introduced since the late 1990s to strengthen coordination among donors, improve the design of programmes, and improve domestic policy implementation include the Poverty Reduction and Growth Facility (PRGF) and the HIPC Initiative. However, they do not seem to have decreased the erratic nature of the availability of funds (Bulír and Hamann, 2005). The effectiveness of increased use of aid to provide budgetary support for countries that have embarked on the PRSP and entered the HIPC Initiative has also been affected by the volatility of aid disbursements.

At the Rome High-level Forum on Harmonization held on 24 and 25 February 2003, a plan of action was elaborated to harmonize aid policies, procedures and practices of donors with those of their developing partner countries. At the second High-level Forum on Joint Progress towards Enhanced Aid Effectiveness, held in Paris from 28 February to 2 March 2005, twice as many countries and new donor countries participated, and for the first time civil society representatives and parliamentarians were also involved. Over 100 countries as well as development institutions committed to a practical blueprint to provide aid in more streamlined ways, and to improve accountability by monitoring the blueprint's implementation. The Paris Declaration on Aid Effectiveness set out five major principles of aid effectiveness: (a) ownership of development strategies by partner developing countries; (b) alignment of donor support with those strategies; (c) harmonization of donor actions; (d) managing for results; and (e) mutual accountability of donors and partners. The Declaration also contained some 50 commitments to improve aid quality which were to be monitored by 12 indicators. Subsequently. the OECD Development Assistance Committee Working Party was able to reach agreement on targets for all of the indicators (see Table II.2).

EU announced its own additional set of targets, including reducing the number of uncoordinated missions by 50 per cent, channelling half of government assistance through country assistance, providing all capacity-building through coordinated programmes, resorting more frequently to multi-donor arrangements, and avoiding the establishment of new project implementation units.

An important implication of the evolving new approach to aid, both in terms of its contribution to achieving the Millennium Development Goals, as well as the full application of the principles of ownership and alignment, is that ODA should be increasingly channeled through the budgets of recipient

Table II.2.
AGREED TARGETS FOR THE 12 INDICATORS OF PROGRESS

Indicators		Suggested targets	
1	Partners have operational development strategies	**At least 75% of partner countries** have operational development strategies.	
2a	Reliable PFM systems	**Half of partner countries** move up at least one measure (i.e., 0.5 points) on the PFM/CPIA scale of performance.	
3	Aid flows are aligned on national priorities	**Halve the gap**—halve the proportion of aid flows to government sector not reported on government's budget(s) (with at least 85% reported on budget).	
4	Strengthen capacity by co-ordinated support	**50% of technical cooperation flows** are implemented through co-ordinated programmes consistent with national development strategies.	
5a	Use of country PFM systems (% of aid)	*Population 'A' countries*— Partner countries with a **score of 5 or above** on the PFM/CPIA scale of performance (see Indicator 2a).	**Reduce the gap by two-thirds** —A two-thirds reduction in the proportion of flows to the public sector not using partner countries' PFM systems.
		Population 'B' countries— Partner countries with a **score between 3.5 and 4.5** on the PFM/CPIA scale of performance (see Indicator 2a).	**Reduce the gap by one-third** —A one-third reduction in the proportion of flows to the public sector not using partner countries' PFM systems.
5a	Use of country PFM systems (% of donors)	*Population 'A' countries*— Partner countries with a **score of 5 or above** on the PFM/CPIA scale of performance (see Indicator 2a).	**All donors** use partner countries' PFM systems.
		Population 'B' countries— Partner countries with a **score between 3.5 and 4.5** on the PFM/CPIA scale of performance (see Indicator 2a).	**90% of donors** use partner countries' PFM systems.
5b	Use of country procurement systems (% of aid)	*Population 'A' countries*— Partner countries with a **score of A** on the Procurement scale of performance (see Indicator 2b).	**Reduce the gap by two-thirds** —A two-thirds reduction in the proportion of flows to the public sector not using partner countries' procurement systems.
		Population 'B' countries— Partner countries with a **score of B** on the Procurement scale of performance (see Indicator 2b).	**Reduce the gap by one-third** —A one-third reduction in the proportion of flows to the public sector not using partner countries' procurement systems.
5b	Use of country procurement systems (% of aid)	*Population 'A' countries*— Partner countries with a **score of A** on the Procurement scale of performance (see Indicator 2a).	**All donors** use partner countries' procurement systems.
		Population 'A' countries— Partner countries with a **score of A** on the Procurement scale of performance (see Indicator 2b).	**90% of donors** use partner countries' procurement systems.

Table II.2 (cont'd)

Indicators		Suggested targets
6	Avoiding parallel PIUs	**Reduce by two-thirds** the stock of parallel PIUs.
7	Aid is more predictable	**Halve the gap**—halve the proportion of aid not disbursed within the fiscal year for which it was scheduled.
8	Aid is untied	**Continued progress over time.**
9	Use of common arrangements	**66% of aid flows** are provided in the context of programme-based approaches.
10a	Missions to the field	**40% of donor missions** to the field are joint.
10b	Country analytic work	**66% of country analytic work is joint.**
11	Results-oriented frameworks	**Reduce the gap by one-third**—Reduce the proportion of countries without transparent and monitorable performance assessment frameworks by one-third.
12	Mutual accountability	**All partner countries** have mutual assessment reviews in place.

Source: OECD/DAC (http://www.oecd.org/dataoecd/57/60/36080258.pdf).

countries. This means, in turn, that the proportion of aid so channeled should become a specific target of international assistance.

In addition to areas covered by the Paris Declaration targets, there are several other areas for improvement in respect of aid effectiveness. First, a follow-up to the commitments made at the World Summit for Social Development (1995), where donors pledged to spend 20 per cent of ODA on basic social services in developing countries, is still needed. Also, despite the evidence on the adverse effects of tied aid which has been available for several decades, this issue remains to be effectively tackled. Although there is an indicator (8) in the Paris Declaration on untying aid, agreement could only be reached on a target of "continued progress over time" in reducing tied aid. While substantial progress has been made in untying aid, it continues to have a high cost: in 2002, it reduced bilateral aid's value by at least $5 billion (Organization for Economic Cooperation and Development, Development Assistance Committee, 2004).

THE MULTILATERAL DEVELOPMENT BANKS

The architects of the post-war international financial system were, in the early years, more concerned with reconstruction than with development finance, but they were clear in their belief that both types of finance should be channelled through multilateral institutions subject to intergovernmental control. The International Bank for Reconstruction and Development (IBRD), established in 1944, was to play this role. IBRD and the International Finance Corporation (IFC) (established 1956), the International Development

Association (established 1960), the Multilateral Investment Guarantee Agency (established 1988) and the International Centre for Settlement of Investment Disputes (established 1966) now constitute the World Bank Group. The World Bank was complemented during the 1950s and 1960s by a number of regional development banks: the Inter-American Development Bank; the Asian Development Bank, the African Development Bank and the European Investment Bank (EIB). The European Bank for Reconstruction and Development (EBRD) was added in 1991. There are also several subregional development banks, particularly in the Latin American and Caribbean region and to a lesser extent sub-Saharan Africa, as well as several Arab institutions, some with a regional reach and others with a broader one.

Regional and subregional development banks experienced major shifts and reforms during the 1990s. In general, the financial base of these institutions grew substantially, allowing them to expand their lending activities and to increase their weight, influence and importance. The expanded role of these institutions led to both enhanced cooperation and partnerships with the World Bank, but also to more competition in the provision of services (Sagasti and Prada, 2006). The implementation of a more systemic perspective in the operations of the multilateral development banks and the World Bank, as well as a division of labour between them, will be of fundamental importance for the future of development finance.

In this regard, paragraph 45 of the Monterrey Consensus highlighted the vital role that multilateral and regional development banks continue to play "in serving the development needs of developing countries and countries with economies in transition". The paragraph went on to make the following observations:

> They should contribute to providing an adequate supply of finance to countries that are challenged by poverty, follow sound economic policies and may lack adequate access to capital markets. They should also mitigate the impact of excessive volatility of financial markets. Strengthened regional development banks and subregional financial institutions add flexible financial support to national and regional development efforts, enhancing ownership and overall efficiency. They also serve as a vital source of knowledge and expertise on economic growth and development for their developing member countries.

Despite this call, and with the exception of the recent recapitalization of IDA and the African Development Bank, only limited commitments have been made to enhancing the role that multilateral development banks play in the international financial system since the International Conference on Financing for Development.

The role of multilateral development banks

Structurally, most multilateral development banks contain a core bank or "hard window" that operates on commercial principles and a "soft-loan" window to support lending to low-income country borrowers. They may also contain private sector financing arms and guarantee agencies (Mistry, 1995). Through these facilities, multilateral development banks fulfil a vast array of financial functions, namely: (a) channelling funds to low-income countries; (b) lending to middle-income countries, and correcting market failures associated with the overpricing of risks, which lead to inadequate access to long-term financing by many middle-income developing countries; (c) acting as a counter-cyclical balance to fluctuations in private capital markets; and (d) facilitating the functioning of private markets by signalling creditworthiness and acting as catalysts for private sector investment. There are also several non-financial functions encompassing: (a) the traditional "value added" of multilateral financing, lending-related technical assistance, and its capacity-building and institutional development effects; (b) knowledge generation and brokering; and (c) the provision of global and regional public goods, including, in the case of most regional and subregional development banks, their support to regional integration processes.

Not each and every multilateral development bank is involved in all these functions, but the multilateral development banks as a whole cover all of them. The central role in satisfying the first function is played by IDA, while several regional development banks play a role in concessional lending, particularly the African Development Bank (44 per cent of total lending) and the Asian Development Bank (27 per cent); the Inter-American Development Bank has also a concessional fund for special operations which amounts to 7 per cent of total lending (see World Bank and International Monetary Fund, 2005).

In contrast with traditional World Bank lending, IDA lending is mainly funded by donor official development assistance, supplemented by IDA loan repayments and net income from IDA lending and from the operations of the World Bank. In its recently completed fourteenth replenishment (IDA-14), donors contributed $18 billion of new funds to the $34 billion that will be available to the world's poorest developing countries under IDA for the period 1 July 2005-30 June 2008. To improve efficiency, IDA policy will take into account the vulnerability to debt problems of the recipient countries through a forward-looking debt sustainability analysis (see chapter III) while the most heavily debt-distressed countries, mainly in sub-Saharan Africa, will receive all of their IDA assistance on grant terms.

The relative roles of loans and grants in development assistance has long been debated. A number of major donors believe that the discipline of loan repayment sharpens the focus on the costs/benefits of prospective projects, and provides an incentive to ensuring that funds are used effectively. Further, timely servicing of loans for development creates a revolving fund that can form a basis for permanent support, while grants require fresh budget allocations by donors which may depend on political and economic conditions. In this respect, it is important that donor countries agree on measures to cushion the effect of the loss of repayment flows (as grants replace loans) on IDA capacity to support the poor developing countries in the future. Forgone reimbursements will be financed through additional donor contributions on a pay-as-you-go basis. Participants in the fourteenth replenishment of IDA have cautioned, however, against the possibility of grants leading to excessive new borrowing from other sources by recipient countries, and warned that they could be disqualified from receiving grants if they are found to have engaged in "excessive or unsustainable" borrowing. Millennium Development Goals-based indicators will monitor overall development progress, thereby making possible a better assessment of country performance as well as aid delivery and management. IDA will make financial support contingent on the performance of the recipient country in the areas of economic policy, governance and poverty reduction efforts.

It is hoped that these measures will enhance the ability of countries to "graduate" from IDA support. Since 1960, 32 countries have graduated but 10 of the 32 countries subsequently re-entered the list at one time or another (these are known as "reverse graduates") and, after re-entry, some graduated again (see table II.3).

Recently, more attention has been given to the possible benefits of combining concessional IDA flows with other types of assistance so as to gain leverage and provide financing tailored to meet different needs between and within countries. Many developing countries receive IDA resources as well as cheap loans and grants from the concessional facility windows of the various regional development banks and from developed-country aid agencies. Concessional loans and grants can help the poorest (IDA-only) countries to scale up investment and spending to meet the Millennium Development Goals without undermining debt sustainability. As highlighted in the *Global Monitoring Report 2005* (World Bank, 2005d), the poorest countries face the largest gaps in financing needs so as to meet the Millennium Development Goals and must rely on external official financing to a substantial extent in covering those needs. There is broad agreement that the poorest countries should receive highly concessional resources, with amounts adjusted to

Table II.3.
GRADUATES FROM IDA ASSISTANCE

	Country	Fiscal year of last IDA credit	Reverse graduate (Year re-entered)
1.	Botswana	1974	-
2.	Cameroon	1981	1994
3.	Chile	1961	-
4.	China	1999	-
5.	Colombia	1962	-
6.	Republic of Congo	1982	1994
7.	Costa Rica	1962	-
8.	Côte d'Ivoire	1973	1992
9.	Dominican Republic	1973	-
10.	Ecuador	1974	-
11.	Equatorial Guinea	1993	-
12.	Egypt	1981, 1999	1991
13.	El Salvador	1977	-
14.	Honduras	1980	1991
15.	Indonesia	1980	1999
16.	Jordan	1978	-
17.	Republic of Korea	1973	-
18.	Mauritius	1975	-
19.	Macedonia, Former Yugoslav Republic of	2002	-
20.	Morocco	1975	-
21.	Nicaragua	1981	1991
22.	Nigeria	1965	1989
23.	Papua N Guinea	1983	-
24.	Paraguay	1977	-
25.	Philippines	1979, 1993	1991
26.	St. Kitts	1994	-
27.	Swaziland	1975	-
28.	Syria	1974	-
29.	Thailand	1979	-
30.	Tunisia	1977	-
31.	Turkey	1973	-
32.	Zimbabwe	1983	1992

Source: IDA, "Countries ceasing to borrow from IDA, 1960-2001" (www.worldbank.org/ida).

take performance and absorptive capacity into account. IDA-only countries with per capita incomes below the IDA cut-off have traditionally received grants from bilateral donors and highly concessional loans from multilateral agencies.

The second and third financial functions of multilateral development banks listed above emphasize the role that official development financing continues to play even for middle-income countries. The evolution of multilateral development bank lending in recent years shows that, whereas financing to low-income countries is steadier, lending to middle-income countries is strongly counter-cyclical: it increased substantially during the first half of the 1980s and during the critical years following the Asian crisis (figure II.8). The strong contraction in recent years, although consistent with the counter-cyclical function, has been very strong, leading to negative net flows to middle-income countries from 2002 to 2005. It is important to emphasize that this counter-cyclical function is distinct from that of IMF, and refers basically to the access of developing countries to long-term borrowing during times of crisis, particularly to maintain critical public sector investment and social spending.

Excellent access to capital markets associated with high capital/asset ratios, a large ratio of subscribed to paid-in capital, and the capacity to draw on the high risk-ratings of developed-country members allow multilateral development banks to offer excellent credit conditions even to middle-income countries. Even those without developed-country members use risk pooling and good risk management practices to achieve better credit ratings and risk premiums than their individual members (for example, the Andean Development Corporation). The preferential relation of multilateral development banks with borrowers, which has resulted in very low loan losses, represents another advantage (The Central American Bank for

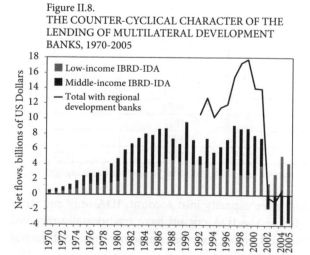

Figure II.8.
THE COUNTER-CYCLICAL CHARACTER OF THE
LENDING OF MULTILATERAL DEVELOPMENT
BANKS, 1970-2005

Source: World Bank, Global
Development Finance Online.

Economic Integration and the African Development Bank are among the few historical exceptions in this regard). The fact that borrowing countries are also investors, that credit costs are low relative to market rates, and that those countries have access to borrowing from multilateral development banks even when access to private capital markets is unavailable or available only at high costs, explains this preferred creditor status. In turn, the high quality of the portfolios and the access to capital markets with minimum premiums are reflected in low costs of funding, which is passed on to their borrowers. In terms of both costs and maturities, these institutions are thus able to lend on much better terms than private agents (see table II.4).

The fourth function, direct financing or co-financing to the private sector (by banks or their associated financial corporations) and provision of guarantee schemes to support public-private partnerships or public infrastructure projects, is of fairly recent origin. However, it has been gaining in importance since the 1990s and should become one of the priorities for multilateral financing in future. It has also been used in recent years in a modest way to support developing countries' efforts to return to markets after crises, but with only limited success in terms of improving the terms of borrowing for developing countries in private capital markets. It could be used to support initial bond issues by developing (particularly poor) countries seeking to position themselves in private capital markets. The full development of these schemes would call for a radical change in the management of guarantees by development banks since their current treatment as being equivalent to lending severely restricts their use.

The services that are bundled with lending also help to support objectives of the global community: poverty reduction, human development, protection of the environment, financial accountability and better public management standards (Gurría and Volcker, 2001). This indicates that these institutions also play a role in the provision of regional and global public goods. Although regional and subregional institutions are not as important as the World Bank in the provision and financing of such goods, in the 1990s the regional development banks entered into the provision of regional public goods (see below).

Structure and trends

The level of resources provided by multilateral development banks to developing countries is low in comparison with other official flows and (during periods of ample external financing) with private financial flows.

Table II.4.
DEVELOPING COUNTRIES: AVERAGE TERMS OF NEW COMMITMENTS, 1995-2004

	1995	1996	1997	1998	1999	2000	2001	2002	2003	2004
Average Maturity (years)										
Official										
All developing countries	19.2	21.6	19.8	16.2	19.7	20.1	20.7	22.7	20.1	23.4
Low income group	28.5	29.4	29.7	31.5	30.8	30.3	30.9	30.1	30.7	32.3
Middle income group	16.9	18.8	17.1	13.3	17.5	16.8	16.6	18.6	16.2	18.4
Private										
All developing countries	7.8	8.3	10.5	10.1	8.7	10.5	9.6	9.6	9.9	10.2
Low income	6.6	7.6	8.7	6.7	10.3	5.5	9.0	7.0	7.2	7.8
Middle income	7.8	8.3	10.6	10.5	8.7	11	9.6	9.7	9.9	10.3
Average interest rate (per cent)										
Official										
All developing countries	5.8	4.8	5.2	5.2	4.3	4.8	3.9	3.1	2.9	2.4
Low income group	2.9	3.1	3.0	2.4	2.3	3.0	2.1	2.4	1.4	1.5
Middle income group	6.5	5.4	5.8	5.7	4.7	5.4	4.7	3.5	3.4	2.9
Private										
All developing countries	6.6	7.3	7.4	7.6	8.1	8.1	7.0	6.7	5.6	5.5
Low income group	6.0	5.7	6.5	3.6	4.8	4.4	4.9	3.1	3.0	3.9
Middle income group	6.6	7.4	7.5	8.1	8.2	8.4	7.1	6.8	5.7	5.5

Source: World Bank, Global Development Finance Online.

The share of different multilateral development banks in total net flows from multilateral sources varies across regions and level of income. Net flows from the World Bank and regional development banks to developing countries represent, respectively, 50 per cent and 41 per cent of total long- and medium-term net flows to developing countries from multilateral sources, with other institutions providing the rest.

However, as table II.5 indicates, there are crucial regional differences with regard to the role played by different multilateral development banks. The expansion of the regional development banks has focused on middle-income countries where their combined net flows surpass those of the World Bank. In turn, the subregional banks make the largest contribution, relative to gross domestic product (GDP), in the medium- and small-sized countries of Latin America and the Caribbean, followed by the Middle East and North Africa. At the subregional level, the Andean region in South America offers the interesting case in which the net flows from a subregional institution totally owned by member countries, namely, the Andean Development Corporation, surpass those of both the World Bank and the Inter-American Development Bank. The Arab financial institutions play an important role, not only in the Middle East and North Africa, but in the Islamic world in general. In contrast, sub-Saharan Africa and South Asia are highly dependent on the World Bank/IDA (International Development Association). East Asia falls somewhere in between, with the World Bank lending slightly more than the Asian Development Bank. The lack of subregional development banks in East and South Asia stands in clear contrast with the situation in other regions. Finally, EIB is the dominant institution in Europe, even when we leave aside the old members of the European Union (EU-15 in table II.5). In the transition economies, however, both the World Bank and the EBRD play an important role (Ocampo, 2006).

The emphasis placed on certain operations by regional and subregional institutions reflects the diversity of their constituencies' financial needs. Institutions serving the African region are more focused on concessional loans and grants. Central Asian and European institutions are more focused on private sector activities; this is particularly true of the European Bank for Reconstruction and Development. These differences among regional development banks also apply at the subregional level. For example, the Caribbean Development Bank operates in some of the poorest Caribbean countries and has a larger proportion of concessional lending in comparison with the Central American Bank for Economic Integration, which has a clear mandate to improve intraregional trade (reflected in its higher proportion of trade finance and infrastructure operations). The Andean Development

Table II.5.
MULTILATERAL DEVELOPMENT BANKS: OUTSTANDING LOANS, 2004
(in millions of current dollars)

	OL	Af	MENA	Asia EAP	Asia SA	Asia CA	Europe EU-15	Europe RE	LAC ABM	LAC RLAC
World Bank Group										
International Bank for Reconstruction and Development (IBRD)[1]	104,401	4,484	8,655	25,981	10,354	4,183	-	15,117	24,523	11,103
International Development Association (IDA)[1]	120,907	48,120	3,561	15,643	43,804	2,654	-	2,521	-	4,604
Regional Development Banks (RDBs)										
European Investment Bank (EIB)[2]	656,578	-	-	-	-	-	597,486	45,960	-	-
Inter-American Development Bank (IADB)[3]	49,800	-	-	-	-	-	-	-	28,138	21,661
Fund for Special Operations (FSO)[3]	7,000	-	-	-	-	-	-	-	1,131	5,869
African Development Bank Group (AfDB + AfDF + NTF)[4]	8,511	6,724	1,787	-	-	-	-	-	-	-
Asian Development Bank (AsDB)	24,159	-	-	15,112	9,047	-	-	-	-	-
Asian Development Fund (AsDF)	27,216	-	-	17,025	10,192	-	-	-	-	-
European Bank for Reconstruction and Development (EBRD)[5]	18,434	-	-	-	-	3,781	7,961	6,693	-	-
Subregional Development Banks (SRDBs)										
Nordic Investment Bank (NIB)[6]	14,125	424	-	847	-	-	11,300	989	565	-
Nordic Development Fund (NDF)[7]	528	240	-	181	-	-	-	-	108	-
Central American Bank for Economic Integration (CABEI)[8]	2,789	-	-	-	-	-	-	-	-	2,789
Caribbean Development Bank (CDB)[9]	2,484	-	-	-	-	-	-	-	-	2,484
Andean Development Corporation (ADC)	7,216	-	-	-	-	-	-	-	433	6,783
FONPLATA[10]	378	-	-	-	-	-	-	-	94	284
North American Development Bank (NADB)[11]	43	-	-	-	-	-	-	-	22	-
East African Development Bank (EADB)[12]	111	111	-	-	-	-	-	-	-	-
West African Development Bank (BOAD)	545	545	-	-	-	-	-	-	-	-

Table II.5, (cont'd)

	OL	Af	MENA	EAP	SA	CA	EU-15	RE	ABM	RLAC
				Asia			Europe		LAC	
Subregional Development Banks (SRDBs) (cont'd)										
Islamic Development Bank Group (IsDB + ICD)[13]	17,929	1,793	8,845	1,076	4,124	239	-	1,853	-	-
Arab Bank for Economic Development in Africa (ABEDA)	606	606	-	-	-	-	-	-	-	-
Arab Fund for Economic and Social Development (AFESD)	11,992	-	11,992	-	-	-	-	-	-	-
Arab Monetary Fund	1,297	-	1,297	-	-	-	-	-	-	-
Total	1,077,050	63,047	36,138	75,865	77,519	10,857	616,747	73,133	54,341	56,251
Total without World Bank Group	851,742	10,442	23,922	34,241	23,362	4,020	616,747	55,495	30,491	39,871
Memo: GDP[14]		511,818	622,396	3,016,618	878,785	645,548	12,167,879	1,154,722	1,432,854	564,519

Sources: The data was collected from the official webpages of each institution. If available, data comes from the Annual Reports of each institution for the year 2004.

Abbreviations: LAC: Latin America and the Caribbean; OL: Outstanding loans; Af: Africa; MENA: Middle East and North Africa; EAP: East Asia and Pacific; SA: South Asia; CA: Central Asia; RE: Rest of Europe; ABM: Argentina, Brazil, Mexico; RLAC: Rest of Latin America and the Caribbean.

Regions: Japan is excluded from East Asia. Europe and Central Asia is divided into Advanced Europe (mainly former EU 15), Rest of Europe (Albania, Belarus, Bosnia & Herzegovina, Bulgaria, Croatia, Czech Republic, Estonia, FYR Macedonia, Hungary, Kosovo, Latvia, Lithuania, Moldova, Poland, Romania, Serbia and Montenegro, Slovak Republic, Slovenia, Turkey, Ukraine, Armenia, Azerbaijan, Georgia) and Central Asia (Kazakhstan, Kyrgyz Republic, Russian Federation, Tajikistan, Turkmenistan). Gulf Cooperation Council members (Saudi Arabia, Bahrain, Kuwait, Oman, Qatar, United Arab Emirates) are excluded from Middle East and North Africa's total GDP.

[1] Country distribution following IBRD and IDA cumulative lending. Data from 2005; [2] They also report credits to ACP (1%) and Asia and Latin America (1%) without further discrimination, not included in the table. Country distribution following loan approvals in 2004. Data from 2005; [3] Country distribution following approved loans 1961-2006; [4] Country distribution following debt outstanding; [5] Country distribution following total project value of EBRD investments; [6] Some relatively small credits go to Russia (Central Asia) without further discrimination. Country distribution following loan portfolio in 2004. Data from 2005; [7] Country distribution following project portfolio; [8] Reported as gross loan portfolio; [9] As reported. Not specified if cumulative, outstanding lending or lending for a specific year; [10] As reported. Not total financing; [11] Country distribution to Mexico (50%) and USA (50%, not included in the table) following loan portfolio; [12] Data from 2003; [13] Country distribution following IsDB net approved operations-sheet. Data from 1425H (2004-2005); [14] GDP data from World Developing indicators World Bank database.

Corporation, operating mainly in middle-income countries, has specialized in other types of operations such as infrastructure projects for regional integration and for improving competitiveness. This supports the general idea behind the creation of regional and subregional institutions: they play specific and localized roles, which are not always covered adequately by global or even by regional institutions (Sagasti and Prada, 2006).

As a result, the loan portfolios of regional and subregional banks also differ. The sectoral evolution of the lending of multilateral development banks has followed two main patterns. The first involves the increasing importance of the social sectors[9] and governance reforms during the 1990s and the current decade, and, to a lesser extent, the environment; and second, the progressive reduction of involvement in the productive sectors through State-owned financial intermediaries which has been partially compensated by the introduction of new financial instruments that directly support private sector investments and private-public partnerships. These include operations with private banks and the development of domestic capital markets that fall under the category of "financial infrastructure", according to the OECD classification.

Along with providing financial sector and capital market support, the regional and subregional banks entered into new areas during the 1990s such as the provision of regional public goods, especially those related to regional transport, energy and communication infrastructure and environmental programmes. ESCAP has proposed the creation of an Asian Investment Bank to finance the region's infrastructure needs (ESCAP, 2005). Initiatives such as the New Partnership for Africa's Development (NEPAD), the Initiative for the Integration of South American Regional Infrastructure and the Plan Puebla-Panama (involving Mexico and Central America) will certainly increase the proportion of such undertakings. This is probably a field for the expansion of regional development banks in the future.

The large and ever-growing role of regional and subregional development banks in the international financial system has received limited attention in the literature on international financial reform.[10] Regional and subregional development banks, even those made up entirely of developing countries, are likely to face lower risks than individual members. On the other hand, competition between world and regional organizations in the provision of development bank services and technical services is undoubtedly a desirable arrangement for small and medium-sized countries. The fact that developing countries are better represented in these banks than in the global financial institutions also creates a strong sense of "ownership" and establishes a special relationship between them and member countries that helps to reduce the risks faced by regional and subregional development banks, further encouraging the virtues of risk pooling (Ocampo, 2002, 2006).

The combination of collective action problems and the absence of supranational institutions indicates how important the regional and subregional development banks can be in supporting regional strategies. They can provide member countries with a coordination mechanism through which to plan and finance the provision of regional transborder infrastructure and other regional public goods requiring large initial investments. They also have the ability to provide a regional public good essential for development: the transmission and utilization of region-specific knowledge. That ability positions them to help countries within their respective regions design specific policies most appropriate to their economic needs and political constraints (Birdsall and Rojas-Suarez, 2004).

The debate around the multilateral development banks

The multilateral development banks came under criticism after the financial crises of the 1990s. In particular, the Meltzer Commission proposed phasing out multilateral bank lending to developing countries with access to private capital markets, and transforming the World Bank into a world development agency focused on low-income countries, with grants as the essential financing instrument (Meltzer and others, 2000). Other analysts argued, in turn, that the occurrence of capital market failures could not be used to defend the existence of the World Bank but only its role as a "knowledge bank", that is to say, a repository of best practices in development assistance (Gilbert and Vines, 2000).

In contrast, the United States Department of the Treasury (2000) defended the *financial* role of multilateral development banks vis-à-vis not only poor but also middle-income countries, given the fragile access of the latter to private capital markets. It also defended large-scale lending during crises to support fiscal expenditure in critical social services and financial sector restructuring. It argued, however, that multilateral development banks should improve coordination among themselves, and should focus their activities on areas of high development priority, be more selective in their lending to emerging economies and encourage eventual graduation of these countries from development assistance. Finally it defended the role of multilateral development banks lending as a catalyst for private lending.

Two independent reports have also underscored the essential role that multilateral development banks will continue to play in the international financial system. The report by the Institute of Development Studies of the University of Sussex (2000) emphasized three essential roles of these institutions: financial resource mobilization; capacity-building, institutional development and knowledge-brokering; and provision of global and regional public goods. It also underscored the need for multilateral development banks to embrace intellectual diversity in their role as knowledge brokers, an issue that has also been emphasized by Stiglitz (1999).

In turn, the report of the Commission on the Role of the Multilateral Development Banks in Emerging Markets (Gurría and Volcker, 2001) emphasized, in terms similar to those of the United States Treasury, that volatility of financial markets implied that the access of emerging markets to private capital markets could be "unreliable, limited and costly". As crises hurt the poor, the counter-cyclical character of multilateral development bank financing is consistent with the role in poverty reduction of the multilateral development banks. The Commission nonetheless suggested that pricing of loans by multilateral development banks should be set in a differential way so as to encourage graduation and correct the pro-cyclical effects of credit ratings. It also emphasized the need to strengthen the relationship between multilateral development banks and the private sector, particularly to encourage private infrastructure financing in developing countries. The catalytic role that multilateral development banks can play in this regard should be based on guarantee schemes, through which multilateral development banks help to cover the government and regulatory risks that private investors are likely to face.

Among other issues that have been the subject of concern to developing countries are the high costs of doing business with many multilateral development banks caused by long negotiation processes and conditionalities attached to lending. Indeed, some developing countries have decided to prepay loans from multilateral development banks with funds borrowed in private capital markets when such financing is available (a mechanism that is equivalent to an automatic "graduation"). This may explain the negative net transfers from several of these institutions in recent years (see figure II.8). Mohammed (2004) has recommended reviewing the pricing of loans, the conditions attached to them and the complex body of safeguard/fiduciary policies that have accumulated over the years for "ring-fencing" the World Bank from risk, as well as the restraints applied to the purposes for which the World Bank lends, in order to reverse the erosion of the competitiveness of the Bank as a development lender.

The Intergovernmental Group of Twenty-Four on International Monetary Affairs and Development, in its communiqué on its April 2005 Ministerial meeting, noted with concern "the sharp increase in recent years in net negative transfers to developing countries from the multilateral development banks, particularly the World Bank" (para. 17). Furthermore, it urged the Bank "to take effective action to reduce the financial and non-financial costs of doing business with the Bank, including by clarifying policies, simplifying procedures, streamlining internal processes, and reducing conditionality in lending operations" (para. 18). The fact that operations of multilateral development banks are financed by net income generated mainly from lending operations conducted with middle-income countries has also been a subject of concern. Retained earnings have also increased their share in the capital of many multilateral development banks, including IBRD, as the share of paid-in capital has declined over the years.

The most controversial issue since the 1980s has been, however, the role of lending-associated conditionalities, particularly structural conditionalities, and the most recent governance conditionalities. A World Bank study recognized in 1998 that conditionality had not influenced the success or failure of its programmes.[11] Nonetheless, and following the debate on aid effectiveness, the report argued that such success or failure was not independent of the economic policies that countries followed.

Of particular interest in this regard are the conclusions of the World Bank Operations Evaluation Department (World Bank, Operations Evaluation Department, 2001) about the World Bank's role in poverty reduction strategies. This report indicated that this initiative had enhanced the focus on poverty reduction of national strategies and the Bank's country programmes, bolstered the role of already robust Governments in aid coordination, and involved new actors in the development dialogue. At the same time, it underscored the fact that there was "an inherent tension in the design of a BWI-driven initiative involving conditionality that is simultaneously meant to foster a country-driven process", and made the following point: "The Bank management's process for presenting a PRSP to the Board undermines ownership. Stakeholders perceive this practice as Washington signing off on a supposedly country-owned strategy." It thus recommended "that management develop a review procedure that is more transparently supportive of ownership and more effectively linked to decisions about the Bank's programme". The Development Committee, in its 17 April 2005 communiqué, recognized once again the significance of these issues, underlining the importance of "aligning assistance better with medium-term country strategies, streamlining conditionality, building institutional capacity and strengthening the focus on development results (para. 12)."

The way forward

The recognition in the Monterrey Consensus of the need to strengthen the role of multilateral development banks in the service of developing countries should lead to concrete actions. They may be associated to past practices, particularly the strong support to low-income countries, but they should also be linked to emerging issues. In respect of the latter, as noted in chapter I, the trade financing facilities of multilateral development banks can play a role, for example, in counteracting the collapse of trade finance during crises. Operations in this area include guarantees of trade instruments issued by local banks and on-lending facilities through commercial banks that have been used in recent crises in Asia, the Russian Federation and Brazil.

This issue is closely associated to the counter-cyclical role of multilateral development banks in financing. However, expanding this role vis-à-vis emerging economies would require a significant increase in resources or a more active use of co-financing and credit guarantees by these institutions. These facilities could be activated in periods of sharp decline in capital flows and could aim to catalyse long-term private financing and investment. Existing guarantee mechanisms may need to be improved or enhanced and/or new mechanisms may need to be created. Existing problems—such as excessive restrictiveness of criteria and approval processes for granting guarantees and other related costs—would need to be addressed. Most importantly, the resources of the multilateral development banks should also be better leveraged in providing guarantees, eliminating the practice of equating guarantees with loans in terms of the accounting of the associated programmes. Guarantees should also be better targeted, for example, by focusing on later stages of long-term projects. Counter-cyclical lending facilities could also be devised, inter alia, by explicitly managing counterpart funds in a counter-cyclical way, or by allowing developing countries to "save" those counterpart funds in the multilateral development banks (for example, for social protection programmes) and use them when they were required during crises.

The role of multilateral development banks as "market makers" has grown in recent years as reflected in the support to public-private partnerships in infrastructure, and in the issuance of long-term bonds in the domestic markets of some developing countries and the subsequent lending to those countries in their own currencies. The Asian Development Bank is already providing extensive support to the ASEAN+3 Asian Bond Markets Initiative. A more active role could be taken in lending in domestic currencies of developing countries, and in extending the benchmark "yield curve" in their domestic bond markets. These market-making activities could be extended to commodity- or GDP-linked bonds; the associated lending could be securitized to be sold in international private capital markets. However, since these institutions are assumed to be "risk-free", it should be emphasized that this innovation, as well as the more active use of guarantees, would involve a major change in the underlying principles involved in the management of multilateral development banks.[12] The expertise developed by the World Bank as market maker for the sale of carbon credits under the provisions of the Kyoto Protocol could provide a basis for these activities. Although the strong portfolio is clearly one of the strengths of multilateral development banks, they also have an essential function in correcting market failures that may involve some risks.

The revealed success of several regional and subregional development banks clearly indicates that this is a promising area of cooperation among developing countries. There are successful financial institutions that have operated with a good credit rating without capital from industrialized countries. Furthermore, more appropriate conditionality makes these institutions attractive to borrowing countries. This should thus become a priority for South-South cooperation (Ocampo, 2006).

SOUTH-SOUTH COOPERATION

Development banking is one form of cooperation among developing countries that has made some progress but has still an untapped potential. The association of the activities of these institutions with trade and other integration processes is particularly promising. The same is true of monetary and macroeconomic cooperation, where initiatives are more limited (see chapter IV). These are thus areas where South-South cooperation can make major strides in the future.

Some developing countries have also been donors of ODA to other developing countries. Among the developing countries in Western Asia, Saudi Arabia has been, for many years, the largest ODA donor, followed by the United Arab Emirates and Kuwait. Total ODA contributions (almost all bilateral ODA) from this group has risen threefold since 1999. The ODA of the Republic of Korea has risen by almost one third since 2002, owing to contributions to the regional development banks and the replenishment of IDA. One third of bilateral ODA went to regions outside of Asia.

The more widespread form of South-South development cooperation is, however, technical cooperation. A recent multinational initiative in this regard is the India-Brazil-South Africa (IBSA) Dialogue Forum. The IBSA Dialogue Forum serves as a mechanism for political consultation and coordination, as well as for strengthening cooperation in particular economic and sectoral areas, and for improving economic relations among the three participating countries.[13]

China is one of the leading proponents among developing countries of South-South cooperation and was the first developing country donor to the Voluntary Trust Fund for the Promotion of South-South Cooperation. With its Technical Cooperation and Development network comprising of 26 centres of excellence, China has begun to establish the appropriate national policy and institutions to advance South-South cooperation. China launched its first South-South Cooperation Demonstration base in Fuzhou with the support of the United Nations Development Programme (UNDP) Special Unit for Technical Cooperation among Developing Countries. China's development cooperation policy with developing countries also focuses on human resource development. As at December 2003, it had trained some 7,000 African personnel in a wide range of professions in a variety of training programmes.[14]

India has spent over $2 billion over the years in wide-ranging programmes in the area of South-South cooperation. Under the India Development Initiative, founded in March 2003, India plans to provide financial and technical support to other developing countries through the sharing of development experiences and institutional capacity. Grants and loans from India to other developing countries have grown markedly, from $83 million to $140 million since 2000 (World Bank, 2005c, p. 100).

Brazil and Morocco underwrite scholarships to various universities and support technical and professional training for students of developing countries. Singapore offers a wide array of training programmes, and Sri Lanka offers training on indigenously developed technology (crab breeding, use of banana fibre, etc.). Cuba has provided medical training as well as experts and support for health-care systems in and outside of Latin America and the Caribbean.

Nigeria, since 1976, has promoted South-South cooperation through the Nigeria Trust Fund, under the administration of the African Development Fund. The South-South development cooperation policy of the Republic of Korea centres on promoting sustainable economic development, through, inter alia, the transfer of technology and information related to its development experiences in human resource and communications. Over the past few years, Turkey has allotted, on average, 80 per cent of its development cooperation budget to South-South initiatives.[15]

Some technical cooperation agreements have been concluded with the support of developed countries. For instance, Japan, through the Japan International Cooperation Agency (JICA), has been an active supporter of the Third Country Training Programme (TCTP) since its introduction in 1975. TCTP activities are located mainly in Central and South America and the countries members of the Association of Southeast Asian Nations (ASEAN).

South-South cooperation can also take the form of providing debt relief to debt-distressed developing countries. For instance, Mexico and Costa Rica have offered major debt relief to the HIPC countries in Central America. In 2000, China provided debt relief of RMB 10.5 billion ($1.27 billion) to 31 African countries and pledged to continue in the future to offer assistance to other developing countries.[16] More recently, China announced that it is expanding its aid programme to the HIPC countries and LDCs by writing off or forgiving within the next two years, all the overdue parts as of end-2004 of the interest-free and low-interest governmental loans owed by HIPCs having diplomatic relations with China. India and many other developing countries have made significant contributions to the HIPC Initiative. In early 2005, developing countries pledged about $200 million in emergency assistance to the victims of the Asian tsunami.

INNOVATIVE SOURCES OF FINANCING

As noted at the beginning of this chapter, the weak political will to meet the official assistance target of 0.7 per cent of GNI as ODA to developing countries was already noticeable in the mid-term review of the Second Development Decade. This led to a search for other sources of financing. In the context of the five-year review of the implementation of the outcome of the World Summit for Social Development, the General Assembly, in its resolution S-24/2 of 1 July 2000, called for a rigorous analysis of the advantages, disadvantages and other implications of proposals for developing new and innovative sources of funding, both public and private (para. 142(g)). Paragraph 44 of the Monterrey Consensus further called upon member States to pursue the consideration of innovative sources of financing.

Significant steps have been taken in response. At the request of the General Assembly, the Department of Economic and Social Affairs of the United Nations Secretariat commissioned the World Institute for Development Economics Research (WIDER) of the United Nations University (UNU) to consider existing proposals, which led to the publication of a study (Atkinson, 2005). At the Summit of World Leaders for Action against Hunger and

Poverty held at United Nations Headquarters in September 2004, a report by the Technical Group on Innovative Financing Mechanisms[17] was presented and is being actively followed up by its members. Other important analyses had been carried out for the Development Committee[18] and were discussed at its 2004 fall and 2005 spring meetings. A report was also presented to French President Jacques Chirac by the Working Group on New International Contributions to Finance Development,[19] on the possible bases, allocation and management of new development resources.

The economic and social impact of the proposals for additional flows, and for aid in general, would be enhanced if they were designed so as to be stable and predictable, with a view to enabling recipient countries to focus on human and physical capital investment needs. Such proposals may be distinguished according to their feasibility and potential revenue. The vertical axis in figure II.9 measures whether a specific initiative can be implemented by an individual country or requires broader participation for success including, at the extreme, universal participation. The horizontal axis measures the time frame required for adoption and implementation, running from most rapid to long-term. The mix of these two dimensions indicates what could be areas of focus so as to allow some proposals to be adopted rapidly without requiring universal acceptance. The size of the circle estimates, in turn, the magnitude of the potential revenue from a given financial source.

Figure II.9.
MAP OF MAIN PROPOSALS ON
INNOVATIVE SOURCES OF FINANCE

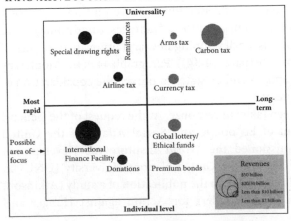

Source: DESA calculations.

Major mechanisms in the short run

As noted by the World Bank and International Monetary Fund (2005), taxing air transport makes economic sense. The level of taxation on air transport is lower than on other means of transport, since aviation fuel is tax-exempt. Aircraft engine emissions play a major role in global warming; however, they are not covered by the Kyoto Protocol[20] to the United Nations Framework Convention on Climate Change.[21] Several options seem to be technically feasible. Taxing aviation fuel would have a major positive environmental impact. A tax on airline tickets could easily be implemented and would present no legal obstacles, as the World Bank points out. The favourable perception by passengers of such a contribution, for which there are reasonable prospects of feasibility in the short term, could be achieved through its being allocated to a fund dedicated to a precise development objective. In view of the small size of this levy, it is expected that there would be minimal impact on the activity of airlines. A 5 per cent rate applied to first-class and business class tickets would yield $8 billion per annum, while a $1 contribution on each ticket issued would yield about $3 billion per annum. Another alternative would involve the indirect taxation of air flight corridors: revenues could reach $10 billion per annum. An indirect tax on passenger transportation could reach $20 billion per annum. Chile and France have both undertaken the legislative steps necessary to introduce a development contribution on air tickets for flights departing from their national airports. The expected dates of implementation are 1 January and 1 July 2006 respectively.

The International Finance Facility (IFF) was initially proposed by the United Kingdom of Great Britain and Northern Ireland in 2003. The Secretary-General called upon the international community to launch it in 2005.[22] It builds on commitments to reach the 0.7 per cent of GNI for ODA target no later than 2015. Its particular feature is that it enables front-loading aid flows through a bond mechanism guaranteed by participating Governments, allowing aid commitments to be spent before they are budgeted. The British proposal shows that with an initial $16 billion payment and regular increases through triennial pledging rounds over a 15-year period, donors can reach a $50 billion financing objective. If disbursements were to begin in 2006 ($10 billion), they would reach $50 billion by 2010, decrease after 2015 and end by 2020, with IFF drawing down donor pledges to pay off its bonds until 2032.

As the IFF mechanism seems to show great potential, it should now be examined experimentally before larger-scale implementation is undertaken. A pilot project announced for 2005 by the public-private partnership Global Alliance for Vaccines and Immunization (GAVI),with the cooperation and support of the British, French, Italian, Spanish, Swedish and Norwegian governments for a small-scale facility ("IFFIm") of $4 billion over 10 years should be scrutinized. The analysis of its financial architecture is likely to show a straightforward absorption by financial markets and a low-cost financing, as issuances of government-backed bonds will certainly obtain the highest ratings (AAA). To insure additionality, longer-term support should be considered to supplement the Facility through refinancing mechanisms.

Donations may also be fostered in the short run, as they account for a small but growing share of funds geared towards development. Voluntary contributions by individuals channelled through non-governmental organizations have doubled since 1990 in nominal terms, from $5 billion to $10 billion. The will of private citizens to participate in global poverty reduction initiatives is strong too, as was recently observed after the Asian tsunami of 2004, which led to the perception of a "globalization of solidarity". Gifts may not, however, be mixed with ODA in as much as they are a complement to, rather than a substitute for, the latter.

Donations can be encouraged through tax deductions: the usefulness of this procedure rests on the assumption that reduction in tax revenues will be more than compensated by the donations they encourage. Mechanisms suggested in this perspective generally include voluntary contributions that are paid together with the income tax slip, either through an opt-in system in which taxpayers choose to pay the tax, or an opt-out in which taxpayers can refuse the tax. Donations on acts of consumption have also been suggested, either through credit card payments or through utility bills. Within EU, the yield of credit card gifts equivalent to 1 per cent of Visa debits would reach $10 billion per annum. It is important to note in this regard that mechanisms linked to voluntary contributions benefit from but do not require international coordination. In early 2006 the rock star Bono promoted the launch of the new product line called Red to help fight AIDS and other diseases that hit hard in impoverished countries. It will include an American Express Red credit card issued to residents of the United Kingdom that contributes an extra 1 percent of spending to the Global Fund.

Using special drawing rights (SDRs) for development purposes (Soros, 2002) would involve the allocation by developed countries of SDRs to a dedicated trust fund, either by gift or through a redistribution of quotas, which would require amending the IMF Articles of Agreement. An amendment was approved in 1997 by the IMF Board of Governors for a special and unique allocation to double cumulated allocations to SDR 43 billion ($65 billion); however, the consensus for a modification has yet to be achieved. Other major innovative financing proposals include a global lottery and global premium bonds, and various taxes that could be earmarked for development objectives.

Major mechanisms in the longer run

Proposals for global taxation in support of development have a long history (Jenks, 1942; Stoessinger, 1964) and are often criticized on grounds of feasibility. Thus, to avert their being perceived as encroachments on participating countries' fiscal sovereignty or as mechanisms triggering new international bureaucracies—which would undermine the possibility of a large consensus among stakeholders—these taxes need to be designed as financing tools that are nationally applied and internationally coordinated, and that entail limited management and process costs. While universal participation is not indispensable, it would serve the interest of development, as more resources would be raised. This should be the ultimate goal, but in the short term, progress can be made with the participation of a smaller group of countries.

One type of tax that has been commonly suggested is the currency transaction tax, for which estimated revenues would range from $30.6 billion to $35.4 billion per annum if it was equivalent to two basis points of market currency transactions, and from $16.8 billion to $19.2 billion if it was equivalent to one basis point (Nissanke, 2003). Another estimates, based on the presumption that the negative impact of the tax on volumes would be minimal or nil, yields an even figure of $60 billion per annum (Clunies-Ross, 2004). However attractive the tax might be in terms of revenue potential its implementation is constrained by a number of obstacles. The tax base will have to be defined so as to exclude transactions by market-makers and special treatment for derivatives to avoid duplicate taxation (Spahn, 2002). It will also have to be protected from erosion, for even if all major financial centers participate, there is a risk that smaller centres will attract an increasing volume of activity from those wishing to evade the tax. Finally, strong opposition by a number of stakeholders must be overcome.

Another suggested tax, which can be recommended on environmental efficiency grounds, would be applied to carbon emissions. It would build on the dynamic launched by the United Nations Framework Convention on Climate Change, adopted on 9 May 1992 by the Intergovernmental Negotiating Committee for a Framework Convention on Climate Change, inviting partner States to decrease greenhouse gas emissions. Carbon dioxide is the main gas at stake and its emissions might be moderated through a tax that would thus have the advantage of correcting negative externalities in addition to being a significant source of development financing. On the basis of a figure of $21 per ton (5 cents per gallon of gasoline), revenues would reach $130 billion per annum and $61 billion per annum in the case where the tax was restricted to rich countries. Governments would levy the tax and dispense it to an international agency, according to a procedure that remains to be defined. However, several challenges would need to be addressed including: the need to consider "free-riding" risks presented by countries not applying the tax and of tax evasion at the company or the country level; the need to coordinate the tax with the current practice involving negotiable emissions permits established by the Kyoto Protocol, adopted by the Conference of the Parties to the Framework Convention at its third session in 1997; and redistributive effects which might require an international agreement on compensations.

A tax on the arms trade could yield between $2.5 billion and $8 billion per annum. This tax is advocated as a means to secure resources to finance development while discouraging military expenditures (Clunies-Ross, 2000). However, if its full potential is to be realized, it is important to ensure that the tax is passed through from the seller to the buyer so that the cost of acquiring arms is effectively increased. Also, if the mechanism is to be efficient, it would be crucial to obtain a large coalition of participants, including all major arms producers and exporters.

NOTES

1 The Development Committee, as it has come to be called, was established by parallel resolutions of the Boards of Governors of the World Bank and the International Monetary Fund at their annual meetings in October 1974.

2 Statement by Richard Manning, Chairman, OECD Development Assistance Committee (DAC), to Development Committee Spring Meeting, Washington, 17 April 2005, para. 5.

3 The problem can be traced to donors' own budgetary procedures. It is linked to the way donors' budgets are approved and administered. In many of the donor countries, there is a disconnect between donor development agencies and those that approve and disburse budgets.

4 Data excludes the Democratic Republic of the Congo for 2003, as important debt relief operations made this country an outlier for that year. (Including the Democratic Republic of the Congo, the share of the top 20 recipients would have been 59 per cent, and 46 per cent of countries would have accounted for 90 per cent of net bilateral aid in 2003.)

5 In this regard, Boone (1996) provides evidence that, on average, aid does not foster economic growth. On the other hand, Burnside and Dollar (2000) and Collier and Dollar (2002) qualify the Boone-type results to indicate that aid promotes growth in good policy environments. Hansen and Tarp (2001) disagree with this view and provide a contrary perspective.

6   At times aid allocations are not guided by development objectives and, in such cases, it
     would be very difficult to establish the links among aid, growth and poverty reduction.
     The discussion in the present section does not focus on such cases. Nor does it focus
     on some extreme cases of leakages through outright corruption and rent-seeking.

7   Critics of this approach question the definition and assessment of good policy implicit
     in the CPIA ratings (see, for example, European Network on Debt and Development
     (Eurodad, 2002). In the view of these critics, performance-based allocation puts too
     much emphasis on old Washington consensus types of policies. The approach ignores
     bad performance due to structural factors such as the inability to withstand commodity
     price shocks.

8   Among these alternative interpretations, we should include the following points:
     (a) Collier and Dollar's model confirms that the impact of reallocating aid on the basis
     of poverty criteria is greater than that of reallocating aid on the basis of policy; (b) World
     Bank evidence that aid is fungible and that ex ante conditionality is ineffective can also
     be questioned; (c) growth is not the only route to poverty reduction nor is growth
     the only benefit of aid: other benefits include, inter alia, health, educational and
     distributional effects, environmental development, empowerment and security and;
     (d) adopting the poverty reduction strategy at the level of each country as opposed to
     having a single global target could significantly alter the pattern of poverty-efficient
     aid allocations.

9   From its creation through the 1960s, the World Bank financed mainly infrastructure
     projects (representing 75 per cent of its total portfolio). The creation of the first
     regional development bank, the Inter-American Development Bank, in 1959, could be
     seen partly as a reaction by Latin American countries to World Bank lending policies
     which had given little attention to the social and agriculture sectors (which represented
     only 3 per cent of the World Bank's portfolio). In the first 10 years of Inter-American
     Development Bank operations, those sectors received almost 50 per cent of total Inter-
     American Development Bank disbursements (Kapur, Lewis and Webb, 1997).

10   Some exceptions are United Nations (2001a), Ocampo (2002), Ocampo and Griffith-
     Jones (2003) and Birdsall and Rojas-Suarez (2004).

11   See World Bank (1998), chap. 2 and appendix 2; and also Gilbert, Powell and Vines
     (1999), Stiglitz (1999) and Gilbert and Vines (2000).

12   Kapur (2003) has argued that the increasingly stringent safeguards that have the
     objective of protecting the World Bank from risk are imposing high financial and
     opportunity costs on the Bank's borrowers, pointing out that "(it) is trivially easy for
     the major shareholders to insist on standards whose costs they do not bear".

13   See "Cape Town Ministerial Communiqué, India-Brazil-South Africa (IBSA) Dialogue
     Forum", press release, 13 March 2005, Republic of South Africa Department of Foreign
     Affairs, available from www.dfa.gov.za/docs/2005/ibsa0311.htm.

14   See "Let us build on our past achievements and promote China-Africa friendly
     relations", address by Wen Jiabao, Premier of the State Council of the People's Republic
     of China, at the opening ceremony of the Second Ministerial Conference of the China-
     Africa Cooperation Forum, Addis Ababa, 15 December 2003, available from http://
     chinaembassy.ru/eng/wjdt/zyjh/t56252.htm.

15   See report of the Secretary-General (A/58/319) entitled "State of South-South
     cooperation", para. 42.

16   See statement by Minister Xiang Huaicheng, Head of the Delegation of the People's
     Republic of China at the International Conference on Financing for Development,
     21 March 2002, Monterrey, Mexico, available from http://www.un.org/ffd/statements/
     china.htm.

17 The September 2004 report, entitled "Action against Hunger and Poverty", was derived from the January 2004 Geneva Declaration signed by the leaders of Brazil, Chile and France, backed by the Secretary-General and endorsed later by Spain, Germany and Algeria.

18 See Development Committee, 25 April 2004 communiqué, para. 7; 2 October 2004 communiqué, para. 9., and background paper DC2004-0012/Add.1 of 29 September 2004 entitled "Aid effectiveness and financing modalities"; and the paper prepared by the Staff of the World Bank and the International Monetary Fund for the 17 April 2005 Spring Meeting, entitled "Moving forward: financing modalities toward the Millennium Development Goals" (SM/05/104, 3/17/05).

19 Report of the Working Group on New International Contributions to Finance Development (Paris, la documentation française, September 2004).

20 United Nations, Treaty Series, vol. 1771, No. 3 08 22.

21 FCCC/CP/1997/7/Add.1, decision 1/CP.3, annex.

22 United Nations (2005b).

Chapter III
External Debt

External finance is meant to supplement and support developing countries' domestic resource mobilization. However, since the nineteenth century, developing countries have experienced repeated episodes of rapidly increasing external indebtedness and debt-service burdens that have brought slower growth or recession and eventually produced renegotiation and restructuring. For this reason, the Monterrey Consensus of the International Conference on Financing for Development (United Nations, 2002b, annex) emphasized the importance of sustainable debt levels in mobilizing resources for development.

The present chapter analyses the current debate on debt and development in historical perspective. It starts with a brief review of the evolution of developing-country debt and rescheduling in the post-war period. The second section surveys measures to deal with the problem of excessive indebtedness, such as the Heavily Indebted Poor Countries (HIPC) Initiative, as well as more recent proposals for additional relief for low-income countries and new Paris Club arrangements for middle-income countries. Efficient use of external resources requires an adequate understanding, and an operative specification, of debt sustainability. The third section presents and critically assesses recent proposals for sustainability to be applied to low-income countries under the fourteenth replenishment of the International Development Association (IDA-14). In the last analysis, when failure to attain sustainability produces default, renegotiation is necessary. The final section reviews recent experience in this area that suggests the need for urgent action for new approaches to the problem, and provides an assessment of various proposals on the table for discussion by the international community.

Debt and development

The post-war approach to lending to developing countries

In the early post-war period, it had been assumed that development finance would take the form of grants or concessional borrowing from multilateral development banks. The potential for private flows was considered limited, given the volatility of such flows in the interwar period and their virtual disappearance (except for trade credits) following the Great Depression. Although official flows were to be multilateral, administered by institutions such as the United Nations Capital Development Fund or through the International Bank for Reconstruction and Development (IBRD), bilateral official flows and private trade credits dominated international financing for development. Multilateral lending tended to be restricted to large project financing of infrastructure, evaluated according to efficient use of capital resources, and based on a notional social rate of return. As a consequence, it did not take into account the ability of the country to generate the foreign-exchange resources required to service the debt. Bilateral lending was carried out on an ad hoc, country-by-country basis with little coordination within different agencies in donor countries and with even less cooperation among lenders, with outcomes dominated by political or domestic concerns through tied aid, and also with little concern for the impact on the country's ability to service the loans.

Similar problems arose–and, if anything, became more acute—when private markets became the dominant source of financial inflows to developing countries in the 1970s. Foreign currency loans with adjustable interest rates were extended to private sector borrowers or public sector enterprises on the basis of domestic performance and creditworthiness, or were driven by competitive pressures on lending banks to retain market shares, without reference to the borrowing country's ability to service the debt. There had been little coordination among private lenders concerning overall foreign currency exposure at the country level or with respect to assessing the implications of possible changes in dollar exchange rates and interest rates before their sharp increase at the end of the decade. Thus, even when external finance had a positive impact on development, it could be frustrated by the lack of capacity to service the loans, irrespective of whether it was official aid or private market financing. Financing for development could become counterproductive if debt service diverted resources from development purposes.

Rapid external borrowing and debt rescheduling in the 1960s and 1970s

Evidence of rapidly increasing indebtedness producing a negative impact on development had already been present during the First United Nations Development Decade. Although developing countries easily achieved the minimum target of an annual rate of growth of gross domestic product

(GDP) of 5 per cent, by 1970 about half of their official foreign-exchange receipts were committed to repayment of debt to official lenders.[1] The decline in official flows during this period, noted in chapter II, made debt servicing even more difficult and required debt rescheduling. The first Paris Club rescheduling was conducted in 1956 and during the 1960s and early 1970s countries accounting for more than half of outstanding developing-country debt were involved in official refunding or rescheduling negotiations.

The continuing decline in official assistance and increasing concentration of multilateral assistance in the poorer developing countries, particularly in sub-Saharan Africa, along with a rapid increase in private sector liquidity due to the expansion of the Eurodollar market in the early 1970s, brought an increase in private market borrowing by a number of fast growing developing countries. Borrowing by non-oil-exporting developing countries in Eurodollars from private banks jumped from $300 million in 1970 to $4.5 billion in 1973, bringing their share of Eurobanks' loans to over 20 per cent. However, the collapse of the commodity price boom that had preceded the 1973 oil crisis quickly created servicing difficulties and by 1974 the Group of 77 were calling for debt cancellation in addition to rescheduling.[2]

The period after the oil crisis and the breakdown of the Bretton Woods system of fixed exchange rates had brought an increase in outstanding non-oil-exporting developing-country debt from $78.5 billion at the end of 1973 to $180 billion in 1976 with about 60 per cent borrowed from private banks through syndicated loans. The result was another round of debt renegotiations (Wellons, 1977) before a final surge of lending at the end of the decade brought the outstanding international indebtedness of developing countries to over $600 billion at the end of 1981. There were to be 50 official or private negotiations leading to debt restructuring agreements between 1978 and 1982, the year of the Mexican default.

The International Monetary Fund (IMF) became increasingly involved in official debt negotiations by providing both estimates of the debtor's ability to pay and a standby programme to countries in debt renegotiation.[3] This usually entailed an estimate of the debtor's external financing gap and the provision of short-term standby credit to finance it, subject to the introduction of an external adjustment programme to ensure that the gap would be eliminated and to permit the country to return to debt servicing.[4]

As a result of the increase in debt problems in the 1970s, both private creditors and IMF formulated statistical techniques to identify factors that would signal an imminent need for debt restructuring. Among the best indicators of rescheduling identified in a survey of 13 of the studies published between 1971 and 1987 were: the ratio of debt service or debt service due to exports, to GDP, and to reserves; the ratio of amortization to debt; and the ratio of debt to exports, and to GDP (Lee, 1993).

Debt resolution in the 1980s

The numerous defaults by Latin American countries in the 1980s changed the nature of the response to debt renegotiations. Initially, debtors had been encouraged to introduce external adjustment policies in the belief that a return to high growth with external surpluses would provide the resources to repay arrears. These policies produced substantial current-account surpluses, but only at the cost of prolonged domestic stagnation and import compression in what came to be called the "lost decade".

The Brady Plan, introduced at the end of the decade, recognized that the debt could not be repaid through current-account surpluses at acceptable levels of growth and sought to induce creditors to accept write-downs, by offering new credit-enhanced assets in exchange for old debts, and to induce debtors to create domestic conditions that would restore their access to international debt markets by offering structural adjustment lending. Creditors accepted write-offs, while the issue of Brady bonds allowed Latin American debtors to return to international capital markets, and effectively created a secondary market for debt issued by emerging economies which facilitated this process. The search for yield generated by low interest rates in the United States of America also contributed on the supply side, while decisions to liberalize financial markets and privatize State-owned enterprises contributed on the demand side. As a result, debt reduction was followed by a new phase of international indebtedness.

While private flows were increasing to middle-income countries, there was an increase in the share of official assistance going to the poorest developing countries, in particular in sub-Saharan Africa. The major proportion was in the form of loans that produced an increase in debt stocks from about $6 billion in 1980 to about $11 billion in the late 1990s. Debt-service growth was less pronounced owing to repeated debt restructuring, increasing debt-service relief and an increasing use of grants. Because multilateral financial institutions did not in general provide debt relief, or provide aid in the form of grants, while bilateral official aid increasingly took this form, the relative share of multilateral institutions in debt service and debt stocks continued to rise from about one seventh to almost one third, while the share of debt service increased from about one tenth to one third.

In addition, as a result of the increasing amounts of official aid, net transfers to these recipients—the poorest developing countries—were positive throughout the 1980s and 1990s, and in most countries constituted as much as ten per cent of national income. Since net official aid flows exceeded debt service, the rise in debt stocks did not cause the difficulties that the rise in private debt stocks caused in middle-income Latin American countries, although it did create problems for bilateral donors. Since an increasing share of bilateral aid was being used to meet the rising debt service due to multilateral institutions, increasing amounts of bilateral aid or relief were required to prevent the debt overhang from having a negative impact on economic performance. Thus, while middle-income countries faced negative net resource transfers in the 1980s, low-income borrowers were faced with an increase in the share of aid used to pay debt service and thus with a decline in real resources for domestic development.[5] Since solutions similar to the Brady initiative were not possible for these borrowers, a more direct approach was required to reduce debt stocks, which eventually took the form of the HIPC Initiative (see below).

Despite substantial differences in their conditions, both low- and medium-income countries reached the 1990s with expanding levels of official and private debt. Figure III.1 shows the sharp increase in the ratio of total debt to gross national income (GNI) that occurred in the last half of the 1970s and its continuation through the mid-1990s when the ratio stabilized, largely owing to the impact of the Brady and HIPC initiatives.

Another measure of the impact of debt is the use of export revenues to meet debt service, since this precludes their use to finance the imports needed for development purposes and implies either increasing indebtedness or

Figure III.1.
RATIO OF TOTAL DEBT TO GROSS
NATIONAL INCOME, 1970-2004

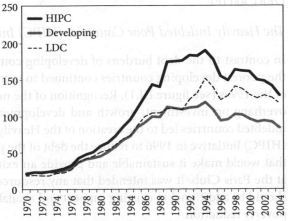

Source: World Bank, *Global Development Finance*, various issues.

slowing of the development process. The severe pressure placed on developing countries by the debt crisis of the 1980s can be seen in figure III.2, with the substantial improvements in the 1990s largely due to the decline in global interest rates during the decade.

Figure III.2.
RATIO OF TOTAL DEBT SERVICE
TO EXPORTS, 1970-2004

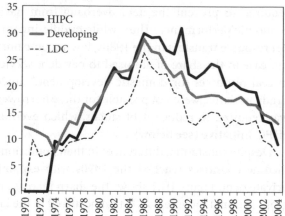

Source: World Bank, *Global Development Finance*, various issues.

The Monterrey Consensus, noting the negative impact of debt service on development expenditures, recognized that the elimination of excessive debt burdens would make available a major source of additional finance for development and therefore called on debtors and creditors to share responsibility for preventing and resolving unsustainable debt situations.

DEBT RELIEF

The Heavily Indebted Poor Countries (HIPC) Initiative

In contrast to the debt burdens of developing countries in general, those of the poorest developing countries continued to increase through the first half of the 1990s (see figure III.1). Recognition of the negative impact of this debt overhang on investment, growth and development in the poorest, heavily indebted countries led to the creation of the Heavily Indebted Poor Countries (HIPC) Initiative in 1996 to reduce the debt of the poorest countries to a level that would make it sustainable and provide an exit from serial rescheduling at the Paris Club. It was intended that any resources freed from debt service should be additional to existing support and available to support growth and poverty reduction.

As the original framework was considered insufficient relief for many poor countries to achieve debt sustainability, an "enhanced" HIPC initiative was introduced in 1999 to provide deeper, broader and quicker debt relief. According to the criterion for eligibility in the enhanced HIPC Initiative, a country should face unsustainable debt even after the full use of traditional relief mechanisms.[6] But the enhanced HIPC Initiative proved in turn insufficient, leading, as we will see in the next section, to a more ambitious solution in 2005.

In an extension of the work noted above that had been undertaken in the 1970s by private banks and IMF on predicting the need for debt renegotiation, the HIPC Initiative used similar variables to determine debt sustainability.[7] As of mid 2006, 29 countries had received debt relief, with 19 countries having reached completion point and 10 countries at decision point.[8] The Initiative was scheduled to expire at the end of 2004, but was extended for two years, leaving open the possibility that additional countries might be included. IMF and World Bank/IDA (2006) have identified 11 additional countries that meet the income and indebtedness criteria on the basis of data available for end-2004 and thus, depending on their performance, could be considered for debt relief under the Initiative before it is concluded at the end of 2006 (Central African Republic, Comoros, Côte d'Ivoire, Eritrea, Haiti, Kyrgyz Republic, Liberia, Nepal, Somalia, Sudan, and Togo). Although Bhutan, Lao PDR, and Sri Lanka meet the eligibility criteria, they have indicated that they do not wish to be considered.

The net present value of the debt stocks of the 29 countries will have been reduced by about two thirds once they have all reached completion point. As a proportion of exports, debt service declined from 16 per cent in 1998-9 to 8 per cent in 2004. Savings from lower debt-service payments provide the potential to increase expenditures targeted to poverty reduction. These expenditures as a share of GDP have risen from 6 per cent in 1999 to about 9 per cent in 2005 and are now about four times higher than debt servicing costs.

Among complementary measures of particular importance are those of the Paris Club whose members have granted debt relief beyond HIPC terms. Overall, reductions have been funded in roughly equal parts by Paris Club and other bilateral and commercial creditors, on the one hand, and multilateral creditors, on the other. The former group contains three HIPC countries which are themselves creditors: the United Republic of Tanzania and Cameroon, which have agreed to provide HIPC relief on all their claims, and Rwanda, which has provided relief to Uganda.

The total cost of providing debt relief to all of the 38 countries currently eligible for assistance under the Enhanced HIPC Initiative has been estimated at $58 billion in 2004 net present value (NPV) terms. A little more than 50 per cent will come from debt forgiveness by bilateral creditors, while the rest will be provided by multilateral lenders, such as IMF, World Bank and the regional development banks. The share of debt relieved by IMF will be financed from income from the investment of the net proceeds from off-market gold sales in 1999 deposited in the Poverty Reduction and Growth Facility (PRGF)-HIPC Trust Fund, plus contributions from member countries. The World Bank has created the IDA HIPC Trust Fund, financed by contribution, to provide funds to reimburse IDA for HIPC debt relief, and to support debt relief provided by eligible regional and subregional creditors. In addition, Paris Club creditors have provided relief to qualifying countries and most have pledged to provide assistance over that required under the HIPC Initiative.

However, resources available to finance IDA's debt relief costs under HIPC were expected to be fully utilized by the end of calendar year 2005, and thus an additional financing of about $1.8 billion will be required during IDA-14 to be able to deliver its agreed debt relief program. Ensuring participation from non-Paris Club bilateral and private creditors has been particularly difficult. Of the 54 non-Paris Club countries participating in the HIPC programme, 28 have committed to deliver some or all of their pledged amounts. Securing the participation of non-Paris Club official bilateral (and private) creditors has been a challenge since the creation of the Initiative and recently there have been setbacks. The Libyan Arab Jamahiriya, has withdrawn its commitment to participate, citing its failure to obtain ratification of the commitment from appropriate authorities. Other creditors complained about obstacles complicating delivery of debt relief, including Algeria, where the majority of debt is in kind, thereby making the valuation of repayment obligations problematic. The costs associated with the Sudan, Somalia and Liberia will need to be met by the IMF HIPC Trust Fund when these countries are ready to benefit from HIPC relief, at a total increased cost of $2.1 billion. Within IMF, low interest rates over the period from 2000 have opened a potential gap in the resources available from the Special Disbursement Account (SDA) to meet IMF costs for HIPC relief.

Paris Club negotiations require a country to seek comparability of treatment from other creditors. However, most commercial creditors have not provided their share of traditional and HIPC debt relief. In the case of at least nine HIPCs, commercial creditors and other bilateral creditors have refused to match Paris Club decisions and have instead pursued full recovery via litigation. In a survey of HIPC countries conducted by IMF in August

2003, nine countries responded that they were facing litigation initiated by commercial creditors and two non-Paris club creditors. Non-delivery of debt relief and resources lost in litigation can substantially affect the debt outlook of HIPCs. Moreover, pending and ongoing litigation can seriously jeopardize the relationship of HIPCs with the international financial community and their access to finance in the future.

It is now generally recognized that most of the debt reduction that was achieved in the HIPC countries took the form of writing off bilateral debts already in arrears, thus freeing up a smaller amount of real resources for poverty reduction spending than had been originally foreseen. Table III.1 shows the nominal debt-service relief for countries that have reached

Table III.1.
DEBT RELIEF AND REDUCTION IN ARREARS FOR
SELECTED HIPC COMPLETION POINT COUNTRIES

	Enhanced HIPC debt relief		Arrears (principal and interests on long-term debt to official creditors)		
	Comple-tion point	Nominal debt service relief[1]	Year before decision point[1]	Year before completion point or last available (2003)[1]	Year after completion point or last available (2003)[1]	Change since decision point (%)
Benin	Mar-03	460	77	20	0	-100%
Bolivia	Jun-01	2,060	21	21	0	-100%
Burkina Faso	Apr-02	930	39	42	41	4%
Ethiopia	Apr-04	3,275	668	593	2	2
Ghana	Jul-04	3,500	13	33	2	2
Guyana	Dec-03	1,353	129	147	122	-6%
Madagascar	Oct-04	1,900	725	699	2	2
Mali	Mar-03	895	589	34	115	-80%
Mauritania	Jun-02	1,100	535	349	333	-38%
Mozambique	Sep-01	4,300	375	898	431	15%
Nicaragua	Jan-04	4,500	1,759	1,014	2	2
Niger	Apr-04	1,190	104	60	2	2
Senegal	Apr-04	850	5	17	2	2
United Republic of Tanzania	Nov-01	3,000	1,748	888	1,050	-40%
Uganda	May-00	1,950	147	147	241	64%
	Total:	31,263	6,934	4,961		
			22%	16%		

Source: GDF 2005, HIPC Initiative Statistical Update, April 2005.

1 In USD Million.
2 Completion point after 2003.

completion point and the arrears at decision point. Nearly 22 per cent of the debt relief classified as aid flows took the form of a write-off of arrears.

Although there are many countries where debt-service ratios and debt management practices have improved, there are others where these debt ratios have deteriorated. Figure III.3 traces debt service before countries had achieved decision point and debt service in 2004 for those of them that had reached completion point. Countries located above the 45-degree line had an increase in debt service and those below had a decrease. Countries located below the -25 per cent and -50 per cent trajectories experienced reduction in debt service of more than 25 and 50 per cent, respectively. Debt service for five of the completion point countries, Bolivia, Mali, Mozambique, Uganda, and Zambia, was higher than it had been before decision point. In Senegal, the reduction in debt service was less than 25 per cent, while seven countries had reductions in the ranging from 25 to 50 per cent and four had reductions of just above 50 per cent.

The success of the Initiative in providing sustainable debt relief has been hampered by the overly optimistic growth and debt-service projections made in assessing country performance. External shocks (commodity price shocks in particular) have not only led to the inability of some countries to meet those projections but also added additional difficulties. In the case of Uganda, the debt-to-exports ratio was 50 per cent higher in June 2003 than before relief had been obtained under the HIPC Initiative. Furthermore, although the Poverty Reduction Strategy Papers (PRSPs) that accompany the HIPC Initiative have been successful in increasing social spending, for some

Figure III.3.
EVOLUTION OF DEBT SERVICE FOR COUNTRIES
THAT HAD REACHED COMPLETION POINT
(Enhanced HIPC initiative, in USD M)

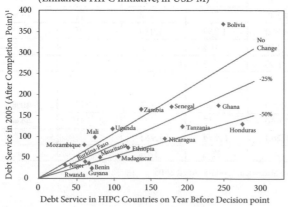

Source: DESA, based on data in World Bank, *Global Development Finance 2005* (Washington, D.C., 2005); and IMF, HIPC Initiative—Statistical Update, 21 March 2006.

countries the commitments on social spending have exceeded the savings on debt service, leading to accumulation of additional indebtedness. On the other hand, since such programmes are not currently embedded in the country's overall development strategy, the higher priority given to their application has led to neglect of other national priorities. In addition, in many cases, the relief provided has been too slow, especially in the interim period between decision and completion points. As a result of all of these factors, there is an emerging consensus that, despite the Initiative, many poor developing countries may continue to suffer from a debt overhang. Further, since the introduction of the original HIPC scheme in 1996, bilateral ODA flows to HIPCs, after deduction of debt forgiveness, food aid and emergency aid have decreased in real terms despite the rise in bilateral aid flows since 2001. This means that project-related grants, which have the largest potential impact for stimulating long-term growth, have declined (see chap. II).

The Multilateral Debt Relief Initiative

The deficiencies identified in the HIPC Initiative spawned a wide range of proposals for augmented debt relief. In line with its objective to front-load the aid resources needed to finance the Millennium Development Goals (see chap. II), the United Kingdom of Great Britain and Northern Ireland proposed 100 per cent reduction of debt service for loans from international financial institutions contracted before 2004; such debt-service reductions would apply for the period 2005-2015 in post-completion point HIPC countries and non-HIPC IDA-only countries with transparent and solid public expenditure management as supported by a Poverty Reduction Support Credit with the World Bank. According to this proposal, donors would contribute in line with their global share of IDA. The cost for IMF would be covered by use of IMF gold reserves. Canada made a similar proposal, but with bilateral donors financing the debt relief. The United States of America made an alternative proposal for full relief for HIPC countries' outstanding debt to IMF, IDA and the African Development Bank African Development Fund with funding for IMF debt forgiveness coming from the reserve account of the PRGF-HIPC Trust Fund and the Special Disbursement Account. IDA and African Development Fund debt would be cancelled without replenishment and funded by reducing the IDA and African Development Fund allocations for each beneficiary country.

Other proposals aimed at enhancing existing relief mechanisms. France proposed to reinforce the HIPC approach by providing liquidity grants, funded by additional bilateral IDA and African Development Fund contributions, for countries facing debt-service problems owing to external factors. Japan suggested lowering the debt-to-export threshold from 150 to 120 per cent (including private and bilateral debt) for pre-completion point HIPC countries, while post-completion point countries would be granted additional relief if they had a high debt overhang after HIPC debt cancellation.

Norway proposed in turn a Millennium Development Goal debt sustainability mechanism[9] based on principles drawn from the existing proposals. The approach stresses that any new initiatives must confirm and fully finance earlier commitments and cover all present and future HIPC costs to IDA and regional and subregional creditors as well as preserve the ability of international financial institutions to provide high levels of concessional loans in future. Such initiatives should ensure equitable treatment and base multilateral debt relief beyond HIPC on debt sustainability analyses as proposed in IDA-14. It also notes that multilateral debt-service reduction seems preferable to debt stock reduction.

Reflecting the concerns with the limitations of the HIPC Initiative, in early June 2005, G-8 Finance Ministers agreed on a proposal for additional debt reduction under HIPC to be submitted for approval by Heads of State and Government at the G-8 Summit in July and by the shareholders of the participating lending institutions at their respective annual meetings in September. Donors agreed to provide additional development resources to provide full debt relief on outstanding obligations to IMF, the World Bank and the African Development Bank, and to IDA and the African Development Fund for HIPC countries that have reached the completion point and to extend similar relief to qualifying countries when they reach the completion point. Donors also agreed to a formula to ensure meeting the full costs of the measures so that they would not reduce the resources available to the lending institutions for support of other developing countries and to ensure the long-term financial viability of international financial institutions. The agreement did not make proposals for dealing with low and middle-income countries that face similar debt burdens but are not eligible for the HIPC process.

At the 2005 Annual Meeting of the World Bank and the IMF, the proposal was endorsed by the International Monetary and Financial Committee (IMFC) as the Multilateral Debt Relief Initiative (MDRI). It would cancel an estimated $55 billion in debt owed to these institutions by qualifying developing countries. The relief provided to these countries was to be in addition to official assistance available and should not impair the lending capacity of the multilateral financial institutions. For relief on IDA and AfDF loans the G-8 pledged in a letter to the President of the World Bank their commitment "to cover the full cost to offset dollar for dollar the foregone principal and interest repayments of the debt cancelled for the duration of the cancelled loans." Compensation from donors for costs of providing this relief will take place via an additional contribution to the current replenishment.

The IMF, on the other hand, agreed to meet the costs of debt relief from its own resources. To abide by a requirement, specific to the IMF, that the use of its resources be consistent with the principle of uniformity of treatment of all shareholders, it was agreed that all countries with per-capita income of $380 a year or less (HIPCs as well as non-HIPCs) would receive debt relief from IMF resources in the Poverty Reduction and Growth Facility (PRGF) Trust. HIPCs with per-capita income above that level would receive the MDRI relief from existing, and if necessary, additional, bilateral contributions to the PRGF Trust. A call for bilateral contributions will be issued in case additional funding is necessary.

While it was agreed that there would be no new conditions applied to countries benefiting from relief, countries would be expected to maintain their existing commitments. For HIPC completion point countries, IDA relief is expected to become effective on 1 July 2006 for debts in existence at end 2003. For the IMF and the AfDF, this implementation, should happen on 1 January 2006 for debt in existence at the end of 2004, subject to approval by the bilateral contributors to the Trust.

While the proposal seeks to resolve known difficulties in ensuring debt sustainability for countries emerging from the HIPC process, it leaves unresolved the debt difficulties of other low and middle-income countries facing severe debt-service burdens not eligible for HIPC relief. Although initial discussions suggested that relief might be extended to non-HIPC low-income developing countries, no action was taken except, as indicated, in the case of low-income IMF debtors.

New measures for official debt relief for middle-income countries (Evian approach)

In October 2003, the G-7 finance ministers agreed to adopt a new initiative, termed the "Evian approach", providing more flexible debt restructuring through the Paris Club for non-HIPC and middle-income countries. The novelty of the approach was the introduction of a debt sustainability framework to provide an orderly, timely and predictable debt workout so as to reduce the occurrence and severity of financial crises. The negotiations are thus carried out on the basis of long-term debt sustainability analysis provided by IMF with specific attention being paid to evolution of debt ratios over time and the debtor's economic potential. The decision on sustainability rests ultimately with the creditors.

It is expected that the analysis will distinguish between liquidity problems and medium- and long-term debt problems. The former will be dealt with under existing arrangements with reductions in debt payments tailored to the debtors' financing requirements. When debtors have medium- and long-term problems that create questions of debt sustainability, a more comprehensive, country-specific treatment that encompasses coordination with private creditors and puts particular emphasis on comparability of treatment with private creditors will be applied. The treatment thus combines flow treatment and debt stock re-profiling or debt stock reduction. It is expected that the treatment will allow exit from the Paris Club and that comparability will be applied by private creditors. Where necessary, the cut-off date, which for many countries may be traced back to the early 1980s, will be moved forward to determine the debts eligible for restructuring. The approach retains the traditional links to IMF conditionality.

The comprehensive treatment of debt will consist of a three-stage negotiation procedure. In the first stage, a flow rescheduling will be provided under a Fund arrangement that could range from one to three years determined by the past performance of the debtor. The second stage will provide exit treatment, with exact terms and approach dependent upon the results of the debt sustainability analysis of the Fund. In the final stage, exit treatment could be provided in a phased manner over the span of a second Fund programme. The debtor's progress and record of payment to the Paris Club would determine the final outcomes of these negotiations.

There are still some technical challenges that need to be worked out so as to make the approach fully operational, such as that posed by the definition of sustainability, in regard to which a transparent framework is required to allow applicant countries to make their own assessments of sustainable debt levels as a basis for negotiation (see the discussion on debt sustainability below). As the Paris Club emphasizes a case-by-case approach to debt restructuring, lack of sufficient transparency in this process could lead to debt-relief outcomes being guided by political considerations. A framework is also needed to enable creditors to distinguish liquidity problems from insolvency. A clear criterion is also needed to determine the new cut-off dates. Finally, clear, transparent principles by which to determine comparability of treatment with private creditors need to be agreed.

The experience with the Evian approach is still limited. Kenya, which applied to the Paris Club for financing for a PRGF programme with IMF, was the first country treated. Assessed as experiencing a liquidity problem, Kenya was therefore granted flow rescheduling under Houston terms.

Iraq was the first country to receive comprehensive treatment under the Evian approach. Iraq's emergence from the conflict that had followed an economic blockade resulted in high demand for investment in critical social areas and an unsustainable debt burden. In September 2004 the IMF granted Emergency Post-Conflict Assistance and in November the Paris Club granted relief on an estimated indebtedness of $120.2 billion, conditional on a promise by Iraq's then interim Government to seek comparable treatment from other creditors, who accounted for more than two thirds of the outstanding debt.

The negotiations were based on a debt sustainability analysis that concluded that an 80 per cent debt stock reduction would be required to produce sustainability. This implied that Iraq would have, in 2015, debt ratios in line with commonly accepted international standards: external debt at 86 per cent of GDP; external debt at 162 per cent of exports; and debt service at 36 per cent of exports.

In October 2005 the Paris Club granted Nigeria comprehensive treatment providing Naples terms debt reduction on eligible debts and a buyback at a market-related discount on the remaining eligible debts. The agreement will be implemented in two phases in consonance with the implementation of an International Monetary Fund Policy Support Instrument (PSI). In the first phase Nigeria will be required to meet all arrears on all categories of its debt, while Paris Club creditors grant a 33 per cent cancellation of eligible debts. In the second phase, which will follow a successful first review of the PSI planned for March 2006, Nigeria will pay debt service on post-cut off date debt, while Paris Club creditors will grant a further tranche of cancellation of 34% on eligible debts, and Nigeria will buy back the remaining eligible debts. In total, this agreement allows Nigeria to obtain a debt cancellation estimated at US$ 18 billion (including moratorium interest) representing an overall cancellation of about 60% of its debt to the Paris Club of around US$ 30 billion.

DEBT SUSTAINABILITY

Debt sustainability analysis for low-income countries

Identifying sustainable levels of debt and debt service is crucial in determining when external finance supports or hinders domestic resource mobilization. During the 1980s and 1990s, despite access to low-cost financing, many low-income countries accumulated high levels of debt that imposed a heavy burden on their economies, a problem whose resolution ultimately required costly debt relief. The fact that many "graduated" HIPCs are experiencing rising debt burdens, and that debt ratios in some other low-income countries are at elevated levels, suggests a need for better understanding of sustainable debt levels. A new approach is particularly important in assessing the appropriate financing of the sizeable social expenditures that will be required to achieve the Millennium Development Goals. Further, as noted in chapter II, one of the major changes introduced in IDA-14 is the use of debt sustainability analysis to determine eligibility for access to grants.[10] The Evian approach, discussed in the previous section, is also centred on debt sustainability analysis.

As noted above, debt sustainability under the HIPC programme had been based on threshold values of standard debt indicators calculated on historical experience, with an ad hoc adjustment in the enhanced Initiative designed to provide a cushion for external shocks. The new approach[11] evolved an analytical country-specific framework grounded in indicative policy-dependent thresholds and a forward-looking analysis of debt dynamics. The basic novelty was to quantify debt sustainability thresholds on the basis of the quality of policies and institutions, reflecting the idea that countries with stronger policies and institutions could support a higher level of debt on a sustainable basis. In contrast with the HIPC approach, which deals with existing debt overhang, the new approach is intended to provide guidance on new borrowing.

The approach proposed threshold values for traditional debt ratios based on the World Bank Country Policy and Institutional Assessments (CPIAs) that could be used to classify countries in "poor", "medium" and "strong" policy performance categories. In assessing policy, governance was given a higher relative weight. As an example, a country classified as a strong policy performer, with a value of the CPIA index above 3.9, would be regarded as having a sustainable debt burden if its ratio of NPV of debt to GDP was below 60, its ratio of NPV of debt to exports below 300, its ratio of NPV of debt to revenue (excluding grants) below 350, its ratio of debt service to exports below 35, and its ratio of debt service to revenue (excluding grants) below 40 (see table III.2, entries for sub-item entitled "Strong policy" under first subheading entitled "Original proposal").

In response to a request for lower threshold ratios, particularly for strong performers, in March 2005, IMF and IDA set out revisions based on a series of options (see also table III.2). Option 1 maintains the original threshold for NPV of debt to exports at 100 per cent for a weak policy performer, but lowers the ratio to 150 per cent for medium performers and to 200 per cent for strong performers. This option would reduce the new lending permitted to strong and medium performers and require an increase in grant resources

Table III.2.
DEBT-BURDEN THRESHOLDS UNDER ALTERNATIVE OPTIONS[1]

	NPV of debt as share of			Debt service as share of	
	Exports	GDP	Revenue[2]	Exports	Revenue[2]
Original proposal					
Weak policy (CPIA < 3)	100	30	200	15	20
Medium policy (3 < CPIA < 3.9)	200	45	275	25	30
Strong policy (CPIA > 3.9)	300	60	350	35	40
Option 1: Narrower band with same lower bound[3]					
Weak policy (CPIA < 3.25)	100	30	200	15	25
Medium policy (3.25 < CPIA < 3.75)	150	40	250	20	30
Strong policy (CPIA > 3.75)	200	50	300	25	35
Option 2: Narrower band with upper bound equivalent to HIPC Initiative threshold[4]					
Weak policy (CPIA < 3.25)	50	20	150	10	20
Medium policy (3.25 < CPIA < 3.75)	100	30	200	15	25
Strong policy (CPIA > 3.75)	150	40	250	20	30
Option 3: Asymmetric threshold adjustment					
Weak policy (CPIA < 3.25)	100	30	200	15	25
Medium policy (3.25 < CPIA < 3.75)	150	40	250	20	30
Strong policy (CPIA > 3.75)	150	40	250	20	30

Source: International Monetary Fund and International Development Association (March 28,2005).

Note: Operational Framework for Debt Sustainability in Low Income Countries – Further Considerations, Table 2, p. 6.

1   All ratios are rounded, in line with the original presentation.
2   Revenue defined exclusive of grants.
3   Implies a probability of distress of about 18-22 percent.
4   Implies a probability of distress of about 16-19 percent.

for the latter to substitute for their lower share of loans in normal assistance flows. Option 2 is even more conservative, setting the thresholds for the ratio of NPV of debt to exports at 50/100/150 per cent, respectively, for weak/ medium/strong. This option would need additional debt relief beyond the HIPC Initiative, as both weak and medium-risk countries would be graduated from the HIPC Initiative with higher debt ratios than these country-specific thresholds. Option 3 proposes a combination of options 1 and 2 by keeping the lower bound of the original threshold range for weak performing countries, while applying the enhanced HIPC threshold to others. The new approach also proposes the use of contemporaneous values for debt burden denominators to avoid the criticism directed at the backward-looking three-year averages used under the original HIPC framework. Another departure is the choice of discount rates for calculation of NPVs in the African Development Fund. Instead of six-month averages of the currency-specific reference long-term commercial interest rates, the new framework relies on aggregate debt-service projections in United States dollars using the corresponding United States dollar discount rate to derive NPVs.

Since the new approach is based on the view that good policy environments enhance the ability to sustain debt and inasmuch as these policy assessments are based on the summary CPIA indicator that includes subjective evaluations of the policy and institutional environment, the approach is not wholly transparent. The World Bank has indicated that it will publish the CPIA indicators. A further improvement would be greater transparency in particular with respect to the information that enters as inputs into the calculation of these indicators. It might be more appropriate if the Bank had discussions on the appropriate inputs and findings with the country concerned.

As noted above, the new approach is designed to serve as a guide to lending and policy advice within IDA and for other donors. This creates the possibility that both multilateral and bilateral creditors will base their lending decisions on the same CPIA-based indicator and thus reinforce the already existing tendency to herding.

Despite the introduction of lower threshold ratios in the new approach, the approval of debt relief for HIPC completion point countries under the MDRI has brought a number of countries below the debt ratio levels at which they would qualify for grant-based financing. This would mean that they would have to access private credit markets to fund additional expenditures on Millennium Develoment Goals. However, the MDRI presumes that beneficiaries should not require substantial new borrowing. There is thus a need to review the new debt sustainability approach in light of the MDRI.

An assessment of debt sustainability analyses

As in previous approaches to debt sustainability the key determinants in the new approach are the existing stock of debt, the development of fiscal and external repayment capacity that is closely linked to economic growth, and the availability of new external financing, both concessional and non-concessional. The accepted methodology is to identify "critical" threshold levels for the ratio indicators, most of which were already identified in the earlier studies mentioned above. In the HIPC process, these threshold levels had been arrived at using historical averages of debt indicators prevailing when the countries experienced debt crises. Later analysis established critical values for debt indicators that caused sharp increases in the incidence of default or market-based indicators of risk (such as the premium over benchmark interest rates on debt securities traded in the secondary market). In recent years, the World Bank and IMF have moved away from the latter approach owing to the wide dispersion of the levels of these indicators in countries experiencing debt crises. While IMF continues to monitor these traditional debt sustainability indicators, the multilateral institutions have recognized the limitations of the indicator approach and the necessity of formulating an alternative approach (IMF, 2003c).

However, in line with the approach to the work in the 1970s taken by private sector lenders and the Fund in their attempt to forecast the probability of rescheduling,[12] debt *sustainability* is still defined "as a situation in which a borrower is expected to be able to continue servicing its debts without an unrealistically large future correction to the balance of income and expenditure".[13] This implies that the focus is on *debt dynamics* rather than on broader concepts of debt sustainability (see below). The calculations thus concentrate on the evolution of the values of the various indicators under alternative assumptions about the future evolution of key internal and external variables and the probabilities of their occurrence.[14] These calculations have been improved by a focus on the components of both historical and projected debt dynamics that attempt to identify whether the stability of debt ratios arises from the behaviour of interest rates, growth rates, inflation or real exchange-rate changes.

The Fund has also made efforts to further elaborate the variables affecting solvency in both the external and public sectors by "unpacking" the endogenous debt dynamics. Much of this research, spurred by emerging market currency crises in the 1990s, attempted to identify significant variables that predict debt crises, such as shares of short-term debt, reserve levels, public sector contingent liabilities, appropriate exchange-rate regimes, market responses such as credit ratings and spreads, and the degree of serial and cross-correlation of major variables during crises. It has also led to increasing scrutiny of existing practice. For example, the use of NPV as the measure of outstanding debt has been questioned owing to lack of a clear criterion for the choice of discount rates that are based on fluctuating interest rates of Organization for Economic Cooperation and Development (OECD) countries. This has led to suggestions that a fixed discount rate would be more appropriate.

Further, recent IMF debt sustainability analyses have included "stress testing" where debt dynamics are evaluated under an increasingly wide variety of conditions. These tests include: (a) *baseline projections* of external debt/ exports and public debt/revenue with macro assumptions at central forecasts; (b) *sensitivity tests* using both two-standard-deviation shocks and historical averages; and (c) an *assessment of the external risks* surrounding the scenario and the particular vulnerability of the country in question.

Given the difficulties in forecasting both the movements of macroeconomic variables and the vulnerability of a given country to cross-correlations between variables in the case of an external shock, the major challenge has been to establish, given simple probabilities, what shocks and scenarios can be considered "reasonable". This has been made more arduous by the fact that recent capital-account crises produced values of debt indicators that exceeded the upper bounds of the stress-test ranges (IMF, 2003c).

An associated difficulty in this respect is how to distinguish a *liquidity* crisis from *insolvency* or, in terms of the objectives of the 1970s forecasting models, how to determine when a restructuring is appropriate, since only insolvency would require debt relief.[15] Based on these earlier models, the evolving approach still regards the inability of a debtor to obtain additional lending as the cause of the inability to service debt, without determining whether this is due to a shortage of liquidity or insolvency.[16] However, such a distinction has serious implications for debt restructuring. The new debt sustainability analysis is based on probabilities of certain outcomes, one of them being the continued ability of the country to obtain additional lending in future periods. Thus, given the difficulties of forecasting the time-path of crucial variables, there are obstacles in making a country-by-country distinction between chronic and transitory resource gaps, and determining the appropriate perspective (short-, medium- or long-term) to apply in a situation of imminent default.[17] As a result, IMF debt sustainability analyses cannot determine the level of debt that may be considered sustainable for individual countries, and thus the point at which a liquidity problem becomes a solvency problem. A liquidity crisis could turn into insolvency if it is not rapidly contained, through decisive action either by domestic authorities or by multilateral lenders.[18]

This lacuna has increased significance since the Evian approach relies on the new debt sustainability analysis to evaluate the amount of debt relief. The negotiations to return countries to sustainable debt paths will be complicated by the fact that the value of an indicative ratio that is good for one country may be a signal of distress for another, or the same value of a ratio may have a different significance at different points of the economic cycle. The solvency-liquidity distinction forms an important basis for considering debt stock treatments rather than debt flow treatments (for example, a deferral or rescheduling of payments). The lack of a strong and consistent analytical tool to separate liquidity from solvency crises remains a fundamental gap in the evaluation of debt sustainability. In addition, an analysis of the link between debt restructuring and debt sustainability based on past debt negotiations is required. Since the interest rates charged on non-ODA debt in the bilateral agreements after a Paris Club negotiation are often higher and at times vary from those stipulated in the original contract, developing countries frequently complain that they more than repay their obligations in terms of the original contract.

Furthermore, the distinction between liquidity and solvency has other policy implications. The policy advice for an insolvent debtor should generally be for it to pursue a debt-reducing strategy, but advice to an illiquid debtor should be for it to borrow so as to make timely interest payments and prevent the loss of creditworthiness that would lead to insolvency. While the new approach has succeeded in giving a broader range to debt dynamics by taking into account variables that have emerged from a study of recent crises, the analysis still falls short of providing an analytical base for defining threshold levels at which debt is to be considered sustainable.

The recent advent of financial crises driven by the build-up of debt underscores the need for analysis and the development of debt sustainability frameworks that are flexible enough to take into account differences across regions and countries. IMF generally regards stable debt ratios as sustainable and rising debt ratios as problematic. Goldstein (2003) points to the difficulties of associating stable debt ratios with debt sustainability. For a middle-income country, the ability to pay depends on the degree of trade openness. Threshold levels for debt-to-export ratios cannot be uniformly applied to all countries. In all of the recent work on debt sustainability, GDP is used as a denominator for threshold levels to reflect the size of the economy. However, the relation between national output and debt sustainability will depend on the ability of the country to divert resources from the non-tradable sector to the tradable sector so as to generate foreign exchange.

Especially since the Asian financial crisis, an additional problem has been the definition of "public debt".[19] Earlier, this was seen as debt contracted by the sovereign, but it now also includes implicit liabilities of the public sector. This inclusion was largely driven by the lessons learned form the Asian crisis where large contingent liabilities due to exorbitant bank recapitalization costs in many cases dwarfed the contractual obligations of the sovereign to its external debtors.[20] Recent research on the strong links between debt and banking crises and the lack of a comprehensive bankruptcy framework in many emerging markets has led to a recognition of the need to consider contingent sovereign obligations under the umbrella of public debt.

In recent years, developing countries have been advised to develop domestic markets for bonds denominated in local currency. This measure is seen as a means not only to deepen domestic financial markets but also to shield debtors from external exchange-rate and interest rate shocks. As a result, domestic debt levels have risen dramatically since the Asian crisis, especially in East Asia. The emergence of liquid domestic debt markets and the increasing domestic debt burdens of sovereign borrowers have added a new dimension to debt sustainability, reflected in the explicit consideration of domestic debt in recent debt sustainability analyses conducted by IMF. There is concern that the rise of domestic indebtedness may lead to a new emerging market debt crisis in the medium term.[21]

Paradoxically, since access to finance appears as an important element of the Fund's approach, the concentration on *debt dynamics* may unintentionally lead to more borrowing. It inadvertently encourages the practice of engaging in new borrowing to meet claims of existing creditors and thus creates the risk of a country's being caught in an endless spiral of increased borrowing to service rising debt levels. Moreover, capital flows are volatile and thus making judgments on a sustainable level of debt based on the access to external financial flows is bound to produce errors.

As noted, both the approach to prediction of rescheduling in the 1970s and the recent efforts at redefining debt sustainability deal with the ability to meet debt service, with an increasing focus on the currency and term structure of the debt. However, this does not in effect deal with the sustainability of debt in terms of the ability of the country to generate the resources necessary to meet debt service without sacrificing its domestic development. A truly viable alternative approach to the problem would place development objectives at the centre of sustainability.[22] The essence of such an approach was reflected in the call by the Secretary-General of the United Nations for debt sustainability to be defined as the level of debt that allowed a country to achieve the Millennium Development Goals and still service its obligations (United Nations, 2005b). In addition to debt dynamics, this would mean that work on debt sustainability should take into account the sources of the capacity to service debt. Thus, more work is needed on defining debt sustainability in terms of:

- The ability to pay.
- The capacity to repay debt taking domestic priorities of human development and poverty reduction into account.
- A level of debt that is growth enhancing, not one that hinders growth.
- Criteria that take the cyclicality of capital flows into account.

DEBT RESOLUTION AND DEBT RELIEF
INVOLVING PRIVATE CREDITORS

New approaches and initiatives

The 1990s saw a series of increasingly large financial crises that required access by members to balance-of-payments support well beyond their normal quota drawings on Fund resources. On the one hand, this raised questions concerning the adequacy of existing credit lines to manage crises that had their origin in the capital account rather than the current account, and the level of Fund resources necessary to preserve global financial stability (see chap. IV). On the other hand, it gave credence to arguments that Fund support of capital-account crises had created a risk of moral hazard among private creditors who had come to depend on large Fund support programmes to protect them from loss.

For this reason, critics as diverse as the Meltzer Commission (Meltzer and others, 2000) and the United Nations Conference on Trade and Development (2001a) argued in favour of strict limits on access to IMF resources. In order to counter the belief that IMF crisis support was simply being used to "bail out" private creditors, leaving the costs of adjustment to domestic residents, many argued in favour of measures to "bail in" the private sector through a new approach to debt crisis and restructuring. This approach reversed normal practice, in which an IMF agreement was considered a precondition for opening negotiations for restructuring in the case of default by requiring the involvement of the private sector in sharing the burden of restructuring in order for it to receive IMF support. However, the experience of debt restructuring following financial crises also led to a number of proposals to provide a more orderly resolution of financial crises caused by excessive external indebtedness.

In 2001, IMF reformulated proposals that had been under discussion since the 1970s[23] for a debt workout mechanism based on private sector bankruptcy legislation and introduced its own proposal for a sovereign debt restructuring mechanism (SDRM).[24] The proposal sought to provide a legal framework within which to deal with restructuring of debt in an orderly manner. It met with opposition from private and Paris Club creditors, as well as from some developing countries that preferred voluntary arrangements. The private sector was concerned about the problem of moral hazard and the Paris Club creditors resisted the proposal to place the ad hoc arrangements of the Paris Club within a new legal structure. IMF was also not regarded by some as a neutral arbitrator because of the presence of a conflict of interest arising from the role of IMF as arbitrator and its preferred creditor status.[25] Some emerging market economies feared that the initiation of the procedure would result in an increase in their borrowing costs or even in a loss of access to international capital markets. In addition, the proposed new insolvency procedure required an amendment to the IMF Articles of Agreement which would then have to feed into national legislations. In the absence of strong support for the measure, attention shifted to the broader use of collective action clauses (CACs) in bond issues, as well as to the drafting of a voluntary framework in the form of a code of conduct for debt resolution that could be agreed on by debtors and creditors.

The increasing use of bond financing to developing countries has been accompanied by an increase in the number of individual creditors, increasing the difficulty in reaching an agreement on resolution in the case of default. CACs provide a solution to this dilemma of collective action and representation by enabling a qualified majority of bondholders to make decisions that become binding on all bondholders and specify voting rules.[26] This allows Governments facing difficulty in servicing their bonds to declare a standstill without exposing themselves to disruptive legal actions. While a CAC, in principle, does not preclude legal action taken against the debtor by the courts, the inclusion of this provision generally prevents a small group of investors or individual investors from taking disruptive legal action, as has been seen in the recent debt workouts for Ecuador and Argentina. By 2004 CACs had become the market standard for emerging market international sovereign bonds issued under New York law. In 2005 more than 95 per cent of new issues, in value terms, included CACs. The rules governing London issues have always allowed for similar clauses. There is still no evidence that they have increased the borrowing costs of developing countries.

Inclusion of a CAC does not necessarily imply that it will be invoked at the time of a debt restructuring. For example, Pakistan in 1999 restructured its international bonds without invoking the CACs included in these bonds, preferring an offer for a voluntary bond exchange. By contrast, Ukraine made use of the CACs included in four of its outstanding international bonds in

April 2000, thereby obtaining the agreement of 95 per cent of its bondholders even though the holders of bonds were widely dispersed. Debt restructuring can also take place using mechanisms different from CACs. In mid-1999, Ecuador carried out a restructuring of its bond debt by inviting eight of the larger institutional holders of its bonds to join a consultative group, with the aim of providing a formal communications mechanism.

Concerns that the inclusion of CACs in bond issues might lead to an increase in the cost of borrowing for the issuer do not appear to be warranted in light of the experiences of Mexico, Brazil, South Africa, Venezuela and Belize. Moreover, a recent study comparing the yield on bonds issued in the Euromarket with CACs, and bonds issued in the United States market and Euromarket without CACs, shows that the inclusion of CACs in bond issues in the Euromarket did not impact secondary market yields as of early 2003 (Gugiatti and Richards, 2003).[27]

One difficulty with CACs as a substitute for a more formal mechanism is that only newly issued bonds would contain CACs, so that the collective action problems could be resolved only once all outstanding bonds were retired. However, the inclusion of CACs in sovereign debt-exchange offers has speeded their expansion and nearly 60 per cent of outstanding issues included CACs as of the beginning of 2006.

In addition, there are perceived risks in the use of the clause, inasmuch as debtors, in alliance with a majority of the creditors, may be able to discriminate against a minority. Another difficulty is that a debtor may be in a position to manipulate the voting process by putting real or fictitious claims in the hands of the creditors that are under the influence of the sovereign. Experience with aggregation thus far has been limited to countries that have issued bonds on a relatively small scale, such as Ecuador, Pakistan, the Republic of Moldova, Ukraine and Uruguay, and it remains to be seen if the problems of aggregation can be resolved for larger sovereign debtors.

The SDRM proposal aimed at a comprehensive framework within which to deal with sovereign debt problems and relied on various statutory instruments to achieve this objective, such as aggregation of claims, targeted stay on litigation, and a dispute resolution forum: CACs constitute an instrument that is targeted at facilitating the restructuring of bonds. In conclusion, the objective of codes of conduct for private creditors and sovereign debtors is to develop a comprehensive voluntary framework within which to address potential debt-servicing problems while preserving to the maximum extent possible contractual arrangements. In its communiqué of 24 April 2004 issued on the occasion of its spring 2004 meeting, the International Monetary and Financial Committee of the Board of Governors of IMF encouraged sovereign debtors and private creditors to continue their work on a voluntary code of conduct, and looked forward to reviewing further work on issues of general relevance to the orderly resolution of financial crises. The finance ministers of the Group of Seven (G-7) have also welcomed efforts at the Group of Twenty (G-20) to develop a code of conduct. The idea is to initiate a voluntary dialogue between debtors and creditors so as to promote corrective policy action to reduce the frequency and severity of a crisis and codes that would lead to an orderly debt workout.

The voluntary code of conduct is perceived by debtors as a framework within which they can formally engage creditors and provide information to them. Creditors, on the other hand, see the code as a framework within which debtors would make stronger commitments to engagement and the provision of information. It is expected that a code of conduct will clarify the roles of the sovereign debtor and creditor, help to avoid disruption in the process of crisis resolution and effect a more balanced distribution of the financial burden.

The Institute of International Finance (IIF) has drafted four key pillars: information sharing and transparency; close debtor-creditor dialogue and cooperation; good faith during a restructuring process; and fair treatment. It is expected that an early dialogue between issuers and investors will lead to a quick rehabilitation of debtors and restore market access. A technical group consisting of Brazil, the Republic of Korea, Turkey and Mexico in association with the IIF and the International Primary Market Association has presented a draft code that has been endorsed by the G-20. Creditors do not consider the code as more robust than current market practices. The increased emphasis on sharing information between investors and debtors and investor-creditor relations, which is being given support under the code of conduct is asymmetric, with debtors providing more information but creditors doing nothing about improving the flow of information from their side.

Whether voluntary efforts, such as those reflected in these principles, can provide a sufficiently strong basis for an effective crisis resolution mechanism has yet to be tested. In the long run, it may have to be combined with internationally sanctioned standstills to be used when needed. It is thus essential that the explorations of debt workout mechanisms, including voluntary codes and international mediation or arbitration mechanisms, continue with full support of all stakeholders. Since it will take time for this to be implemented, a transitional framework may also be needed. Overall, there has been less progress in providing institutional mechanisms for the debt problems facing middle-income countries. The experiences of some of these countries are analysed in the next section.

Experiences of alternative debt restructuring mechanisms[28]

In the absence of the implementation of a multilateral framework for debt restructuring like those outlined above, debt crises in the 1990s relied increasingly on voluntary country-by-country negotiations between debtors and creditors. At the same time, resolution moved farther away from the pattern of the Brady Plan. As noted above, the initial response to the Mexican default of 1982 had been voluntary rescheduling and domestic adjustment policies, complemented in the Baker plan by additional IMF and private financing. It was only when the Brady Plan added substantial debt write-downs backed by credit enhancements in the form of collateral for the new Brady bonds that debtors managed to meet their debt service through a return to international credit markets. During the 1990s, the fear that large IMF lending, such as that provided to Mexico in 1994, would create moral hazard led to the view that the market mechanism should be allowed to determine restructuring, as IMF assistance was cut back. This was evident first in the withdrawal of the debt enhancements as part of IMF support in the Russian default.

Under an IMF facility arrangement, the Russian Federation had implemented a domestic stabilization through control of the money supply that required its fiscal deficit to be financed through market sales of treasury securities (known by the acronyms GKO and OFZ) at interest rates substantially above international levels. This led to a rapid increase in debt service that reached about one third of federal spending in the first quarter of 1998. The major buyers were Russian banks which borrowed dollars through repurchase agreements using the bonds as collateral, earning substantial profits from the large interest rate differential. Given IMF support for a stable exchange rate, the risk of devaluation was considered to be low. Non-residents accounted for about a quarter of the subsequently defaulted debt, financing their purchases with rubles received from repurchase agreements with Russian banks. These investors hedged their currency risks with forward contracts from Russian as well as from Western banks. Falling export revenues due to the collapse of commodity prices after the Asian crisis reduced government revenues and external earnings. Attempts to offset the decline with higher interest rates failed to attract sufficient external inflows to finance government deficits and caused rising debt service that the Government could no longer meet. In August 1998, the Russian Federation suspended payment of debt service and payments on forward contracts. This meant that the collateral behind the repurchase agreements was worthless and banks and foreign investors faced losses of 100 per cent of their investments. The situation was aggravated by the suspension of payment on forwards by Western banks. Russian banks' attempts to repay borrowed dollars increased downward pressure on the exchange rate and international reserves led to the collapse of the currency and brought technical insolvency for the banks.

In March 1999, a novation scheme accepted by over 99 per cent of creditors (by value) offered 10 per cent of par value in cash, 20 per cent in 3- and 6-month debt securities and 70 per cent in 4-to-5-year securities. The proceeds received by non-residents were deposited into special ruble-denominated accounts that were not freely convertible into foreign exchange or cash rubles. Owing to the complexity of the scheme, there is no reliable estimate of the loss incurred by investors. In a strategy that would later be followed by Ecuador, the Russian Federation suspended service on former Soviet Union foreign debt and began accumulating arrears, but stayed current on all its Eurobond issues and other external debt denominated in foreign currencies contracted by the Russian Federation.

A new agreement with IMF in 1999 contained even more stringent conditionality, but it seems that the major purpose of the new loan was to allow the Russian Federation to stay current on its payments to IMF and to reach agreements with other creditors. In August 1999, a rescheduling was agreed with the Paris Club and in August 2000 with the London Club, exchanging obligations of the Bank for Foreign Economic Affairs for Eurobonds issued by the Russian Federation.

This multistage process of write-offs and renegotiation, accompanied by a recovery in commodity prices, in particular petroleum, rising fiscal receipts, and external budget surpluses along with growth rates in excess of 5 per cent, led international credit rating agencies to classify Russian sovereign debt as investment grade by the end of 2004.

In Ecuador, debt enhancement was not offered and the support of IMF remained questionable in the early stages of its debt renegotiation process. Following a series of climatic, external earnings and political shocks that had led to a banking crisis in August of 1999, Ecuador missed payment of interest on the Brady bond portion of its $13.6 billion external debt. A month later it announced that it would default only on the Discount Brady bonds, since these bonds had credit-enhanced interest collateral that could be invoked on a 25 per cent vote by holders. When this decision was taken, it activated cross-default clauses in other bonds and made automatic default on the principal of the $6 billion in Brady bonds, as well as the $500 million in Eurobonds.

Unable to agree a support programme with IMF, Ecuador initially attempted a domestic stabilization programme based on dollarization. By April 2000, the Government had been granted a one-year IMF standby loan for about $306 million accompanied by nearly $2 billion in additional multilateral support.

In July, about 97 per cent of Brady investors accepted an offer to exchange the defaulted bonds for about $4 billion in new 30-year bonds and about $1 billion in cash to cover accrued interest and amortization. Since the Brady bonds did not contain CACs, any change in terms required the unanimous decision of all the creditors. In order to induce creditors to participate in the restructuring, Ecuador used carefully crafted exit consents that required only a supermajority, plus upfront cash disbursements and principal reinstatement clauses to encourage participation. The haircut of approximately 40 cents on the dollar was marginally larger than the 36 per cent estimated for the Russian default. The restructuring resulted in a reduction of Ecuador's Brady bond and Eurobond stock by 40 per cent and a reduction in service of $1.5 million over the first five years of the exchange. It also opened the way for a Paris Club agreement restructuring 100 per cent of its $887 million official debt.[29]

Ecuador's restructuring provides an example of a successful voluntary restructuring of securities held by a heterogeneous group of bondholders with competing interests in the absence of CACs. However, it is not clear that this market-based approach dependent on the relative bargaining strengths of debtors and creditors has provided long-term debt sustainability, given that Ecuador's current ratios of debt to exports of 180 per cent and debt to GDP of nearly 50 per cent in 2004 place it in the high-risk category according to the new approach to debt sustainability.

In contrast to both the Russian Federation and Ecuador, Argentina was not even provided with additional multilateral financial support after its default in 2001. Argentina had already received exceptional access to IMF resources of 800 percent of quota when IMF suspended a review of an existing arrangement, halting disbursement and effectively declaring to financial markets that it no longer considered Argentina's external debt sustainable. The government default declaration less than a month later made rollover of maturing Fund borrowing the equivalent of "lending into arrears",[30] and thus subject to "good faith" negotiations with creditors. This meant that Argentina was subject to IMF conditionality on its recovery programme and debt renegotiations without receiving any additional resources to support them. This was a clear application of the new approach of refusing to use Fund resources to bail out external creditors,[31] and to leave restructuring to voluntary market processes.

The decision to suspend current programmes, along with the Fund's position as a preferred creditor, meant that Argentina faced its creditors in very different conditions from those of previous debt renegotiations and thus that debt sustainability required a substantially larger debt reduction. Further, Argentina was denied new support to avoid moral hazard problems but at the same time, under lending-into-arrears principles, was required to provide a settlement with creditors to avoid having to repay maturing programmes. Under these conditions, it was difficult or outright impossible to follow a market solution.

On the grounds that about 50 per cent of the population was below the poverty line as the result of the crisis that it had been undergoing, Argentina argued that it had made sufficient contribution and that the only equitable debt renegotiation was one that allowed a rate of growth that provided for a recovery of the living conditions of the population and offered the assurance that the solution was sustainable on a long-term basis. Rather than view the negotiation as providing the means by which it could borrow what was required to meet post-restructuring debt service, Argentina argued that the solution would have to make it possible to meet debt service without additional borrowing. Thus, the break with the Brady solution of providing additional funding, write-offs and debt enhancement to ensure a return to capital markets was met in Argentina with a refusal to consider the return to international borrowing as a solution to its debt sustainability. After a series of adjustments to unilateral proposals to creditors, Argentina made an exchange offer at the end of 2004 that implied about a 75 per cent haircut which was accepted by over 75 per cent of creditors.

Although it is still unclear if major creditor countries consider this result to have met the good-faith conditions that would allow rollover of existing credits, and although some outstanding creditors have attempted to achieve full consideration through challenges in the courts, the Argentine experience may herald a new post-Brady era in debt renegotiations that highlights the difficulties of the market-based approach and reinforces the need for a new multilateral approach to default resolution.

NOTES

1   Concessional bilateral credits accounted for about 60 per cent of funds loaned to developing countries, with 6 per cent multilateral credits and a third in direct investment and trade credits in the period. See D'Arista (1979, pp. 57-58).
2   An assessment of the pre- and post-debt rescheduling experience of seven developing countries notes that a majority experienced slower growth, investment and net resources transfers after rescheduling, suggesting the need for more susbstantial relief measures. See United Nations Conference on Trade and Development (1974).
3   See United Nations Conference on Trade and Development (1975), where the tendency for creditors to require an IMF standby arrrangement as a prior condition for renegotiation is noted.

4 United Nations Conference on Trade and Development (1975) notes that the main focus of IMF assessments was on short-run economic problems.

5 See Birdsall, Claessens and Diwan (2004, pp. 59-62). These authors show that the result has been for countries with higher debt stocks to receive higher aid flows, irrespective of the policies they follow, thus limiting the policy selectivity that is supported by official donors.

6 Regarding the eligibility criteria, it has been argued by some authors that eligibility ratios are not based on a comprehensive measure of either poverty or indebtedness, and that as a result some poor and some heavily indebted countries are not HIPC-eligible. The scope of country selection is also regarded by some analysts as too narrow, as the "IDA-only" criterion disqualifies some otherwise debt-strapped non-IDA countries. It has also been asserted that political and cost factors excluded countries that met eligibility criteria (see Gunter, 2001; G-24 Secretariat, 2003; United Nations Conference on Trade and Development, 2004b).

7 These threshold levels were largely based on empirical work undertaken by Underwood (1990) and Cohen (1996). A critique of HIPC using market-based indicators can be found in Cohen (2001).

8 In 2005, Honduras, Rwanda and Zambia and in 2006 Cameroon and Honduras reached completion point. In 2005 Burundi and in 2006 the Congo reached decision point.

9 See Kingdom of Norway, Ministry of Foreign Affairs (2005).

10 This reassessment process was initiated in the International Monetary Fund (2002b).

11 In a series of papers by IMF and International Development Association (2004 and 2005).

12 The Fund's analysis of how outstanding stocks of liabilities evolve over time includes projections of the flows of revenue, expenditure and debt servicing, current account and exchange-rate changes. Assessments of fiscal sustainability are an important element of the debt sustainability exercise and include indicators of public debt and deficits and medium-term fiscal projections. The projected debt *dynamics* in turn depends upon macroeconomic and financial market developments. A key variable is the availability of financing.

13 International Monetary Fund (May 2002b), p. 4.

14 The distinction between an analysis of debt dynamics and a broader view of debt sustainability is elaborated in Schneider (2007).

15 Debt relief here refers to a write-off of debt leading to a reduction in the stock of debt. Much confusion arises from the fact that the term is commonly used for both debt write-off and debt rescheduling which allows the debtor grace periods before repaying the amount treated in the rescheduling.

16 "Sustainability thus incorporates the concepts of solvency and liquidity, without making a sharp demarcation between them" (International Monetary Fund, 2002b, p. 4).

17 This distinction is examined in detail in Roubini (2001).

18 As has been stressed by Kenen (2001), and explored further using a more theoretical formulation by Haldane and Kruger (2004).

19 See Goldstein (2003) for a discussion within the Brazilian context.

20 See figure 3.1 on "Public debt in emerging market economies" in International Monetary Fund (2003a).

21 See International Monetary Fund (2003a).

22 See Schneider (2007). This issue was consistently addressed in the Multi-stakeholder consultations on sovereign debt for sustained development, held in New York in March 2005 and in Maputo, Mozambique, also in March 2005, and undertaken by the Department of Economic and Social Affairs of the United Nations Secretariat as part of the financing for development process.

23 In 1978, the United Nations Conference on Trade and Development raised the question of debt relief, proposing a mechanism of debt reorganization that would be "carried out within an institutional framework that would ensure the application of the principles of international financial cooperation and protect the interests of debtors and creditors equitably" (see UNCTAD, 1978, annex II, p. 2). A more detailed proposal was made in 1980 to create "a multinational forum agreed upon by the debtor and the creditors", see the annex to section B of Trade and Development Board resolution 222 (XXI) of 27 September 1980 which endorsed a set of features to guide members in future operations relating to the debt problems of interested developing countries. The United Nations Conference on Trade and Development subsequently proposed a mechanism based on the 1978 reform of United States bankruptcy law; see annex to chapter VI of *Trade and Development Report, 1986* (United Nations Conference on Trade and Development, 1986) which contains a proposal based on the analysis provided by a New York law firm. Similar proposals have also been made in the 1998 and 2001 editions of the *Trade and Development Report* (United Nations Conference on Trade and Development, 1998 and 2001a).

24 For a survey of the various prior proposals in this area, see Rogoff and Zettelmeyer (2002) who curiously do not refer to the prior proposals by UNCTAD.

25 A recent proposal seeks to remedy this by using the G-20 to create an independent entity to oversee the mechanism. See Berensmann and Schroeder (2005).

26 The use of CACs in bond issues governed by English, Japanese and Luxembourg law has been an established practice. Historically, such bonds issued under United States, German, Italian or Swiss law did not include such clauses. The largest market for sovereign bonds is in New York; however, bonds issued under New York law have traditionally included only majority enforcement provisions, not majority restructuring provisions.

27 There is as yet no evidence how CACs may perform if a major sovereign defaults on its bonds that include CACs. The Emerging Market Credits Association has largely remained silent on the type of CAC that should be included.

28 For a more complete discussion, see United Nations (2001a), sect. 3.

29 Ecuador's default was not well received by private creditors who objected that Ecuador's Brady Plan had already involved a 45 per cent write-down and was supposed to have provided permanent resolution. In addition, some accused IMF of having precipitated the default in order to test its new approach to "bailing in" private sector creditors. See BradyNet Forum (http://www.bradynet.com/ bbs/bradybonds/100090-0.html).

30 Conceived in the late 1980s as a means of resolving the debt crisis, the scope of the Fund's policy concerning lending into sovereign external payments arrears to private creditors required the debtor to pursue appropriate policies and make a good faith effort to reach a collaborative agreement with its creditors. See IMF (2002c).

31 Although some suggested that the exceptional access granted in 2001 allowed foreign creditors to bail out before the crisis (see Cafiero and Llorens, 2002). This is confirmed by the large increase in capital outflows reported in November of 2001 (see Comisión Especial de la Cámera de Diputadas, República Argentina, 2005).

Chapter IV
Systemic Issues

The systemic agenda addressed by the Monterrey Consensus covers two broad groups of issues. The first relates to the structural features of the international monetary system, and the possible vulnerabilities that they pose for the world economy or for specific groups of countries. The second is associated with the institutional design of the current international financial system.

With respect to the first set of issues, the analysis undertaken in the present chapter starts with the major macroeconomic imbalances that characterize the world economy today, which many observers fear may become unsustainable. This issue relates, at least in part, to the design of the international reserve system, particularly to the role of the United States dollar as the major international currency. The second issue has to do with the potential vulnerability to systemic risk generated by the evolving structure of private international financial markets. A particular source of concern is the potential interaction between the macroeconomic risks associated with the current global imbalances and the potential vulnerabilities generated by the financial innovations and market consolidation that are taking place. A third issue relates to the asymmetries that characterize the international financial system which not only subject developing countries to pro-cyclical private capital flows, but also limit their room for manoeuvre in adopting counter-cyclical macroeconomic policies. The major implications of this problem were dealt with in chapter I; this chapter considers its implications for the role of the international financial institutions in crisis prevention and resolution.

The analysis of these problems includes some issues relating to institutional design, such as the role of multilateral surveillance, the possible role of the International Monetary Fund (IMF) in the coordination of macroeconomic policies among major industrialized nations, the surveillance of domestic policies and emergency liquidity provision during crises. The last three sections deal with a selected set of additional institutional issues: the role of special drawing rights (SDRs), the only genuinely international reserve asset in the current system; the role of regional reserve funds and other regional monetary arrangements; and the voice and representation of developing countries in decision-making in the international financial system.

GLOBAL MACROECONOMIC IMBALANCES
AND THE INTERNATIONAL RESERVE SYSTEM

The global economy has large and widening imbalances across regions, reflected in the large current-account deficit in the United States of America which is matched by an aggregate of surpluses in a number of other countries, mainly in Asia and Europe, as well as oil-exporting countries. These imbalances are continuing to widen and policymakers worldwide are increasingly concerned about their sustainability, about the risks associated with various adjustment processes and, ultimately, about their implications for global financial stability and the growth of the world economy. Even if the imbalances are sustainable or if there is a smooth adjustment, questions remain on whether such large and skewed imbalances constitute an efficient and equitable allocation of global resources across countries.

The current-account deficits of the United States have been the rule for most of the past three decades, with only a brief period of balance (see figure IV.1), and have risen rapidly since 2000 to a record high of more than $800 billion in 2005. As a result, the United States, the world's largest economy, has accumulated net international debts of about $3 trillion, making it the world's largest debtor. These changes in national holdings of international assets are both a counterpart to the current-account deficits and their mirror image in national savings-investment imbalances. The external deficit of the United States corresponds to a shortfall of its savings in relation to its investment and surpluses of savings over investment elsewhere, with the United States

Figure IV.1.
UNITED STATES CURRENT-ACCOUNT
DEFICITS, 1970-2005

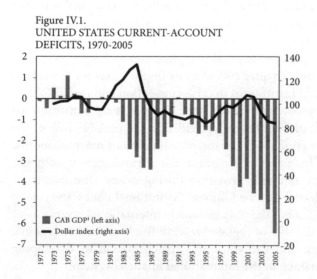

CAB GDP¹ (left axis)
Dollar index (right axis)

Source: United States Department of Commerce, Bureau of Economic Analysis, and United States Fed.

1 The ratio of current-account balance to GDP.

absorbing at least 80 per cent of the savings that other countries do not invest domestically. The solution to the problem of the global imbalances can therefore be seen either from the trade perspective or from the point of view of rebalancing savings and investment across countries.

These chronic large United States imbalances are closely related to the nature of the current international reserve system and international monetary arrangements. A central feature of the international reserve system is the use of the national currency of the United States as the major reserve money and instrument for international payments. Other major currencies, the euro and the yen, play a supplementary and slightly larger role than in the past, with their exchange rates floating relative to the dollar.

As early as the 1960s, Robert Triffin (1960) focused on a dilemma facing the international reserve system. He pointed out that the increase in the supply of international liquidity necessary to support expanding international trade depended on balance-of-payment deficits in the United States. However, when the US deficit rose, the supply of dollars relative to the US gold stock increased, eroding confidence in the ability of the US to preserve the gold-dollar peg on which the Bretton Woods system was founded and weakening the dollar's role as the world's reserve currency. Attempts to counter this dilemma led to a perpetual cycle of expansion and contraction in the external deficit of the United States, along with its effects on world economy growth.

Although the dilemma posed by Triffin was set in the context of the fixed exchange rates that characterized the Bretton Woods system, and presaged its collapse, it remains broadly relevant to the current international monetary arrangements. One important difference is that the origin of the external imbalances of the United States has changed. In the 1960s, they were the counterpart of the attraction of low interest rates in US capital markets to foreign borrowers, whereas now they are the consequence of large foreign investments in US real and financial assets.

Under the Bretton Woods system, stability of exchange rates relative to the dollar depended on exchange market intervention by all central banks, except the US. Thus the US had no need to hold international reserves, while all other central banks had to hold dollars. The US only had to guarantee the dollar price of gold, and thus held gold reserves. As Triffin predicted, the system broke down when the amount of outstanding claims on the US so exceeded its gold reserves that it became clear that the dollar price of gold could not be guaranteed.

In the current system there is no longer any peg to gold, But, as the issuer of international reserve money, the United States still has no need for international reserves since it is able to finance persistent external deficits with its own currency. The absence of an external constraint allows the United States to adopt policies that are more stimulatory than those of other countries. In contrast, most other, particularly developing countries cannot use their own national currencies in their international transactions and as a medium for accumulating foreign-exchange reserves, are constrained in their capacity to run external deficits by their accumulated reserves and their access to global credit markets, both of which are limited.

The United States also profits more concretely from its role as the world's banker. A large part of its liabilities are the foreign-exchange reserves accumulated by other countries, usually held in a combination of cash, and short-term and liquid longer-term securities paying a relatively low interest rate, while its assets consist mostly of its long-term loans and equity investment in foreign countries, which yield higher returns. In addition, dollar depreciation produces an increase in the value of US-owned foreign assets and income relative to foreign claims on the US. Thus, despite its position as a net international debtor, the United States continues to have a positive net inflow of investment income from abroad.

Historically, adjustments to the large external deficits of the United States have involved considerable volatility in foreign exchange and world financial markets and a contractionary effect on both the United States and the global economy. In the early 1970s, adjustment led to the collapse of the Bretton Woods system and the transition to a floating exchange-rate system among major currencies, including a major downward correction of the dollar (see figure IV.1). It was also one of the factors that contributed to the end of the "golden age" of post-war economic growth in the developed countries.

During the 1980s, the United States faced the combination of "twin" fiscal and external deficits and an appreciating dollar. The adjustment was initiated by the 1985 Plaza Accord which sought to reverse the appreciation. However, the market response produced a sharp fall in the value of the dollar of about 40 per cent against a basket of other major currencies, despite efforts at international policy coordination among the major developed countries, such as the Louvre Accord of 1987.[1] Although this period saw two sharp equity market falls in the United States in 1987 and 1989 this did not dampen domestic activity and the correction of the deficit only occurred after the slowdown in growth of gross domestic product (GDP) in the United States produced by the collapse of the domestic real estate bubble and recession in 1990. The United States slowdown led, in turn, to a global economic slowdown in 1989-1991.

The adjustment of the deficit in the United States during the late 1980s was matched by a rebalancing of surpluses in Germany and a few other developed countries, a number of developing countries in Asia and, as a result of falling petroleum prices, in some oil-exporting developing countries. In contrast, Japan's large external surplus declined only marginally and rebounded in the following years, even though the yen had appreciated significantly against the dollar since the mid-1980s. In this period Japan engaged in policies to improve domestic productivity and then turned to outsourcing of production in the US and South East Asia to retain international competitiveness despite appreciation. The experience of Japan during the 1980s and the 1990s shows that currency revaluation in a surplus country may not necessarily result in the necessary adjustment in the external imbalance; this is contrary to the conventional wisdom, which relies exclusively on exchange rates to adjust current-account imbalances, that still underpins some analyses.

Today's global imbalances have become larger and lasted longer than experienced in the 1980s. Some analysts argue that increasing global economic integration, particularly deepening global financial integration, have made current imbalances different from those of the 1970s and 1980s in terms of their sustainability and their implications for the world economy. The difference, however, can be only in quantity, not in quality. As the imbalances continue to increase, the risks of an abrupt and disorderly reversal also rise, suggesting risks of larger adjustment costs for the world economy in the future.

Other analysts have argued that current imbalances could be sustained for a long time (see Dooley, Folkerts-Landau and Garber, 2003; 2004a; 2004b). This school of thought contends that the maintenance of exchange market intervention by Asian countries to stabilize their currencies will continue to provide an important part of the financing needed by the United States to continue its current-account deficits. According to this point of view, for many developing countries, the economic benefits of stable and weak exchange rates exceed the costs of reserve accumulation.[2] In turn, continued reserve accumulation by some Asian and other central banks allows the United States to rely on domestic demand to drive its growth and to run the resulting large current-account deficits. After a decline from 70 per cent in the 1960s to almost 50 per cent in the early 1990s, the share of United States dollar assets in total world official holdings of foreign exchange has since rebounded, to about 66 per cent (see table IV.1); the share of the euro remains around 25 per cent and that of the Japanese yen less than 4 per cent.[3]

However, an increasing number of observers fear that three features may cause the rising United States current-account deficit to become unsustainable in the next few years. First, in difference from the 1990s, the deficit is now financing domestic consumption and military expenditures, rather than

TABLE IV.1.
SHARE OF NATIONAL CURRENCIES IN IDENTIFIED OFFICIAL HOLDINGS OF FOREIGN EXCHANGE, END OF YEAR[1], 1995-2004
(Percentage)

All Countries Currency	1995	1996	1997	1998	1999	2000	2001	2002	2003	2004
U.S. dollar	59.0	62.1	65.2	69.4	71.0	70.5	70.7	66.5	65.8	65.9
Japanese yen	6.8	6.7	5.8	6.2	6.4	6.3	5.2	4.5	4.1	3.9
Pound sterling	2.1	2.7	2.6	2.7	2.9	2.8	2.7	2.9	2.6	3.3
Swiss franc	0.3	0.3	0.3	0.3	0.2	0.3	0.3	0.4	0.2	0.2
Euro[2]	—	—	—	—	17.9	18.8	19.8	24.2	25.3	24.9
Deutsche mark	15.8	14.7	14.5	13.8	—	—	—	—	—	—
French franc	2.4	1.8	1.4	1.6	—	—	—	—	—	—
Netherlands guilder	0.3	0.2	0.4	0.3	—	—	—	—	—	—
ECUs[3]	8.5	7.1	6.0	1.2	—	—	—	—	—	—
Other currencies[4]	4.8	4.3	3.8	4.5	1.6	1.4	1.2	1.4	1.9	1.8

Source: International Monetary Fund, Annual Report of the Executive Board for the financial year ended 10 April, 2005.

1   The currency shares are calculated for the reserves of member countries that report the currency composition of their foreign exchange reserves to the International Monetary Fund.

2   Not comparable with the combined share of euro legacy currencies in previous years because it excludes the euros received by euro area members when their previous holdings of other euro area members' legacy currencies were converted into euros on January 1, 1999.

3   In the calculation of currency shares, the ECU is treated as a separate currency. ECU reserves held by the monetary authorities existed in the form of claims on both the private sector and the European Monetary Institute (EMI), which issued official ECUs to European Union central banks through revolving swaps against the contribution of 20 percent of their gross gold holdings and U. S. dollar reserves. On December 31, 1998, the official ECUs were unwound into gold and U.S. dollars; hence, the share of ECUs at the end of 1998 was sharply lower than a year earlier. The remaining ECU holdings reported for 1998 consisted of ECUs issued by the private sector, usually in the form of ECU deposits and bonds. On January 1, 1999, these holdings were automatically converted into euros.

4   Foreign exchange reserves that are reported to be held in currencies other than those listed above.

investment; second, United States investment is shifting towards non-tradable sectors; and third, the deficit is increasingly being funded by short-term flows rather than direct investment (Summers, 2004). It is such factors that increase the risk of a reversal of capital flows and a sharp adjustment of the dollar that would make current-account deficits less likely to be sustainable, as has been the past experience in both developed and developing countries. In addition, during some recent periods an increasing share of the financing needed by the United States to sustain its deficits has been provided by the world's central banks, not by private investors (Higgins and Klitgaard, 2004).

For these reasons, many argue that there is an increasing risk that the value of the dollar could fall significantly: the financing required to sustain United States current-account deficits may be increasing faster than the willingness of the world's central banks to continue to build up dollar reserves given the potential sources of instability built into the current international financial system (see, for instance, Williamson, 2004; International Monetary Fund, 2005g; Roubini and Setser, 2005). One of these sources of instability is the tension between the growing need of the United States for financing to cover its current-account and fiscal deficits and the losses that those lending to the United States in dollars are almost certain to incur from further dollar depreciation. There are also concerns that rising trade deficits will lead to protectionist pressures, especially against Chinese products; indeed signs of a new burst of protectionism are already apparent. These growing signs that the system is under stress raise doubts that the present massive rate of reserve accumulation can continue for an extended period.

Globally, owing to the particular role that the dollar plays in the world economy, the income and wealth effects that the devaluation of the dollar generates tend to run counter to the relative price effects, resulting in limited overall adjustment. Dollar depreciation may therefore counteract the more fundamental rebalancing of growth rates among major economies which is required to correct the global imbalances (United Nations, 2005a). In particular, currency appreciation in Europe and the economies of Asia is likely to lead to reduced investment demand and growth,increasing, rather than reducing, the savings surplus of these regions. The fact that the wealth effects of dollar depreciation are also adverse for those holding dollar assets is likely to reduce their spending, particularly where those assets are held by private agents (as is the case in Europe). Appreciation of the yen may also slow the effort of Japan to overcome price deflation and a large-scale appreciation of other currencies could eventually generate deflation in the economies concerned.

Until recently, concerns about the deficit of the United States have been reflected mainly in foreign exchange markets, but not in bond and equity markets. While individual regions have adjusted their US investments, the decline of the dollar in the foreign-exchange market in the past few years has not been accompanied by overall sales of the foreign holdings of United States government bonds or stocks during the same period. The risk is that this dichotomy between the foreign-exchange market and the capital market may be a short-run anomaly, as the volatility is stock markets in May 2006 showed, and that there could eventually be a large movement away from dollar-denominated securities by foreign holders. This, as well as the fear of inflation, could increase interest rates in the United States, as well as in the global capital market; which in turn, could have negative effects on the United States economy and on the rest of the world, particularly on the developing countries.

This highlights the need to mitigate the risks of an abrupt adjustment of the global economy. In this regard, there is a large degree of agreement that measures should be taken simultaneously in two broad areas (see, for example, International Monetary Fund, 2005g; United Nations, 2005a). First, the United States should reduce its fiscal deficit; and second, the surplus countries in Europe and Asia should adopt more expansionary policies to stimulate their aggregate demand. Despite the growing consensus on these priorities, implementation has been very limited. Further delay could cut short the present period of improved widespread global growth.

Smooth global rebalancing requires more international policy cooperation and coordination. Given the systemic risks associated with global imbalances, purely national approaches to the macroeconomic policies of major economies are inadequate. In choosing their policy stance, national policymakers should take into account the interdependence and spillover effects of their policies on others. Consequently, their domestic policies should at least be based on mutually consistent assumptions and preferably be designed in a cooperative manner that recognizes global interdependence.

Reinforcing the role of IMF in surveillance of major economies and in surveillance of developments in the international financial system—one of the most important innovations introduced during the Asian crisis—are as important as ever. These roles could be complemented by its more prominent role as an honest broker in policy coordination among major economies (Ocampo, 2002). Despite the problems of representation addressed below, IMF is the only institution where developing countries have a voice on macroeconomic imbalances of major economies and could eventually have a voice on global macroeconomic policy coherence.

It has thus been suggested that there is a need to rethink the role of the Fund in the management of the international monetary system (King, 2005). With the advent of financial globalization, surveillance should focus not only on crisis-prone countries but, increasingly, on the stability of the system as a whole and on major economic challenges that require a global cooperative approach (IMF, 2006). Consequently, rather than be confined to occasional lending to middle-income countries hit by financial crises and balance-of-payments financing for low-income countries, the Fund should play a more active role in supporting the management of the world economy. This role should be reinforced by the agreement of the International Monetary and Financial Committee (IMFC) in April 2006 that IMF will introduce multilateral surveillance of groups of countries and regions to assess the interaction of the domestic policies of individual countries.

Compared with the Bretton Woods system, the current international reserve system has the merit of flexibility. However, such a system can hardly be considered efficient if it consistently fails to correct large balance-of-payments disequilibria across countries. Nor can the arrangement be deemed equitable when adjustment of the global imbalances often places heavy burdens asymmetrically on many developing countries. The international community should begin to address the long-term and ultimate goal of the reform of the international reserve and international monetary system so as to overcome these systemic weaknesses. More urgent and decisive cooperative action is required to ensure that the imbalances do not result in the derailment of global growth in the short term, an occurrence that itself would have substantial adverse long-term effects.

CHANGES IN THE STRUCTURE OF GLOBAL FINANCIAL MARKETS

Risk implications of changes in global financial markets

The global financial system has undergone a profound transformation over the past decades. Many of the impediments to the free flow of capital across borders have been dismantled and domestic financial markets deregulated. The collapse of the Bretton Woods system of fixed parities among major currencies has brought increased volatility to exchange rates. This, together with interest-rate fluctuations, has generated a rapid expansion of new financial instruments aimed at managing the risks to specific financial institutions or investors dealing in these instruments. While this has provided the possibility for greater risk diversification, it has also led to the transfer of risk across different segments of the financial system. In addition, advances in data processing and telecommunications technologies have radically reduced costs of financial transactions required for risk diversification. As a result of all of these factors, financial activity now represents a much larger share of aggregate economic activity than it did 20 or 30 years ago.

The increase in securitization—brought about, in part, by the response to the introduction of risk-based capital requirements—has moved many financial assets off the balance sheets of regulated financial institutions and transferred the monitoring of debt relationships to the capital market. This process has led to the growing role of non-bank institutional investors as well as to an increase in trading activities of all financial institutions. It has also made the debt relationships more anonymous, and increased the sensitivity of all market agents to short-term variations in the valuation of assets.

Another important change has been the consolidation of the financial industry. In the United States, this is the result of new financial regulations that eliminated the segmentation of commercial and investment banking. As a result, the top five United States domestic bank holding companies now concentrate about 45 per cent of banking assets, almost twice the share that they held 20 years ago. At the same time, as a result of increased securitization, and despite their increased size and scale, depository institutions now hold only about one fifth of all assets held by United States financial institutions, or less than half the share that they held in 1984. The reduction in their traditional deposit and commercial lending business, in part due to the introduction of risk-based capital adequacy requirements, and the elimination of restrictions on other activities, has led banks to replace lost income from net interest margins on lending with expansion in other activities that generate fee and commission incomes, such as loan originations, and the provision of specialized over-the-counter derivative structures. The notional value of outstanding derivatives held by the five largest United States banks is more than half of the global total and 95 per cent of the total held by all United States banks. The degree of concentration in the market for credit derivatives—the newest and fastest growing segment—is even greater, with one bank holding more than half of the total notional value of United States holdings. As a result, there has been a sharp increase in the share of assets that are not on the balance sheets of institutions subject to consolidated risk-based capital frameworks (Geithner, 2004).

However, the fact that there is less risk concentrated in banks in the current US system implies that the probability of systemic financial crises may be lower than in traditional bank-based financial systems. The increase in the diversity of nonbank financial institutions holding risk may also provide a stabilizing force in credit markets (Geither, 2006).

Increasing concentration has been observed in all regions, including emerging market countries. At the same time, the diminishing obstacles to capital flows and foreign establishment, as well as improved communication and information, have facilitated the expansion of these financial conglomerates across borders. Given the size and reach of such institutions into national markets and financial systems around the globe, the phrase "too big to fail" has acquired a stronger and more urgent connotation than in the past decade.

Alongside these changes, there has also been substantial convergence in the type of financial transactions performed by bank-centred and non-bank affiliated financial intermediaries. With the growing marketability of assets produced by increased securitization and the development of secondary markets, portfolio investors, such as insurance companies and pension funds, have diversified into areas that used to be the exclusive domain of banks. For their part, commercial banks have increased their involvement in the securities business.

The trends towards consolidation and a broadening of the range of activities performed by any given player have culminated in the formation of a rather small group of dominant global financial institutions. In addition to being engaged in different forms of intermediation in many countries, these firms are the main trading partners of, and most important providers of lending to highly leveraged institutions (HLIs). These institutions have been largely unregulated in the past but are coming within the purview of regulatory authorities.[4]

These structural trends have manifested themselves in greater convergence and growing linkages among different segments of the global financial system—between financial institutions and markets, among different types of financial institutions, and among different countries. They have important implications for the transformation of financial risk. The fact that a much larger, more complex and interlinked financial sphere has emerged, in which the market has replaced government regulators, means that problems in the financial system can have larger consequences for the real economy than in the past.

The growing size of large financial institutions and the diversity of their activities probably make them less vulnerable to shocks. However, combining commercial and investment banking operations, as well as insurance and brokerage services raises potential concentration risks. In these large, internationally active financial institutions, a common capital base underpins an increasing number of activities such as on-balance sheet intermediation, capital market services and market-making functions. Losses in one activity could put pressure on other activities of the firm, and a failure of one of them could have a broader impact than in the past and be considerably more difficult to resolve. In sum, the systemically significant financial institutions are larger and stronger than in the past, but they are not invulnerable and the impact of a failure would be greater.

Also, numerous new financial instruments, including derivatives, tailored to a broader set of investors, have permitted the independent pricing of risk factors that were previously bundled together in the same instrument (see chapter I). As a result, risk transfer mechanisms have become more efficient at the microeconomic level. To the extent that new financial instruments have improved the technology of risk management, they improve the climate for real and financial investment.

However, the unbundling process does not necessarily eliminate or reduce risk, and may simply transform and redistribute it among different holders. The development of risk transfer markets has strengthened the links between different types of risk. For the same reasons, the similarities of underlying risks are becoming more apparent, regardless of the type of financial firm incurring them. Owing to the layering of direct and indirect links through the markets, assessment of true underlying risks becomes difficult (Knight, 2004b). Besides, the increased opportunities for risk transfer mean that more risk may end up in parts of the financial system where supervision and disclosure are weaker, or in parts of the economy less able to manage it. Despite the positive effects of financial innovations, it is necessary to ask whether they could have the same destabilizing impact in the present cycle that deregulation had in earlier ones (*Financial Times*, 2005).

Recent macroeconomic events have also introduced specific implications for financial risk. While the extent of leverage is now lower than in 1998, when its perils became obvious amid the collapse of a large United States hedge fund, increases in liquidity in response to the recent recession have provided more funds to borrow. Indeed, the search for yield in the low interest rate environment characteristic of recent years resembles the period after the recession of the early 1990s and has prompted a yield famine that has led financial institutions and their customers to take positions in swaps and options in derivatives markets for the purpose of making bets on changes in interest and exchange rates. As the spread between short- and long-term interest rates narrowed, institutions borrowed more in order to take the larger positions needed to bolster shrinking profit margins.

In their 2004 reports, both the Bank for International Settlements (BIS) and IMF pointed out that increased speculation had made the financial sector more vulnerable to unexpected shifts in economic activity or interest rates. IMF also noted that hedge fund assets had grown by 20 per cent globally in 2004 as large banks and brokers, as well as institutional investors increased their presence in the hedge fund business (International Monetary Fund, 2005g, pp. 50-51). This movement of regulated entities into less regulated hedge fund activities suggests that leveraged risk-taking has expanded and may continue to expand over time. Activities by institutions such as hedge funds have clearly increased swings in asset and commodity prices.

Implications for prudential regulation and supervision

The evolution of the financial system and the changing nature of financial risk have had profound implications for prudential regulation and supervision. The major trend in this area has been towards improving risk sensitivity of regulatory arrangements at both the national and the international level. Risk-focused supervision implies that supervisors are expected to concentrate their efforts on ensuring that financial institutions use the processes necessary to identify, measure, monitor and control risk exposures. The first Basel Capital Accord (Basel I) and the New Basel Capital Accord (Basel II) are considered to constitute a major step in that direction. It is still unclear, however, whether improvements in risk management practices can more than compensate for the dangers implicit in the changes in the financial structure. Furthermore, most regulation applies to financial institutions, but not to the markets in which they trade. This is especially true of over-the-counter derivatives.

Another important development has been the move towards an indirect approach to financial regulation, which is considered to be more consistent with the evolving financial environment. This involves the establishment of a framework of rules and guidelines intended to set minimum standards of prudent conduct within which financial institutions should be freer to take commercial decisions. In other words, there has been a move away from codified regulation and towards supervision, that is to say, towards an assessment of the overall management of a financial firm's business and the multiple sources of risk that it is likely to confront (Crockett, 2001a).

Within this approach, special attention is being paid to large, systemically important financial firms. It has been argued that large financial firms should maintain capital cushions over and above those stipulated by regulatory standards. Also, the internal risk management regime needs to meet a more exacting standard (Geithner, 2004). However, it is hard to know what constitutes an adequate cushion when so much financial activity that could pose a systemic threat is outside the banking system, and the degree of leverage in finance is so hard to gauge.

Another notable development is the convergence in prudential frameworks across functional lines. The growing similarities of underlying risks call for greater consistency in the supervisory treatment of financial risk across functional segments of the industry. For instance, by now, capital adequacy, supervisory review of risk management processes, and enhanced public disclosure are all emerging as common elements of regulation in both the banking and insurance industries (Knight, 2004a). Also, the United States Securities and Exchange Commission (SEC) has outlined a framework that provides a form of consolidated supervision of the major investment banks with a risk-based capital framework based on Basel II. The proposed new regime will add a consolidated approach to risk-based capital and an intensified focus on the risk management regime to the traditional SEC focus on enforcement for investor protection and market integrity. This will be similar to the European Union (EU) implementation of Basel II, which will be applied to all financial institutions.

The trend towards convergence has also manifested itself in the consolidation of financial sector supervision into a single agency in over 30 countries. Internationally, this trend has led to the creation of the Joint Forum, which brings together representatives of regulatory authorities in banking, securities and insurance. With globalization of financial activity, the pressure to adopt similar regulatory and financial reporting arrangements across countries has also intensified (Knight, 2004a).

It is also worth noting that, with the advent of liberalization, the financial sector, at both the national and the international level, has tended to become much more pro-cyclical. Having realized this, supervisors are searching for techniques that can help make financial systems more resilient to the financial cycle.

The transformation of the financial system has increased the likelihood of boom-bust cycles. Those cycles have common features. Credit and debt levels rise in the upturn, with lenders and investors becoming increasingly vulnerable to the same shocks owing to common risk exposures. As a result, the "endogenous" component of risk, which reflects the impact of the collective actions of market participants on prices and liquidity of financial assets, and on system-wide leverage, becomes more prominent. In the downswing, this process goes into reverse with significant and long-lasting costs to the economy.

In this regard, it has been argued that, at least in part, the financial problems of the past 15 years or so are the result of the sustained period of credit expansion and increasing asset prices in the industrialized countries in the 1990s (White, 2003). An important development in this respect is that, while inflation in the prices of goods and services has become less of a problem in the developed countries, increases in liquidity tend to be reflected in increases in asset prices. These excesses, combined with overvalued exchange rates and currency mismatches in many emerging market economies, have contributed to the financial crises both in developed and in developing economies.

Consequently, policymakers in developed countries should pay more attention to preventing harmful feedback effects of financial excesses. The existing tools, however, are not very useful for that purpose. Indeed, regulators rarely consider the probability of shocks generated endogenously in the system. The risk assessments of rating agencies are highly pro-cyclical (Reisen, 2003) and tend to react to the materialization of risks rather than to their build-up, in relation to both sovereign and corporate risk. Most risk models rely heavily on market-determined variables like equity prices and credit spreads that may be biased towards excessive optimism when imbalances are emerging. Furthermore, the use of similar market-sensitive risk models, together with other features of financial markets (for example, benchmarking and evaluation of managers against competitors), may increase herding behaviour (Persaud, 2000).

Improving the safeguards against instability for a financial system that is larger and more interconnected, and whose endogenous component of risk is more prominent, calls for a modified approach to prudential regulation with a system-wide perspective and a focus on endogenous components of risk. This systemic or macro orientation of prudential regulation requires a shift away from the notion that the stability of the financial system is simply a consequence of the soundness of its individual components.

The importance of this macroprudential perspective as a complement to the more traditional microprudential focus is widely recognized (see, for instance, Crockett, 2000, 2001a; Knight, 2004b; Ocampo, 2003a). Its objective is to limit the risk of episodes of financial distress with significant losses in terms of real output for the economy as a whole. Consequently, it stresses the need to establish cushions as financial imbalances build up during the upswing in order to both restrain excesses and give more scope to supporting losses in the downturn. This implies introducing some counter-cyclicality into financial regulation, which would compensate for the tendency of financial markets to behave in a pro-cyclical manner (see chapter I).

An important impediment to implementing macroprudential policies in practice is uncertainty about the significance of potential systemic problems. Relevant analyses are now carried out in various forums, including IMF, the World Bank, the Financial Stability Forum (FSF) and the Bank for International Settlements. The process of convergence within the global financial system across markets, institutions and national jurisdictions makes it very important to have appropriate institutions for this purpose.

Among existing institutions, the Financial Stability Forum stands out in its capacity to ensure macroprudential monitoring and appropriate policy response. However, the Forum has no power to propose or to sanction, and insights gained from its deliberations may not necessarily be turned into policy actions. The need for stronger international governance institutions in the area of financial regulation has been suggested by several analysts (see, for instance, Eatwell and Taylor, 2000), but these proposals face constraints associated to the desire of major countries to retain sovereignty over national financial regulations and supervisory systems and the persistence of differences in the structure of national financial markets.

The regulatory approach will be seriously tested for the first time during and after the implementation of the New Basel Capital Accord (Basel II), which, according to many observers, may increase pro-cyclicality of bank lending especially for developing countries, because of its increased risk-sensitivity (see chapter I). To alleviate these concerns, the architects of Basel II have noted that supervisory oversight and market discipline should reinforce the incentive for banks to maintain a cushion of capital above the minimum so as to have a margin of protection in downturns. Financial institutions are also urged to adopt risk management practices that take better account of the evolution of risk over time (thus taking better account of the full business cycle) and that are not excessively vulnerable to short-term revisions. It has also been argued that because of greater disclosure built into Pillar 3 of Basel II, markets may become less tolerant and more suspicious of risk assessments that are too volatile and lead to substantial upgrades in good times (Borio, 2003). However, as noted above, rating agencies and other market actors themselves often have strong pro-cyclical biases. More broadly, the regulators' success in dealing with the problem of the pro-cyclicality of the New Accord remains an issue of serious concern.

CRISIS PREVENTION AND RESOLUTION

Avoiding financial crises is crucial to ensuring that the benefits of capital inflows create permanent increases in national welfare. Since the Asian crisis, increased attention has been given to the design of measures at the national and international levels aimed at better managing external shocks and preventing financial crises.

Domestic macroeconomic policies

Developing countries have the primary responsibility for their own macroeconomic policies and thus for crisis prevention. In this regard, important progress has been made since the Asian crisis. Inflation rates have tended to fall and stabilize at historically low levels in all developing-country regions. Also, despite setbacks and variations across countries, fiscal policy has become more prudent in its general thrust. Strong external accounts have led to a reduction in external debt ratios and the accumulation of foreign-exchange reserves. Greater global liquidity and reduced risk aversion have contributed to declining spreads between emerging market sovereign borrowing rates and developed-country benchmark interest rates. All these factors, together with strong growth in world trade and high commodity prices, have led to rapid economic growth in all developing-country regions in 2004 and 2005, for the first time in three decades (United Nations, 2005a).

However, owing to higher and more volatile interest rates paid by emerging market Governments, their budgets are more vulnerable to interest rate shocks than those of developed countries. Also, many developing countries depend heavily on commodity exports and thus are much more vulnerable to risks of sharp external price swings. Indeed, improved terms of trade due to high commodity and energy prices of recent years might have made underlying fiscal and external positions in some countries look healthier than they actually are.

There has also been a gradual shift of developing countries towards more flexible exchange rates. Greater exchange-rate flexibility is considered by some observers to have contributed the most to the reduction of the risk of future crises (Fischer, 2002) but it also carries the risk of exchange-rate instability in the face of volatile capital flows.

In this regard, there is now strong evidence that capital-account liberalization has increased growth volatility, without clear benefits in terms of more rapid growth (Prasad and others, 2003). Vulnerability to capital-account shocks is compounded by the tendency to adopt pro-cyclical macroeconomic policies that reinforce rather than mitigate the effects of external financial cycles (Kaminsky and others, 2004). Despite some advances (for example, the introduction of structural benchmarks for fiscal policy and the design of fiscal stabilization funds by some countries), limited progress has been made in introducing explicit objectives of counter-cyclical management of macroeconomic (that is to say, fiscal, monetary and exchange rate) policies, or in designing instruments that cushion developing borrowers against adverse economic developments by linking debt payments more directly to the borrower's ability to pay (see chapter I).

Given the evidence that capital-account liberalization increases macroeconomic volatility, many developing countries have continued to use capital controls. The evidence shows that there has been a slowdown in the removal of capital controls in developing countries since 1998 (International Monetary Fund, 2003a). To reduce currency mismatches, which have been a prominent feature of every major emerging market financial crisis of the past decade, local currency bond markets have expanded in developing countries. At the same time, lending by foreign banks has shifted from largely dollar-denominated cross-border loans to local currency loans through local affiliates. As a result, in many emerging economies, currency mismatches were reduced (see also chapter I).

There has also been progress in strengthening financial regulation and supervision. Supervisory and regulatory regimes of many developing countries have been brought in line with international practices as codified in the Basel Core Principles for Effective Banking Supervision. Also, in spite of the fact that there is no implementation timetable for non-Group of Ten (G10) members, many developing and emerging market countries have already begun to deal with implementation of the new capital adequacy framework (Basel II). It is expected that, by 2010, almost 75 per cent of banking assets in the developing world will be covered by Basel II arrangements (Bank for International Settlements, 2004b).

Irrespective of the exchange-rate regime adopted, to ensure themselves against sudden shifts in market sentiment, most emerging economies have kept increasingly high stocks of international reserves. This "self-insurance" option entails significant costs and could constrain global growth as it reduces global aggregate demand. Nevertheless, in the absence of efficient market-based private alternatives or appropriate international official facilities, and given the enormous costs of financial crises, reserve accumulation remains a reliable, although costly, option for coping with volatility.

Surveillance of national macroeconomic policies

Surveillance of national macroeconomic and, since the Asian crisis, financial policies remains at the centre of IMF crisis prevention efforts. It has been argued, however, that increasing complexity of financial markets may have rendered the existing instruments of surveillance such as the Article IV consultations, the Financial Sector Stability Assessments and programmes, and the reviews of the observance of international codes and standards, less effective than assumed so far in identifying and preventing crises (Commonwealth Secretariat, 2004).

In July 2004, the IMF Executive Board concluded the latest biennial review of the surveillance activities. The review identified key priorities for further strengthening surveillance. It has been agreed that surveillance activities should be focused on improving analytical tools for early identification of vulnerabilities, including more rigorous assessments of balance-sheet weaknesses and stress-testing in regard to possible macroeconomic shocks.

To raise the effectiveness of surveillance, increased focus on country-specific areas of vulnerability is considered necessary. This requires surveillance that is tailor-made for addressing mainly those macroeconomic issues that are relevant in each member country. In addition, there is a need to better understand the constraints on a country's ability to take certain actions. It is therefore necessary to consider institutional, social and political realities in order to offer realistic policy advice.

As in the case of national efforts, more attention should be given to increasing the room for manoeuvre to enable countries to adopt counter-cyclical macroeconomic policies in the face of trade and, particularly, capital-account shocks. Greater attention within IMF surveillance on ways to enhance such room for manoeuvre would improve the effectiveness of crisis prevention efforts and financial support.

To increase the transparency of surveillance, IMF moved from voluntary to presumed publication of Article IV surveillance reports and programme documents. Increased transparency is thought to help improve both countries' policies and the quality of the Fund's work. However, there could be a potential tension between greater transparency and the Fund's role as a provider of candid and frank advice. Hence, in the handling of sensitive topics during surveillance exercises, there is a need for an appropriate balance between candour and confidentiality.

The Fund's ability to influence policies through surveillance is most limited with regard to large non-borrowing, mostly developed countries. At the same time, some of those countries have the greatest global impact. As was emphasized in the first section of this chapter and agreed by the IMFC in April 2006, the role of IMF in macroeconomic surveillance of major economies and as an honest broker in policy coordination among these countries thus deserves special attention.

The role of emergency financing and precautionary financial arrangements

At the country level, central banks have acted for many decades as lenders of last resort, to prevent systematic banking or other financial crises, and to prevent their deepening when they do occur. Equivalent international mechanisms are still at an embryonic stage, with the current IMF arrangements operating more under the principle of the "emergency financier". However, this function is different from that of the lender of last resort as performed at the national level, since there is no automatic provision of liquidity during crises (Ocampo, 2002). Enhanced provision of emergency financing at the international level in response to external shocks is essential to lowering unnecessary burdens of adjustment. Appropriate facilities should include a liquidity provision to cover volatility in export earnings—particularly that caused by fluctuations in commodity prices—sudden stops in external financing and, as recently emphasized, natural disasters.

The evidence of the adverse effects of terms-of-trade shocks on economic growth is strong. Particularly important is the finding that their negative effects on growth and poverty reduction can be very large (Collier and Dehn, 2001). However, the major IMF facility designed to compensate for terms-of-trade shocks, the Compensatory Financing Facility (CFF), has become increasingly ineffective. Since its modification in early 2000, which basically tightened conditionality for access, the CFF has not been used, in spite of the additional shocks affecting developing countries (International Monetary Fund, 2003a).

During the 1990s, capital-account liberalization and large capital-account volatility greatly increased the need for official liquidity to deal with sudden and large reversals of flows. There is an increasing consensus that many of the recent crises in emerging markets have been triggered by self-fulfilling liquidity runs, rather than by fundamental disequilibria or incorrect policies (see, for instance, Hausmann and Velasco, 2004). Indeed, capital outflows could be provoked by many factors not related to countries' policies. Among those factors are changes in financial conditions in industrialized countries and the pro-cyclical behaviour of capital markets, as well as contagion effects.

The enhanced provision of emergency financing in the face of capital-account crises is important not only to manage crises when they occur, but to prevent such crises and to avert contagion (Cordella and Yeyati, 2004; Griffith-Jones and Ocampo, 2003). Indeed, lending of last resort at the national level is basically conceived as a tool for crisis *prevention*, particularly prevention of systemic crises.

To address this obvious need, IMF has made efforts in recent years to improve its lending policy during capital-account crises. In 1997, the Supplemental Reserve Facility (SRF) was established. The SRF provides larger and more front-loaded financing to countries hit by a capital-account crisis, at a higher interest rate than that of other Fund facilities. Also, in some cases, the Fund softened its requirements and accelerated the approval process in the renewal of credits extended under this Facility, as was the case for Brazil in 2003 and 2004.

However, large-scale access by certain emerging economies led to criticism by some IMF members who considered that such large-scale lending should be more strictly limited. To a large measure, these debates have been provoked by cases of exceptional access to Fund resources not accompanied by an agreement on the conditions that should determine eligibility for such special treatment. In February 2003, the IMF Executive Board approved a new framework for exceptional access in capital-account crises, which included the following criteria for eligibility: exceptionally large need; a debt burden that would be sustainable under reasonably conservative assumptions; good prospects of regaining access to private capital markets during the period of the IMF loan; and indications that the country's policies had a strong chance of succeeding.

A major problem of many recent Fund-supported programmes, especially in cases of capital-account crisis, has been the lower-than-expected levels of private financing, resulting in sharper and more abrupt current-account adjustment and steep output declines (International Monetary Fund, 2004a). Past experience has shown that the catalytic effects of IMF financing on private capital flows may work only in rather rare situations when there is no doubt about debt and exchange-rate sustainability. This means that a further analysis of the optimal mix between financing and adjustment, as well as of the catalytic effects of Fund-supported programmes, is required (International Monetary Fund, 2005d).

The evidence that even countries with good macroeconomic fundamentals might be subject to sudden stops of external financing also gave broad support to the idea that a precautionary financial arrangement, closer to the lender-of-last-resort functions of central banks, had to be added to existing

IMF facilities. The goal was to create a mechanism to prevent self-fulfilling liquidity crises.

In response to these demands, in 1999 the IMF had introduced the Contingent Credit Line (CCL). The facility was never used, however, and was discontinued in November 2003. Among the factors that may have contributed to the fact that countries failed to avail themselves of the CCL, observers have emphasized the "entry" and "exit" problems (Buira, 2005). Contrary to what was desired, access to the CCL was seen as an announcement of vulnerability that could harm confidence. Another problem was that, even with a CCL, the country had to go back to the IMF Executive Board to secure a loan. There was also a lack of clarity regarding the amount of support that would be available and its timing.

Since the expiration of the CCL, IMF has been exploring other ways to achieve its basic objectives. In its Mid-Term Strategic Review it has proposed a new High Access Contingent Financing Vehicle. The new instrument would be available to members with strong macroeconomic policies, sustainable debt, transparent reporting, but which still face balance-sheet weaknesses and vulnerabilities. Access would normally be up to 300 percent of quota, automatically available in a single up-front purchase, and augmentable upon subsequent review. This strikes a balance between providing some assurance of financing and limiting exposure before the size and policy response to a crisis are known. Financing beyond the initial drawing would take into account the emerging needs and policy requirements. Conditionality would target policies to maintain macroeconomic stability and reduce vulnerabilities. Conditionality would focus on addressing underlying vulnerabilities, and performance criteria set to broadly indicate when policies go off-track, not to capture minor deviations from projections.

A related recent proposal suggests the creation of a country insurance facility (CIF) to help stop and reverse liquidity runs (Cordella and Yeyati, 2005). Through this facility, eligible countries would have automatic access to a line of credit at a predetermined interest rate to cover short-term financing needs. Automaticity, which is essential for pre-empting liquidity runs, would distinguish the CIF (or any similar facility) from the late CCL, which required a pre-qualification process. The eligibility suggested would focus primarily on Maastricht-type rules, with a debt-to-GDP ratio not higher than 60 per cent and a fiscal deficit of 3 per cent or less being natural candidates for eligibility criteria. This has many merits, although the level of reserves should also be included, so that net indebtedness may be considered. Following lender-of-last-resort principles, the proposal envisages short-term lending (up to one year) at a penalty rate relative to pre-crisis levels.

It is assumed that, by replacing the standard *ex post* conditionality with voluntary *ex ante* conditionality, more countries would have the incentive to adopt sustainable policies conducive to solvency and eligibility. Furthermore, a well-designed CIF, or a similar facility designed to prevent liquidity runs, would be used very infrequently or, possibly, never. However, its impact should be visible in an increasing number of eligible countries and lower emerging market risk premiums. Indeed, the essential advantages of such a facility is that, by offering instant liquidity, it "would place a ceiling on rollover costs— thus avoiding debt crises triggered by unsustainable refinancing rates, much in the same way as central banks operate in their role of lenders of last resort" (International Monetary Fund, 2005d).

The additional demand for IMF lending facilities that was evident during the succession of the Asian, Russian and Latin American crises in the late 1990s also made evident the fact that a significant strengthening of the resource base of IMF might be needed, and that the potential loss to the global economy of failing to act was much higher than the opportunity costs of a larger Fund size (Kelkar, Chaudhry and Vanduzer-Snow, 2005). Existing mechanisms, which allow the Fund to borrow from major economies when such exceptional demands arise, may be suboptimal relative to the option of strengthening the resource base of the Fund, via SDRs. This issue is explored below.

Strengthening IMF financing of poor countries

In September 1999, the IMF transformed the previously existing Enhanced Structural Adjustment Facility (ESAF) into the Poverty Reduction and Growth Facility (PRGF) for lending operations to its low-income member countries. PRGF-supported programmes are framed around Poverty Reduction Strategy Papers (PRSPs), the major policy instrument of concessional lending from both IMF and the World Bank, as well as of debt relief under the Heavily Indebted Poor Countries (HIPC) Initiative. In the case of IMF, PRGF-supported programmes are designed to cover mainly areas that constitute the primary responsibility of the Fund, such as exchange-rate and tax policy, fiscal management, budget execution, fiscal transparency, and tax and customs administration.

Concessional lending under the PRGF is administered by IMF through the PRGF and PRGF-HIPC Trusts. The PRGF Trust borrows resources from official institutions at market-related interest rates. The difference between the market-related interest rate paid to PRGF Trust lenders and the rate of interest of 0.5 per cent per year paid by the eligible borrowing members is financed by contributions from bilateral donors and the International Monetary Fund's own resources. As of September 2005, 78 low-income countries were eligible for PRGF assistance. In May 2006, total loan resources provided by PRGF creditors amounted to SDR 15.8 billion, of which SDR 13.0 billion have already been committed and SDR 12.1 billion disbursed under 29 arrangements.

A major issue under debate is how to improve existing arrangements so as to assist low-income countries in dealing with shocks. One of the most appropriate mechanisms could be to increase significantly access under the PRGF arrangements (called PRGF augmentation in recent IMF analysis) and diminish conditionality, as well as make the conditionality more supportive of growth and poverty reduction. This could be done, for example, by allowing post-stabilization countries with low levels of inflation more flexibility to use fiscal policy to offset the impact of negative external shocks on domestic demand (see Oxfam, 2003).

Given that about half the eligible low-income members have PRGF arrangements this would be an important channel for the provision of liquidity support at subsidized rates. Augmentation of the PRGF has in fact been the main vehicle the Fund has used to provide financing for low-income countries hit by shocks.

In late 2005 a new Exogenous Shocks Facility (ESF) was created to provide policy support and financial assistance to PRGF eligible low-income countries facing exogenous shocks that do not have a PRGF program in place. Financing terms are equivalent to a PRGF arrangement and more concessional than under other IMF emergency lending facilities. However, conditionality is high, which is inappropriate in a facility to finance exogenous shocks.

Low-income countries are also vulnerable to natural disasters. In early 2005, IMF agreed to subsidize emergency assistance for natural disasters to PRGF-eligible members. However, the total amount allocated has been very limited, and was to an important extent used up in the first few months.

Conditionality of IMF lending

As important as the lending facilities of IMF is the conditionality attached to them. Conditionality in IMF-supported programmes had been introduced in the 1950s and incorporated as a requirement into the Articles of Agreement in 1969. Until the 1980s, conditionality mainly focused on monetary, fiscal and exchange-rate policies. However, in the late 1980s, and especially in the 1990s, in addition to traditional quantitative targets for macroeconomic variables, IMF financing was increasingly made conditional on structural changes, involving changes in policy processes, legislation and institutional reforms. This resulted in a significant increase in the average number of structural conditions in Fund-supported programmes. These climbed from 2-3 per year per programme in the mid-1980s to 12 or more per year per programme by the second half of the 1990s, and to as high as 117 in the case of Indonesia after its financial crisis in 1997 (International Monetary Fund, 2003a). This change was also reflected in increasing numbers of performance criteria, structural benchmarks and prior actions.

The increase in the number of structural conditions raised concerns that IMF was exceeding its mandate and expertise. It has also been argued that the number and detail of structural policy conditions attached to IMF loans were too extensive to be fully effective (United Nations, 2001b). In this regard, it has been observed that the rate of member countries' compliance with Fund-supported programmes fell from over 50 per cent in the late 1970s and early 1980s to about 16 per cent in the 1990s, if compliance is defined as that which permitted the full disbursement of the loan (Buira, 2003).

There were also concerns that excessive conditionality might have undermined the national ownership of programmes thereby impeding their implementation. Indeed, following closely the arguments related to external assistance in general (see chapter II), it has become clear that lack of real domestic ownership is the most important obstacle to effective programme implementation, and that conditionality is not a substitute for government commitment. In this regard, it has also been argued that "ownership" can be promoted only by an effective plural discussion of the virtues of alternative types of "structural reforms" (Griffith-Jones and Ocampo, 2003).

In response to these concerns, in September 2002, the IMF Executive Board approved new conditionality guidelines, the first revision since 1979. A review of the new guidelines took place in 2005 (IMF, 2005h). It noted that the basic objectives of the 2002 guidelines to streamline conditionality and enhance programme ownership had been met. However, despite a shift towards greater focus on critical core areas and better specificity in formulating conditions, there had been little actual decline in the number of structural conditions of programmes. It recommended further efforts in streamlining the coverage of structural conditionality by setting structural benchmarks only in critical core areas and to delineate programme strategies more clearly in IMF staff reports. It also suggested improving the *ex ante* formulation of structural conditions to provide policy space, rather than having to introduce it *ex post* policy space in the form of flexibility on timing.

The progress in implementing new guidelines is rather difficult to assess. There may still be a temptation to use IMF financial leverage when the country is in a difficult situation, but this temptation needs to be resisted (Allen, 2004). Also, it has been noted that since 2000-2001, the first phase of the "streamlining" initiative, the number of conditions in programmes has not declined but stayed fairly constant, with about 15 conditions per year per programme (IMF, 2004b; Allen, 2004), which is similar to the average of the 1990s.

A key challenge is to determine which actions are critical to the success of programmes. There appears to be no consensus among IMF Executive Directors regarding the extent to which structural conditionality should be streamlined (IMF, Independent Evaluation Office, 2005). IMF staff may have different views on the new policy (Killick, 2004). This can explain, at least partly, why conditionality streamlining has been so slow.

Another concern is that the reduction of the number of structural conditions in Fund-supported programmes may lead to an expansion of conditionality by the World Bank with the aggregate conditionality burden remaining unchanged or even increasing. There are differences between the two organizations in terms of mandates, cultures and structures (Commonwealth Secretariat, 2004). Finding the appropriate collaborative framework is an issue of great priority.

THE ROLE OF SDRs IN THE INTERNATIONAL FINANCIAL SYSTEM

The creation of SDRs in 1969, as a result of international financial debates in the 1960s concerning the impact of the Triffin dilemma on the provision of sufficient liquidity for the international trading system was a major advance in the design of the international financial system. It represented an initial step in the creation of a true world money, with the potential to generate a more balanced distribution of powers of seigniorage. In a world characterized by the use of the national currencies of major industrialized countries as international monies, the accumulation of reserves and their cost generate, in fact, a redistribution of income from developing economies to the major industrialized countries, a large flow of so-called reverse aid (see Zedillo report United Nations, 2001d).

Unfortunately, no allocations of SDRs to IMF member countries have been made since 1981. The IMF Board of Governors did approve in 1997 a special one-time allocation of SDRs that would have doubled cumulative SDR allocations to SDR 42.9 billion and would have corrected the fact that new

IMF members (since 1981) had never received an SDR allocation. However, this decision has not yet become effective.

The cessation of SDR allocations had negative effects for developing countries, as it coincided with a growing demand for international reserves. In recent years, in particular, many developing countries (especially, but not only, in Asia) accumulated substantial foreign-exchange reserves, partly to protect themselves against the risk of future financial crises due to reversible capital flows. However, holding such high levels of reserves with the aim of "self-insurance" implies high costs which are particularly onerous for low-income countries. Polak and Clark (2005) estimate the significant cost of the holding by low-income countries of about SDR 90 billion of reserves at about US$ 10 billion per year; this is about one sixth of total annual net official development assistance (ODA).

Such high demand for reserves also reduces aggregate world demand and therefore has a deflationary effect at the global level. There are therefore clear benefits to be derived from internationally issued reserves which, together with emergency financing during crises, would provide developing countries with a "collective insurance" that was cheaper and therefore more efficient than "self-insurance" via foreign-exchange reserve accumulation.

Proposals to renew SDR allocations have been increasing in recent years. They follow two different models. The first calls for SDRs to be issued in a temporary way during episodes of financial stress and destroyed once financial conditions normalize (United Nations, 1999; Camdessus, 2000; Cooper, 2002; Ocampo, 2002). This would develop a counter-cyclical element in world liquidity management, as sudden drops in private lending would be partly compensated by increased official liquidity; furthermore, total long-term liquidity would not increase, since normalization of private lending would imply a cancellation of those SDRs issued during the preceding crisis. Output in developing countries currently lowered by temporary shocks would be higher than otherwise, and the risk of additional world inflation would be minimal.

This proposal would solve the problems of adequately financing needs for extraordinary and temporary official liquidity but not the distributive issues associated with uneven distribution of seigniorage powers. The solution to this problem requires permanent allocations. Such allocations could go (directly or indirectly) to developing countries only or to the entire Fund membership. The advantage of the former is that it would focus SDR issues on the countries that need them the most. Furthermore, it would avoid the risk of creating more SDRs than the membership would collectively want to have. Alternatively, allocations of SDRs to industrialized countries could be used to finance important international objectives, particularly increased international development cooperation (see chapter II).

For developing countries, holding additional SDR reserves would have a zero net cost or even a net benefit, as payment by the country for its reserves would be equal to or lower than the interest earned if they did hold them (Polak and Clark, 2005). There would also be no fiscal cost to industrialized countries if IMF issued SDRs, and they held them. Indeed, if an industrialized country is allocated SDRs, it will also have either zero net costs, or even a small positive net benefit (see UK Treasury and IMF, 2003).

Currently, greater SDR liquidity could allow other countries, including developing countries, to relax their efforts directed at increasing current-account surpluses (Williamson, 2004). Furthermore, it would help somewhat to reduce the massive dependence of the United States on the foreign central banks financing its deficit, a dependence that may be or could become problematic for the United States authorities.

One of the main reasons for traditional opposition of some industrialized countries to SDR issues is that those issues could increase inflation globally. This concern seems exaggerated, as the amount of SDRs that were issued would constitute an extremely small proportion of the world's total money supply. For example, in the most recent allocation of SDRs approved in 1997, but not yet ratified, an issue was proposed of SDR 21 billion, or approximately US$ 31 billion at mid-2006 exchange rates. If we compare this with the total money supply (M2) of the United States, of over US$ 6,000 billion, the amount of possible SDR issue is less than 0.5 per cent, and therefore represents an even smaller proportion of the world's total money supply (Griffith-Jones and Gottschalk, 2004). Furthermore, if SDRs were issued in a counter-cyclical way, the risk of inflationary impact would be even smaller, as they would be compensating for a decline in private liquidity.

THE ROLE OF REGIONAL FINANCIAL ARRANGEMENTS

A strong case can also be made for the creation and development of regional reserve funds, which can provide a valuable complement to multilateral and national mechanisms in the case of capital-account crises. The large currency crises of the last decade have been regional in nature. Therefore, neighbouring countries have a strong incentive to extend financial assistance to each other in the face of potentially contagious threats to stability "to help put out a fire (a financial crisis) before it spreads to them" (Ito, Ogawa and Sasaki, 1999). Also, despite contagion, critical demands for funds do not coincide exactly in time, a fact that generates the possibility of a useful role for regional reserve funds as a first line of defence during crises. Besides, regional institutions can and should play a stronger role in relation to small and medium-sized countries, which will usually receive less attention and have a weaker bargaining position than larger countries with multilateral institutions. Indeed, a case could even be made that they could provide full support to the small and medium-sized countries within some regions, as well as part of the financing for larger countries. Furthermore, greater attention—especially in East Asia—to the formation of regional financial arrangements reflects frustration with the slow reform of the international financial system, and particularly the limitations of multilateral official emergency lending (Park, 2006). In its Medium-term Strategy Review, the IMF has proposed formal support for regional pooling of reserves.

Looking into the future, an organizational structure for crisis prevention and regulation could be conceived entailing the establishment of a dense network of multilateral, regional and subregional financial institutions to provide official financing, basically on a complementary basis (Ocampo, 2002, 2006). This model could be extended to macroeconomic surveillance, again with regional institutions complementing multilateral ones, whereas regional arrangements might be especially suitable for macroeconomic policy coordination. Such a network of institutions would be more similar to federal arrangements, like those of the United States Federal Reserve Board, or the slightly less formal structure of the European Central Bank. Indeed, the post-war European experience of building financial cooperation, combined with growing macroeconomic surveillance, may offer some interesting lessons at the global level.

Despite these potentialities, existing regional financial arrangements among developing countries are only in an embryonic stage. The valuable role that regional reserve funds can play is illustrated by the Andean Reserve Fund, created in 1978, which became the Latin American Reserve Fund (FLAR) when Costa Rica joined in 1989. It operates essentially as a foreign exchange reserve pool and its main function is the provision of short-term liquidity support to countries in crises. Since 1978, this Fund has provided such financing to member States, equivalent to 60 per cent of that of IMF, benefiting in particular two of its smallest members, Bolivia and Ecuador.

Disbursements of loans have always been rapid and its financing has been clearly counter-cyclical. FLAR's "preferred-creditor status" has been reflected in its healthy portfolio, even in the face of two major crises in the region, when some member countries accumulated arrears in their public sector obligations. This zero default and preferential creditor status contributes to the very high credit ratings of the Reserve Fund, well above the rating of the countries that constitute it. It also shows that the fear that "soft conditionality" would result in major losses by an institution providing emergency liquidity financing is exaggerated (Titelman, 2006).

After the East Asian crisis, Japan had proposed the creation of an Asian monetary fund. Though the proposal was well received throughout the region, the idea was shelved owing to objections from outside the region. However, a more modest version was created in 2000, when the Association of Southeast Asian Nations (ASEAN), China, Japan and the Republic of Korea created a system of bilateral currency swap arrangements known as the Chiang Mai Initiative (Park, 2006). They also institutionalized meetings of finance ministers for policy dialogue and coordination In May 2005, the Initiative was increased significantly from its previous $39 billion level, reaching $71.5 billion by February 2006. It is based on 16 bilateral swap arrangements, and thus any country in need of short-term liquidity must discuss activation with all swap-providing countries individually.

Disbursement of 20 per cent of the maximum drawing would be automatic; a country drawing more than 20 per cent is placed under an IMF programme. In this sense, the Initiative is of somewhat limited size and clearly complementary to IMF lending facilities. Its efficacy in firefighting crises has not yet been tested. In the meantime, efforts are being undertaken to overcome potential problems, such as the bilateral nature of swap arrangements, which could reduce the speed of response of the mechanism, so essential in times of speculative attacks. There is an understanding that the multilateralization of the bilateral swap arrangements would require a more formalized and rigorous surveillance system, upon which it has been difficult to agree (Park, 2006).

ENHANCING THE VOICE AND PARTICIPATION OF DEVELOPING COUNTRIES IN INTERNATIONAL FINANCIAL DECISION-MAKING

The Monterrey Consensus stressed the need to broaden and strengthen the participation of developing countries and countries with economies in transition in international economic decision-making and norm-setting. It encouraged the Bretton Woods institutions to continue to enhance the participation of all developing and transition economies in their decision-making. However, the Monterrey Consensus goes beyond the Bretton Woods institutions and highlights the need to extend the discussion of voice and participation to other policymaking bodies, including informal and ad hoc groups. Although the discussion below will focus on two of those institutions, the Basel Committee on Banking Supervision and the Financial Stability Forum, the principle is applicable to similar organizations. These include the Bank for International Settlements, the Financial Stability Forum and financial standard-setting bodies, such as the Basel Committee on Banking Supervision, the International Association of Insurance Supervisors, the International Accounting Standards Board, the International Organization for Standardization and the International Federation of Stock Exchanges.

There were two main reasons behind the position adopted at Monterrey. It seemed necessary to review the governance of these institutions in the light of the vast changes that had taken place since their creation, in particular the increasing importance of emerging economies. Also, these institutions would be more effective and efficient if their agenda and decisions better reflected the needs and issues of the majority of the countries affected by them.

The Bretton Woods institutions have taken some limited action to make more effective the participation of developing countries, leading, *inter alia*, to strengthening the offices of African Directors in IMF and establishing an Analytical Trust Fund to support the African Executive Directors at the World Bank. Modalities for consultations in the Basel Committee and the Financial Stability Forum have also widened; yet, in respect of the crucial issue of participation of developing countries in decision-making, there has been no progress.

In the Basel Committee and the Financial Stability Forum, developing countries are not represented at all. The Basel Committee defines regulations— including the capital adequacy regulations and the Core Principles for Effective Banking Supervision— that strongly influence, in turn, the cost and distribution of bank lending, as well as banking stability, in developed and developing countries. Lack of any representation by developing countries makes their analysis incomplete in crucial aspects, as shown by the new Capital Accord (Basel II) (see chapter I).

All members of the Basel Committee are developed countries: 10 Western European countries, Canada, Japan and the United States. There is no representation of developing countries in this Committee. Notwithstanding, the Basel Committee does liaise with developing and transition economies. However, consultations are no substitute for having a seat at the decision-making table. A Basel Committee with a more appropriate representation from the world economy could result not only in a fairer system, but also in better regulation leading to a more stable financial system with welfare-enhancing effects for all.

The question of strengthening representation of developing countries is now clearly on the agenda of the Bretton Woods institutions. The voting structure and composition of the Executive Board of IMF determine to a large extent the policies of the Fund, in particular those that affect the use of IMF resources. Yet, policy discussions and policy formulation in the Board and the International Monetary and Financial Committee often involve areas in which IMF resources are not directly involved. Such discussions and the policy orientations that they provide deal mostly with international economic and financial cooperation, but they also touch upon policy orientations of individual countries or groups of countries. In fact, such policy orientations exert a significant influence on the scope for autonomous policy formulation. This illustration relates to IMF, but the same arguments are applicable to the World Bank.

The report of the IMF Executive Board to the International Monetary and Financial Committee on quotas, voice and representation of 24 September 2004 (IMF, 2004d) lays out the elements that would need to be considered to make additional progress on these questions: a general quota increase with a relatively large selective element allocated by means of a new quota formula; ad hoc quota increases with the objective of addressing the clearest cases where the relation between quota and economic size is significantly out of line; and an increase in basic votes to correct the erosion of voting power of countries with small-sized economies, such as many in Africa. Informal proposals dealing with revision of quotas and the broader question of representation were discussed at the Spring 2006 meeting of the Committee, and more formal proposals are expected at the Fall meeting to be held in Singapore in September, 2006.

The way in which quotas are calculated is central to the relative voting power of individual countries and country groupings. Also, the individual country quota determines the amount of financing the country can obtain from the Fund. A central consideration in determining the quota is the capacity to contribute. Thus, the economic size of a country largely determines its quota level. From the perspective of a potential user of IMF resources, the eventual need to finance its balance of payments is a key factor to be considered. Currently, the formula to calculate the quota includes GDP or gross national income (GNI), current-account transactions, official reserves and a measure of variability of receipts in foreign currency (for example, exports of goods and services plus income revenues).

Even without a change in the IMF Articles of Agreement,[5] there are several changes in the method of calculating the quota that would lead to a comparatively larger quota for developing countries as a whole. Those widely mentioned in current discussions include: using the GNI measured in purchasing power parity (PPP) instead of GNI at average exchange rates as a measure of economic size in the quota formula; excluding the amount of trade among EU members that adopted the euro, as it does not generate potential balance-of-payments difficulties; and increasing the coefficient assigned in the quota formula to the indicator of variability of receipts.

The first of the aforementioned factors could be the most critical in redefining quotas. Purchasing power parities (PPPs) represent an effort to apply a common set of prices to the same activities in all countries so that measures of aggregate output and similar variables are comparable. For a variety of reasons, market exchange rates do not necessarily achieve this comparability. Particularly for developing countries, they do not necessarily reflect market conditions, as they sometimes experience long periods of misalignment and are often volatile. PPP exchange rates provide a more accurate reflection of the relevant weight of individual countries in the world economy and, correspondingly, are more stable (since economic weight does not itself change much in the short term). For these reasons, several international organizations prefer to use GNI/PPP directly when making cross-country comparisons or to use them indirectly as weights when aggregating certain country data. For example, the Organization for Economic Cooperation and Development (OECD) incorporates GNI/PPP in much of its statistical and analytical work. GNI/PPP is also used to determine budget allocations for the structural funds used to reduce economic disparities among the members of EU (McLenaghan, 2005). Of particular relevance to the matter of voice in the Bank and the Fund is the fact that IMF utilizes the GNI/PPP to estimate rates of growth at regional and world levels in its *World Economic Outlook*. Even more pertinently, because of the shortcomings of official exchange rates for these purposes, a PPP conversion factor was adopted by IMF in the 1980s and 1990s when the economies in transition joined IMF and their quota levels had to be decided. This suggests that there is a strong case for using PPPs for quota calculations in IMF. If they were used, developing countries' share of IMF quotas would be 41 per cent, compared with 31 per cent at present (see table IV.2).

As table IV.2 indicates, the use of purchasing power measures of GNI would increase substantially the quota of developing countries. Most of the increases in the quota share would go to developing Asian countries, particularly China, India and the Republic of Korea. Indeed, the quota share of developing Asia is barely 17 per cent while its share of GNI/PPP is 29 per cent. This would require, as the table also suggests, a significant adjustment of the share of the European countries whose quota share as a whole is 1½ times its GNI/PPP share.[6]

TABLE IV.2.
IMF QUOTAS AND SHARES OF GNI/PPP IN WORLD TOTAL

	IMF quota share (Percentage of total IMF quotas as of May 9, 2006)	GNI/PPP Share (Percentage of world GNI/PPP 2003)
Industrial economies	63.2	54.7
United States	17.4	21.4
Japan	6.2	7.1
EU-25	32.2	22.3
Other European	2.5	0.8
Australia, Canada, New Zealand	4.9	3.1
Economies in transition	5.6	4.2
Developing countries	31.2	41.2
Asia and Pacific	16.7	29.0
Latin America and Caribbean	7.5	7.5
Middle East and North Africa	2.7	2.2
Subsaharan Africa	4.4	2.5

Source: IMF webpage (http://www.imf.org/external/np/sec/memdir/members.htm) and WDI World Bank online database.

On the other hand, enhanced representation of countries with small size economies can be increased only by restoring basic votes to close to their original weight. There are also strong arguments to do so. Basic votes initially constituted about 11 per cent of total voting power in the Fund; with the increases in quota since the creation of the Fund and no adjustment in basic votes, the latter represent only 2 per cent of total voting power. This figure of 2 per cent becomes even more insignificant when the size of the IMF membership—which grew—is taken into account.

In any event, a sizeable quota increase with a large selective component would be necessary to move in the desired direction. The adjustment in relative positions can be implemented only by measurable increases in countries whose calculated quota is higher than actual quota, unless those countries with calculated quota lower than actual quota accept a lower absolute quota.

In the end, the way the variables are defined and the magnitude of the coefficients used for each variable in the quota formula will depend on their acceptability to the members of the IMF Executive Board and the IMFC—and, by extension, the Executive Board of the World Bank and the Development Committee. This would require an essentially political decision.

Representation in other international financial institutions, particularly those setting international norms, requires additional political determination. Because democracy has become such an important aim of nations and of the international community, it is to be hoped that such political agreement can be reached.

NOTES

1 According to some analysts, the Plaza Accord might have exacerbated the downturn of the dollar, contrary to its initial objective of achieving an orderly devaluation of the United States currency. The purpose of the Louvre Accord was to stabilize the dollar. For a detailed account of policy coordination during the late 1980s, see Frankel (1994).

2 This view, that maintaining weak exchange rates to fuel export growth should be the goal of exchange-rate interventions in Asia, ignores certain facts behind recent foreign-exchange pressures in Asia, particularly the fact that the largest accumulation has taken place in Japan, a country that has already experienced a sizeable appreciation of its currency, that some countries have also allowed their exchange rates to strengthen and, particularly, that the pressure on others (including China) come more from the capital account than from current-account surpluses. See, in this regard, Genberg and others (2005).

3 Japan's holdings of foreign exchange reserves, approaching $1 trillion, are much larger than foreign holdings of Japanese yen as foreign-exchange reserves, suggesting that the "net" role of Japanese yen as an international reserve money is limited.

4 In the United States, the Securities and Exchange Commission (Rule 203(b)(5)-2) that required certain advisers to hedge funds to register with the Commission under the Investment Advisers Act of 1940 has been vacated and remanded by a US Court of Appeals opinion.

5 A decision to increase the number of basic votes would also lead to an increase in the share of the voting power of developing countries, in particular the countries of small economic size (see below). However, such a decision would require an amendment to the Articles of Agreement.

6 Several observers have suggested this should be seen in the context of EU policies and the possibility of one chair representing the Union.

Bibliography

Adam, Christopher, Ben no Ndulu and Nii Kwaku Sowa (1996). Liberalisation and seigniorage revenue in Kenya, Ghana and Tanzania. *Journal of Development Studies*, vol. 32, no. 4, pp. 531-553.

Agosin, Manuel (2000). Corea y Taiwan en la crisis financiera asiática. In *Crisis financieras en economías 'exitosas'*. Ricardo Ffrench-Davis ed. ECLAC/McGraw-Hill, Santiago.

_____, and Ricardo Mayer (2000). Foreign investment in developing countries: does it crowd in domestic investment? UNCTAD Discussion Paper No. 146, February. Geneva: United Nations Conference on Trade and Development.

Allen, Mark (2004). IMF conditionality and ownership. Remarks prepared for the Development Policy Forum on "Conditionality Revisited" organized by the World Bank, Paris, 5 July.

Andriamananjara, Soamiely (1999). On the size and number of regional integration arrangements: a political economy model. Department of Economics, University of Maryland at College Park, Maryland.

Asian Development Bank (2004). *Asian Development Outlook, 2004*. Manila.

Atkinson, Anthony (ed.) (2005). *New Sources of Development Finance*. Oxford University Press, New York.

Atta-Mensah, Joseph (2004). Commodity-linked bonds: a potential means for less-developed countries to raise foreign capital. Bank of Canada Working Paper No. 2004-20, Ottawa.

Akyut, Dick, and Dilip Ratha (2004). South-South FDI flows: how big are they? *Transnational Corporations*, vol. 13, no. 1 (April), pp. 149-176.

Azam, Jean-Paul (1998). Politiques macro-économiques et réduction de la pauvreté. Communication à l'atelier 'Pauvreté, répartition des revenus, et questions relatives au marché du travail' du Centre de recherche en économie appliquée (CREA), Algiers.

_____, Augustin Fosu and Njuguna S. Ndung'u (2002). Explaining slow growth in Africa. *African Development Review*, vol. 14, no. 4 (December), pp. 177-220.

Bank for International Settlements (2001). *71st Annual Report*. June, Bank for International Settlements, Basel.

_____ (2003). *Quarterly Review* (September). Bank for International Settlements, Basel.

_____ (2004a). *Quarterly Review* (June). Bank for International Settlements, Basel.

_____ (2004b). Implementation of the new capital adequacy framework in non-Basel Committee member countries. Financial Stability Institute Occasional Paper no. 4 Bank for International Settlements, Basel.

_____ (2005). *Quarterly Review* (March). Bank for International Settlements, Basel.

_____ (2006). *Quarterly Review* (March). Bank for International Settlements, Basel.

Basu, Anupam, and Krishna Srinivasan (2002). Foreign direct investment in Africa? Some case studies. IMF Working Paper No. WP/02/61, March, International Monetary Fund, Washington, DC.

Berensmann, Kathrin, and Frank Schroeder (2005). A proposal for a new international debt framework (IDF) for the prevention and resolution of debt crisis in middle-income countries. Paper for the Multistakeholder Consultation on Systemic Issues in Lima, 17 and 18 February. Available from http://www.new-rules.org/docs/ffdconsultdocs/berensmanna-shroeder.pdf.

Berensztein, Eduardo, and Paulo Mauro (2004). The case for GDP-indexed bonds. *Economic Policy*, vol. 19, pp. 165-216.

Beynon, J. (2003). Poverty efficient aid allocations: Collier/Dollar revisited. ESAU Working Paper No. 2, Economics and Statistics Analysis Unit, Overseas Development Institute, London.

Bhinda, Nils, and others (1999). *Private Capital Flows to Africa: Perception and Reality.* Forum on Debt and Development (FONDAD), The Hague.

Bigsten, Arne, Jorgen Levin and Hakan Persson (2001). Debt relief on growth: a study of Zambia and Tanzania. Paper prepared for the WIDER Development Conference on Debt Relief, Helsinki.

Birdsall, Nancy (2004). Seven deadly sins: reflections on donor failings. Center for Global Development Working Paper No. 50, December, Washington, D.C. Also available from http://www.cgdev.org/content/publications/detail/2737.

_____, and Liliana Rojas-Suarez, eds (2004). *Financing Development: The Power of Regionalism.* Center for Global Development, Washington, DC.

_____, Stijn Claessens and Ishac Diwan (2004). Policy selectivity forgone: debt and donor behaviour in Africa. In *Debt Relief for Poor Countries*, Tony Addison, Henrik Hansen, and Finn Tarp, eds. Palgrave Macmillan, New York, in association with the United Nations University.

Bonin, J. P., and István Ábel (2000). Retail banking in Hungary: a foreign affair?. Background paper for *World Development Report, 2002*. Wesleyan University, Middletown, CT.

Boone, Peter (1996). Politics and the effectiveness of foreign aid. *European Economic Review*, vol. 40, no. 2, pp. 289-329.

Borio, Claudio (2003). Towards a macroprudential framework for financial supervision and regulation? BIS Working Paper No. 128, Bank for International Settlements, Basel.

Borio, Claudio, Craig Furfine and Philip Lowe (2001). Procyclicality of the Financial System and Financial Stability: Issues and Policy Options. In *Marrying the Macro- and Micro-Prudential Dimensions of Financial Stability*. BIS Paper No. 1, March, Bank for International Settlements, Basel.

Bosworth, Barry, and Susan M. Collins (2003). The empirics of growth: an update. *Brookings Papers on Economic Activity*, no. 2, pp. 113-206.

Boughton, James M. (2001). *Silent Evolution: The International Monetary Fund 1979-1989.* International Monetary Fund, Washington, DC.

BradyNet Forum. Http://www.bradynet.com/bbs/bradybonds/100090-0.html.

Buira, Ariel (2003). An analysis of IMF conditionality. G-24 Discussion Paper no. 22, August, UNCTAD, Geneva. UNCTAD/GDS/MDPB/G24/2003/3.

_____ (2005). Financial crises and international cooperation. Briefing note prepared for "The Orderly Resolution of Financial Crises: A G20-led Initiative", Mexico City, 30 January. Available from: www.globalcentres.org.

Bulír, Aleš, and A. Javier Hamann (2001). How Volatile and Unpredictable are Aid Flows, and What are the Policy Implications? WIDER Discussion Paper no. 2001/143. United Nations University World Institute for Development Economics Research, Helsinki.

_____ (2003). Aid volatility: an empirical assessment. _IMF Staff Papers_, vol. 50, no. 1, pp. 64-89. Also available from http://www.imf.org/External/Pubs/FT/staffp/2003/01/bulir.htm.

_____ (2005). Volatility of development aid: From the frying pan into the fire? International Monetary Fund paper presented at the Seminar on Foreign Aid and Macroeconomic Management, Maputo, 14 and 15 March.

Burnside, Craig, and David Dollar (1997). Aid, policies and growth. Policy Research Working Paper, no. 1777. Development Research Group, World Bank. June.

_____ (2000). Aid, policies and growth. _American Economic Review_, vol. 90, no. 4 (September), pp. 847-868.

Cafiero, Mario, and Javier Llorens (2002). _La Argentina Robada_. Buenos Aires: Ediciones Macchi.

Camdessus, Michel (2000). An agenda for the IMF at the start of the 21st Century. Remarks at the Council on Foreign Relations, New York. February.

Caprio, Gerard, Jr., and Aslï Demirgüç-Kunt (1997). The role of long term finance: theory and evidence. Policy Research Department, World Bank. February.

Caruana, Jaime (2004). Hacia un efectiva implementación del Nuevo Acuerdo de Capital de Basilea. Remarks to the International Seminar El Nuevo Acuerdo de Capital de Basilea: retos y oportunidades para las Américas, organised by Asociación de Supervisores Bancarios de las Américas (ASBA), Centro de Estudios Monetarios Latinoamericanos (CEMLA) and Federación Latinoamericana de Bancos (FELABAN), México D.F., 12 July.

Chauvet, L., and P. Guillaumont (2002). Aid and growth revisited: policy, economic vulnerability and political instability. 7 July 2002 version of paper presented at the Annual Bank Conference on Development Economics, ABCDE-Europe, Oslo, 24-26 June.

Chew, Lillian (1996). _Managing Derivative Risks: The Use and Abuse of Leverage_. John Wiley, New York.

Clarke, George, Robert Cull and Maria Soledad Martinez Peria (2001a). Does foreign bank penetration reduce access to credit in developing countries? Evidence from asking borrowers. World Bank Development Research Group. Policy Research Working Paper No. 2716, November, World Bank, Washington, DC.

Clarke, George, Robert Cull, Maria Soledad Martinez Peria and Susana M. Sanchez (2001b). Foreign bank entry: Experience, implications for developing countries and agenda for further research. Policy Research Working Paper No. 2698, World Bank, Washington, DC.

Clemens, Michael, Steven Radelet and Rikhil Bhavnani (2004). Counting chickens when they hatch: the short-term effect of aid on growth. Working Paper, no. 44, Center for Global Development, Washington, DC.

Clunies-Ross, Anthony (2000). A tax on foreign-exchange transactions: report of a consultation held by Coopération Internationale pour le Développement et la Solidarité (CIDSE) in collaboration with the University of Antwerp (UFSIA), 22 October 1999. February.

_____ (2004). Imminent Prospects for Additional Finance: What Might Be Done Now or Soon and Under What Conditions. Research Paper No. 2004/45. United Nations University World Institute for Development Economics Research, Helsinki.

Cohen, Daniel (1996). The sustainability of African debt. Policy Research Working Paper No. 1621, July, International Finance Division, International Economics Department, World Bank, Washington, DC.

_____ (2001). The HIPC initiative: true or false promises. International Finance, vol. 4, no. 3, pp. 363-380.

Collier, Paul, and Jan Dehn (2001). Aid, shocks and growth. Policy Research Working Paper No. 2688, Development Research Group, World Bank, Washington, DC.

Collier, Paul, and David Dollar (1999). Aid allocation and poverty reduction. Policy Research Working Paper No. 2041, Development Research Group, World Bank, Washington, DC.

_____ (2001). Can the world cut poverty in half? How policy reform and effective aid can meet the international development goals. World Development, vol. 29, no. 11, pp. 1787-1802.

_____ (2002). Aid allocation and poverty reduction. European Economic Review, vol. 46, no. 8, pp. 1475-1500.

Collier, Paul, and Anke Hoeffler (2002). Aid, policy and growth in post-conflict countries. Policy Research Working Paper No. 2902, Development Research Group, World Bank, Washington, DC.

Comisión Especial de la Cámara de Diputados, 2005, República Argentina (2005). Fuga de Divisas en la Argentina: Informe Final. Comisión Latinoamérica de Ciencias Sociales (Clacso) and Siglo XXI, Buenos Aires.

Commission for Africa (2005). Our Common Interest: Report of the Commission for Africa. Available from http://www.commissionforafrica.org/english/report/thereport/cfafullreport_/.pdf (accessed 13 June 2005).

Commonwealth Secretariat (2004). Review of IMF/World Bank issues. Paper prepared by the Commonwealth Secretariat, London.

Cooper, Richard (2002). Chapter 11 for countries? Foreign Affairs, vol. 81, no. 4.

Cordella, Tito, and Eduardo Levy Yeyati (2004). Country insurance. IMF Working Paper no. WP/04/148, International Monetary Fund, Washington, DC.

_____ (2005). A (new) country insurance facility. IMF Working Paper no. WP/05/23, January, International Monetary Fund, Washington, DC.

Council of Economic Advisers (2004). Growth-indexed bonds: a primer. 22 November, Council of Economic Advisers, Washington, DC.

Crockett, Andrew (2000). Marrying the micro- and macro-prudential dimensions of financial stability. 21 September. Available from www.bis.org.

_____ (2001a). Banking supervision and regulation: international trends. Remarks at the 64th Banking Convention of the Mexican Bankers' Association, 30 March. Available from www.bis.org.

_____ (2001b). Monetary policy and financial stability. 13 February. Available from www.bis.org.

Dalgaard, Carl-Johan, and Henrik Hansen (2001). On aid, growth and good policies. *Journal of Development Studies*, vol. 37, no. 6, pp. 17-41.

Dalgaard, Carl-Johan, Henrik Hansen and Finn Tarp (2002). On the empirics of foreign aid and growth. CREDIT Research Paper no. 02/08. University of Nottingham Centre for Research in Economic Development and International Trade, Nottingham, UK.

D'Arista, Jane (1979). Private overseas lending: too far, too fast? In *Debt and the Less Developed Countries*. Jonathan David Aronson, ed. Westview Press, Boulder, pp. 57-58.

Dobson, Wendy, and Gary Hufbauer, assisted by Hyon Koo Cho (2001). *World Capital Markets: Challenge to the G-10*. Institute for International Economics, Washington, DC.

Dodd, Randall (2004). Protecting developing economies from price shocks. *Special Policy Brief* 18. Financial Policy Forum, Washington, DC.

_____ (2005). The consequences of liberalizing derivative markets. Processed, Initiative for Policy Dialogue, Columbia University. To appear in *Capital Market Liberalization*. Joseph Stiglitz and Jose Antonio Ocampo eds. Oxford University Press, New York (forthcoming).

Dollar, David, and Aart Kraay (2001). Trade, growth, and poverty. Policy Research Working Paper No. WPS 2615, Development Research Group, World Bank.

Dooley, Michael P., David Folkerts-Landau and Peter Garber (2003). An essay on the revived Bretton Woods system. NBER Working Paper No. 9971, National Bureau of Economic Research, Cambridge, MA.

_____ (2004a). The revived Bretton Woods system: the effects of periphery intervention and reserve management on interest rates and exchange rates in center countries. NBER Working Paper No. 10332, National Bureau of Economic Research, Cambridge, MA.

_____ (2004b). The US current account deficit and economic development: Collateral for a total return swap. NBER Working Paper No. 10727, August, National Bureau of Economic Research, Cambridge, MA.

Easterly, William (2001). *The Elusive Quest for Growth: Economists' Adventures and Misadventures in the Tropics*. The MIT Press, Cambridge, MA.

Eatwell, John, and Lance Taylor (2000). *Global Finance at Risk: The Case for International Regulation*. The New Press, New York.

Economic and Social Commission for Asia and the Pacific (ESCAP) (2005). Implementing the Monterrey Consensus in the Asian and Pacific Region: Achieving Coherence and Consistency. Sales No. E.05.II.F.8, United Nations, New York.

Economic Commission for Africa (2004). *Economic Report on Africa 2004: Unlocking Africa's Trade Potential on the Global Economy*. Sales No. E.04.II.K.12. United Nations, Addis Ababa.

Economic Commission for Latin America and the Caribbean (1994). *Open Regionalism in Latin America and the Caribbean: Economic Integration as a Contribution to Changing Production Patterns with Social Equity.* LC/G.1801/Rev.1-P/I. Sales No. E.94.II.G.3. ECLAC, Santiago.

_____ (2003). *Foreign Direct Investment in Latin America and the Carribean 2002.* ECLAC, Santiago.

_____ (2004). *Foreign Investment in Latin America and the Caribbean 2003.* Sales No. E.04.II.G.54. ECLAC, Santiago.

_____ (2005). *Foreign Investment in Latin America and the Caribbean 2004.* Sales No. E.05.II.G.32. ECLAC, Santiago.

Eichengreen, Barry (2004a). Financial instability. In *Global Crises, Global Solutions*, Bjorn Lomborg, ed. Cambridge University Press, New York.

_____ (2004b). Global imbalances and the lessons of Bretton Woods. NBER Working Paper No. 10497, National Bureau of Economic Research, Cambridge, MA.

_____ (2005). Preparing for the next financial crisis. Briefing note prepared for "The Orderly Resolution of Financial Crises. A G-20 led Initiative", 29 and 30 January 2005, Mexico City. Available from www.globalcentres.org.

_____, Ricardo Hausman and Ugo Panizza (2003). Currency mismatches, debt intolerance, and original sin: why they are not the same and why it matters. NBER Working Paper No. 10036, National Bureau of Economic Research, Cambridge, MA.

_____, and Ricardo Hausman (eds) (2005). *Other People's Money. Debt Denomination and Financial Instability in Emerging Markets Economies.* University of Chicago Press, Chicago.

Emmerij, Louis, Richard Jolly and T.G. Weiss (2001). *Ahead of the Curve? UN Ideas and Global Challenges.* Indiana University Press, Bloomington.

Epstein, Gerald, Ilene Grabel and Jomo Kwame Sundaram (2003). Capital management techniques in developing countries: an assessment of experiences from the 1990s and lessons for the future. Paper presented at the XVIth Technical Group Meeting of the G-24 in Port of Spain, Trinidad and Tobago, 13 and 14 February.

Escaith, Hubert (2004). El crecimiento económico en América Latina y sus perspectivas más allá del sexenio perdido. *Problemas del Desarrollo* (Mexico), vol. 35, no. 139 (October-December).

Euromoney (2004). December, pp. 92-99.

European Central Bank (2005). Financial flows to emerging market economies: changing patterns and recent developments. *Monthly Bulletin* (January), pp. 59-73.

European Network on Debt and Development (Eurodad) (2002). Moving beyond good and bad performance. Brussels, 26 June.

Fernández de Lis, Santiago, Jorge Martínez and Jesús Saurina (2001). Credit Growth, Problem Loans and Credit Risk Provisioning in Spain. In *Marrying the Macro-and Micro-Prudential Dimensions of Financial Stability*, BIS Paper No. 1, March, Bank for International Settlements, Basel.

Ffrench-Davis, Ricardo, and Stephany Griffith-Jones (2003). *From Capital Surges to Drought: Seeking Stability for Emergency Economies.* UNU-WIDER Studies in Development Economics and Policy Series. Palgrave Macmillan Basingstoke, UK.

Financial Times (2005). Shock of the new: a changed financial landscape may be eroding resistance to systemic risk. Comment and analysis. 16 February.

Fischer, Stanley (2002). Financial crises and reform of the international financial system. NBER Working Paper, No. 9297. Cambridge, Massachusetts: National Bureau of Economic Research. October.

Fraga, Arminio, Ilan Goldfain and Andre Minella (2003). Inflation targeting in emerging market economies. NBER Working Paper No. 10019, National Bureau of Economic Research, Cambridge, MA.

Frankel, Jeffrey (1994). Exchange rate policy. In *American Economic Policy in the 1980s*. Martin Feldstein, ed. University of Chicago Press, Chicago, pp. 293-341.

Geithner, Timothy (2004). Changes in the structure of the U.S. financial system and implications for systemic risk. Remarks before the Conference on Systemic Financial Crises at the Federal Reserve Bank of Chicago, 1 October.

_____ (2005). Further investments to strengthen the financial system. Remarks before the Economic Club of Washington, Washington, DC, 9 February. Available from www.bis.org.

_____ (2006). "Implications of Growth in Credit Derivatives for Financial Stability," Remarks at the New York University Stern School of Business Third Credit Risk Conference, May 16, New York City.

Gemmell, N., and M. McGillivray (1998). Aid and tax instability and the government budget constraint in developing countries. CREDIT Research Paper No. 98/1, University of Nottingham Centre for Research in Economic Development and International Trade, Nottingham, UK.

Genberg, Hans, Robert McCauley, Yung Chul Park and Avinash Persaud (2005). *Official Reserves and Currency Management in Asia: Myth, Reality and the Future*. Geneva Reports on the World Economy no. 7, International Center for Monetary and Banking Studies, Geneva.

Genberg, Hans, A. Powell and D. Vines (1999). Positioning the World Bank. *Economic Journal*, vol. 109 (November).

Genberg, Hans, and D. Vines (2000). *The World Bank: Structure and Policies*. Cambridge: Cambridge University Press.

Gilbert, Christopher L., A. Powell and D. Vines (1999). Positioning the World Bank. *Economic Journal*, vol. 109 (November).

_____ and D. Vines (2000). *The World Bank: Structure and Policies*. Cambridge, United Kingdom: Cambridge University Press.

Goldstein, Morris (2003). Debt sustainability, Brazil and the IMF. Institute for International Economics wp 03-1, February, Washington, DC.

_____ (2005). A note on improving the international financial architecture. Briefing note prepared for "The Orderly Resolution of Financial Crises. A G-20 led Initiative", 29 and 30 January, Mexico City. Available from www. globalcentres.org.

Goodhart, Charles, and J. Danielsson (2001). The inter-temporal nature of risk. Presented at the 23rd European Money and Finance Forum (SUERF) Colloquium on "Technology and finance: challenges for financial markets, business strategies and policy makers", October, Brussels. Available from www.bis.org.

Gorton, Gary B., and K. Geert Rouwenhorst (2005). Facts and fantasies about commodity futures. Yale International Center for Finance Working Paper No. 04-20. 28 February. Available from the Social Science Research Network Electronic Paper Collection website http://ssrn.com/abstract=560042 (accessed 13 June 2005).

Griffith-Jones, Stephany (1998). *Global Capital Flows: Should They be Regulated?* St. Martin's Press, New York.

_____ (2004a). Basilea II: los países en desarrollo y la diversificación de la cartera. In *Revista de la CEPAL*, August, pp. 153-169.

_____ (2004b). CAD3 and developing countries: the potential impact of diversification effects on international lending patterns and pro-cyclicality. Institute of Development Studies, University of Sussex. August. Available from www.stephanygj.com.

_____, and Ana Fuzzo de Lima (2005). Alternative loan guarantee mechanisms and project finance for infrastructure in developing countries. In *The New Public Finance, Responding to Global Challenges*, Inge Kaul and others, eds. Oxford University Press, New York.

_____, and Ricardo Gottschalk (2004). Costs of currency crises and benefits of international financial reform. Currently available from www.stephanygj.com.

_____, and José Antonio Ocampo (2003). What progress on international financial reform? Why so limited? Prepared for the Expert Group on Development Issues. Sweden.

_____, Stephen Spratt, and Miguel Angel Segoviano (2003). Submission to the Basel Committee on Banking Supervision: CP3 and the developing world. Institute of Development Studies, University of Sussex, Brighton, United Kingdom. Available from www.stephanygj.com.

_____ (2004). CAD3 and Developing Countries: the Potential Impact of Diversification Effects on International Lending Patterns and Pro-cyclicality. Available from www.stephanygj.com.

_____ (2004). CAD3 and Developing Countries: the Potential Impact of Diversification Effects on International Lending Patterns and Pro-cyclicality. Available from www.stephanygj.com.

_____, and Krishnan Sharma (2006). GDP-Indexed Bonds: Making It Happen, UN DESA Discussion Paper no. 21, April, United Nations, New York.

Groupe de travail présidé par Jean-Pierre Landau (2004). *Les nouvelles contributions financièrs internationales*. Paris: La documentation française.

Gugiatti, Mark, and Anthony Richards (2003). Do collective action clauses influence bond yields? New evidence from emerging markets. Research Discussion Paper, RDP 2003-02, Reserve Bank of Australia, Sydney. Guillaumont, P., and L. Chauvet (2001). Aid and performance: a reassessment. *Journal of Development Studies*, vol. 37, no. 6, pp. 66-92.

Gunter, Bernhard G. (2001). Does the HIPC Initiative achieve its goal of debt sustainability? United Nations University/World Institute for Development Economics Research (UNU/WIDER) Discussion Paper, no. 2001/100. September. Available from www.wider.unu.edu/publications/dps/dp2001-100.pdf.

_____ (2003). Achieving long-term debt sustainability in all heavily indebted poor countries (HIPCs). Discussion paper prepared for the Intergovernmental Group of 24 (G-24) XVI Technical Group Meeting in Trinidad and Tobago, 13 and 14 February.

Gurría, José Angel, and Paul Volcker (2001). *The Role of the Multilateral Development Banks in Emerging Market Economies*. Carnegie Endowment for International Peace, EMP Financial Advisors, LLC, and the Inter-American Dialogue, Washington, DC.

G-24 Secretariat (2003). Heavily Indebted Poor Country (HIPC) Initiative. Briefing paper No. 2, March, G-24 Secretariat, Washington, DC.

Haldane, Andrew G., and Mark Kruger (2004). The resolution of international financial crises: an alternative framework. In *The IMF and its Critics: Reform of Global Financial Architecture*. David Vines and Christopher L. Gilbert, eds. Cambridge University Press, New York.

Hansen, H., and F. Tarp (2000). Aid effectiveness disputed. *Journal of International Development*, vol. 12, pp. 375-398.

Hanson, Gordon H. (2001). Should countries promote foreign direct investment? G-24 Discussion Paper Series No. 9, February, Center for International Development, Harvard University, Cambridge, MA, and UNCTAD, Geneva.

Hausman, Ricardo, and Ugo Panizza (2003). The mystery of original sin. Kennedy School of Government, Harvard University, and Inter-American Development Bank, Washington, DC

Hausman, Ricardo, and Andres Velasco (2004). The causes of financial crises: Moral failure versus market failure. December, Kennedy School of Government, Harvard University, Cambridge, MA. Available from http://ksghome.harvard.edu.

Higgins Matthew and Thomas Klitgaard (2004) Reserve Accumulation: Implications for Global Capital Flows and Financial Markets . *New York's Current Issues in Economics and Finance*, vol. 10, no. 10, Federal Reserve Bank of New York, September/October.

Hindustan Times (2003). Developing muscles. 13 November.

International Development Association (2005). Countries ceasing to borrow from IDA, 1960-2001. Available from www.worldbank.org/ida (accessed on 8 June 2005).

International Labour Organization (2005). *World Employment Report, 2004-05*. International Labour Office, Geneva.

International Monetary Fund (2000). Debt and reserve-related indicators of external vulnerability. Paper prepared by the Policy Development and Review Department in consultation with other Departments, 23 March, International Monetary Fund, Washington, DC.

_____ (2001). The challenge of maintaining long-term external debt sustainability. Paper prepared by the Staff of the World Bank and the International Monetary Fund, 20 April, Washington, DC.

_____ (2002a). *Global Financial Stability Report, December 2002*. International Monetary Fund, Washington, DC.

_____ (2002b). Assessing sustainability. Paper prepared by the Policy Development and Review Department, 28 May, International Monetary Fund, Washington, DC.

_____ (2002c). Fund policy on lending into arrears to private creditors: further consideration of the good faith criterion. Paper prepared by the International Capital Markets, Policy Development and Review and Legal Departments, 30 July, International Monetary Fund, Washington, DC.

_____ (2003a). *Global Financial Stability Report: Market Development and Issues: September 2003*. International Monetary Fund, Washington, DC.

_____ (2003b). *IMF Survey*, vol. 32 (Supplement).

_____ (2003c). Debt sustainability in low-income countries: towards a forward-looking strategy. Paper prepared by the Staff of the Policy Development and Review Department, 23 May, International Monetary Fund, Washington, DC.

_____ (2003d). Sustainability assessments: review of application and methodological refinements. Paper prepared by the Policy Development and Review Department in collaboration with the Monetary and Financial Systems Department and in consultation with other Departments, 10 June, International Monetary Fund, Washington, DC.

_____ (2003e). The restructuring of sovereign debt: assessing the benefits, risks, and feasibility of aggregating claims. Paper prepared by the Legal Department, September, International Monetary Fund, Washington, DC.

_____ (2004a). *Global Financial Stability Report, April 2004*. International Monetary Fund, Washington, DC.

_____ (2004b). *Global Financial Stability Report, September 2004*. International Monetary Fund, Washington, DC.

_____ (2004c). Communiqué of the International Monetary and Financial Committee of the Board of Governors of the International Monetary Fund. Press release No. 04/84, 24 April, International Monetary Fund, Washington, DC

_____ (2004d). Report of the Executive Board to the International Monetary and Financial Committee (IMFC) on quotas, voice and representation. Prepared by the Finance and Secretary's Departments, 24 September, International Monetary Fund, Washington, DC. Available from www.imf.org.

_____ (2004e). Progress report to the International Monetary and Financial Committee on crisis resolution. International Monetary Fund, Washington, DC, 20 April.

_____ (2004f). Fund conditionality: a provisional update. IMF Staff Paper (June), International Monetary Fund, Washington, DC. Available from www.imf.org.

_____ (2004g). IMF Executive Board discusses financial sector regulation: issues and gaps. Public Information Notice (PIN) No. 04/131. 22 November, International Monetary Fund, Washington, DC. Available from www.imf.org.

_____ (2004h). IMF Executive Board discusses "Fixed to float: operational aspects of moving toward exchange rate flexibility". Public Information Notice (PIN), no. 04/141. 30 December, International Monetary Fund, Washington, DC. Available from www.imf.org.

_____ (2004i). The design of Fund-supported programs: overview. Policy Development and Review Department, 24 November, International Monetary Fund, Washington, DC.

_____ (2004j). Debt sustainability in low-income countries: proposal for an operational framework and policy implications. Prepared by the Staff of the IMF and the World Bank, 3 February, International Monetary Fund, Washington, DC.

_____ (2004k). Sovereign debt structure for crisis prevention. Discussion paper prepared by the Research Department, 2 July, International Monetary Fund, Washington, DC.

_____ (2005a). Heavily Indebted Poor Countries (HIPC) Initiative: Statistical Update. 11 April, International Monetary Fund, Washington, DC.

_____ (2005b). IMF Executive Board approves proposal to subsidize emergency assistance for natural disasters for PRGF-eligible members. Public Information Notice (PIN), no. 05/8, 27 January, International Monetary Fund, Washington, DC. Available from www.imf.org.

_____ (2005c). IMF Executive Board discusses balance sheet approach to analysis of debt-related vulnerabilities in emerging markets. Public Information Notice (PIN), no. 05/36, 22 March, International Monetary Fund, Washington, DC. Available from www.imf.org.

_____ (2005d). IMF Executive Board discusses program design. Public Information Notice (PIN), no. 05/16, 8 February, International Monetary Fund, Washington, DC. Available from www.imf.org.

_____ (2005e). *IMF Survey*, vol. 34, no. 5 (21 March).

_____ (2005f). Subsidization of IMF emergency assistance for natural disasters. Press release, no. 05/90, 22 April, International Monetary Fund, Washington, DC.

_____ (2005g). *Global Financial Stability Report, April 2005*. International Monetary Fund, Washington, DC.

_____ (2005h). Review of the 2002 Conditionality Guidelines Prepared by the Policy Development and Review Department in consultation with other Departments. March 3, International Monetary Fund, Washington, DC. http://www.imf.org/external/np/pp/eng/2005/030305.pdf

_____ (2006). "The Managing Director's Report on Implementing the Fund's Medium-Term Strategy". April 5, International Monetary Fund, Washington, DC. Available from http://www.imf.org/external/np/pp/eng/2006/040506.pdf.

_____ Independent Evaluation Office (2003). Evaluation of fiscal adjustment in IMF-supported programs. 9 September, International Monetary Fund, Washington, DC.

_____ Independent Evaluation Office (2005). Draft issues paper for an evaluation on structural conditionality in IMF-supported programs. 18 March, International Monetary Fund, Washington, DC. Available from www.imf.org.

_____, and International Development Association (2004). Debt sustainability in low-income countries: further considerations on an operational framework and policy implications. Prepared by the Staff of the IMF and the World Bank, 10 September, International Monetary Fund, Washington, DC.

_____ (2005). Operational framework for debt sustainability assessments in low-income countries: further considerations. Prepared by the Staff of the IMF and the World Bank, 28 March, International Monetary Fund, Washington, DC.

_____, and International Development Association (2006). Heavily Indebted Poor Countries (HIPC) Initiative—List of Ring-Fenced Countries that Meet the Income and Indebtedness Criteria at end-2004. April 11.

_____ (2006). "The Managing Director's Report on Implementing the Fund's Medium-Term Strategy". April 5, International Monetary Fund, Washington, DC. Available from http://www.imf.org/external/np/pp/eng/2006/040506.pdf.

Ito, Takatoshi, Eiji Ogawa and Yuri Sasaki (1999). Establishment of the East Asian Fund. In *Stabilization of Currencies and Financial Systems in East Asia and International Financial Cooperation*. Institute for International Monetary Affairs, Tokyo: chap. 3.

Jenks, C. Wilfred (1942). Some legal aspects of the financing of international institutions. *Transactions of the Grotius Society*, vol. 28, pp. 87-132.

Johnson, S., and A. Subramanian (2005). Aid, governance, and the political economy: growth and institutions. International Monetary Fund paper presented at the Seminar on Foreign Aid and Macroeconomic Management, Maputo, 14 and 15 March.

Kaminsky, Graciela L., Carmen M. Reinhart and Carlos A. Végh (2004). When it rains, it pours: procyclical capital flows and macroeconomic policies. NBER Working Paper No. 10780, National Bureau of Economic Research, Cambridge, MA.

Kaplan, Ethan, and Dani Rodrik (2001). Did the Malaysian capital controls work? John F. Kennedy School of Government, Harvard University, Cambridge, Massachusetts.

Kapur, Devesh (2003). Do as I say not as I do: a critique of G-7 proposals on reforming the Multilateral Development Banks. G-24 Discussion Paper Series No. 20, February, UNCTAD, Geneva.

_____, John Lewis and Richard Webb (1997). *The World Bank: Its First Half Century, vol. 1. History*. The Brookings Institution, Washington, DC.

Kelkar, Vijay, Praveen Chaudhry and Marta Vanduzer-Snow (2005). Time for change at the IMF. *Finance & Development* March.

Kenen, Peter (2001). *The International Financial Architecture: What's New? What's Missing?* Institute for International Economics, Washington, DC.

_____ (2005). Stabilizing the international monetary system. Contribution presented at the Annual Meeting of the American Economic Association, Philadelphia, Pennsylvania. 8 January.

Keynes, John Maynard (1936). *General Theory of Employment, Interest and Money. Collected Writings of John Maynard Keynes, vol. 7: The General Theory*. Donald Moggridge, ed. Macmillan, London, for the Royal Economic Society, 1973.

Killick, Tony (2004). Did conditionality streamlining succeed? Remarks prepared for the Development Policy Forum "Conditionality Revisited", organized by the World Bank, Paris, 5 July.

Kindleberger, Charles P. (1978). *Manias, Panics, and Crashes: A History of Financial Crises*. Basic Books, New York.

King, Mervyn (2005). The international monetary system. Speech at the "Advancing Enterprise 2005" Conference, London, 4 February. Available from www.bis.org.

Kingdom of Norway, Ministry of Foreign Affairs (2005). Pursuing the MDGs: the contribution of multilateral debt relief. Oslo. 14 April.

Knight, Malcolm (2004a). Regulation and supervision in insurance and banking: greater convergence, shared challenges. Speech at the International Association of Insurance Supervisors (IAIS) 11th Annual Conference, Amman, 6 October. Available from www.bis.org.

_____ (2004b). Markets and institutions: managing the evolving financial risk. Speech delivered at the 25th European Money and Finance Forum (SUERF) Colloquium, in Madrid, 14 October.

Kregel, Jan (1996). Some risks and implications of financial globalization for national policy autonomy. *UNCTAD Review*, pp. 55-62.

_____ (1998). "Derivatives and Global Capital Flows: Applications to Asia," *Cambridge Journal of Economics*, Nov., pp. 677-692.

_____ (2004). External financing for development and international financial instability. G-24 Discussion Paper Series No. 32 (October), United Nations Conference on Trade and Development and Intergovernmental Group of Twenty-four, UNCTAD, Geneva.

Lakonishok, J., A. Shleifer and R. V. Vishny (1992). The impact of institutional trading on stock prices. *Journal of Financial Economics*, vol. 32 (August), pp. 23-43.

Lee, Boon-Chye (1993). *The Economics of International Debt Renegotiation: The Role of Bargaining and Information*. Westview Press, Boulder.

Lensink, Robert, and Oliver Morrisey (2000). Aid instability as a measure of uncertainty and the positive impact of aid on growth. *Journal of Development Studies*, vol. 36 (February), pp. 31-49.

_____ (2003). On the welfare cost of economic fluctuations in developing countries. *International Economic Review*, vol. 44 (May), pp. 677-698.

Levy-Yeyati, Eduardo, Ugo Panizza and Ernesto Stein (2003). The cyclical nature of North-South FDI flows. Inter-American Development Bank Research Department Working Paper No. 479, January, Washington, DC.

Lewis, W. Arthur (1954). Economic development with unlimited supplies of labour. *The Manchester School*, vol. 22, no. 2, pp. 139-191.

Lipsey, Robert E. (2001). Foreign direct investors in three financial crises. NBER Working Paper No. 8084, National Bureau of Economic Research, Cambridge, MA.

Ma, Guonan, Corrinne Ho and Robert N. McCauley (2004). The markets for non-deliverable forwards in Asian currencies. *BIS Quarterly Review* June.

Manning, Richard (2005). OECD/DAC statement to the Development Committee Spring Meeting, 17 April, Washington, DC.

McLenaghan, John B. (2005). Purchasing power parities and comparisons of GDP in IMF quota calculations. Paper presented to the G24 Technical Group Meeting, Manila, 17 and 18 March.

Mead, Russell Walter, and Sherle R. Schwenninger (2000). A financial architecture for middle-class-oriented development: A report of the Project on Development, Trade, and International Finance. Council on Foreign Relations, New York.

Mehmet, Ozay, and M. Tahiroglu (2003). Globalization and Sustainability of Small States. *Humanomics*, vol. 19, no. 1/2, pp. 45-59.

Meltzer, A. H. (Chair) and others (2000). Report to the United States Congress of the International Financial Institutions Advisory Commission, March, Washington, DC.

Minsky, Hyman P. (1982). *Inflation, Recession and Economic Policy*. Sussex, United Kingdom: Wheatsheaf Books.

Mistry, Percy S. (1995). *Multilateral Development Banks: An Assessment of their Financial Structures, Policies and Practices*. Forum on Debt and Development (FONDAD), The Hague.

Mohammed, Aziz Ali (2004). Who pays for the World Bank? Working paper presented to the G-24 Technical Group Meeting, Geneva, February.

Morrissey, Oliver (2001). Does aid increase growth? *Progress in Development Studies*, vol. 1, no. 1, pp. 37-50.

Nissanke, Machiko (2003). Revenue potential of the Tobin tax for development finance: a critical appraisal. Paper presented at the WIDER Conference on Sharing Global Prosperity, Helsinki, 6 and 7 September. Available from http://www.wider.unu.edu/conference/conference-2003-3/conference2003-3.htm (accessed 23 June 2005).

Nkusu, Mwanza, and Selin Sayek (2004). Local financial development and the aid-growth relationship. IMF Working Paper No. WP/04/238, International Monetary Fund, December, Washington, DC.

Ocampo, José Antonio (2001). *International Asymmetries and the Design of the International Financial System*. Serie Temas de Coyuntura no. 15. Sales No. E.01.II.G.70. Economic and Social Commission for Latin America and the Caribbean, Santiago.

_____ (2002). Recasting the international financial agenda. In *International Capital Markets: Systems in Transition*. John Eatwell and Lance Taylor, eds. Oxford University Press, New York.

_____ (2003a). Capital account and counter-cyclical prudential regulations in developing countries. In *From Capital Surges to Drought: Seeking Stability for Emerging Economies*. Ricardo Ffrench-Davis and Stephany Griffith-Jones, eds. UNU-WIDER Studies in Development Economics and Policy Series. Palgrave Macmillan, Basingstoke.

_____ (2003b). International Asymmetries and the Design of the International Financial System. In *Critical Issues in Financial Reform: A View from the South*. Albert Berry and Gustavo Indart, eds. Transaction Publishers, New Brunswick, NJ.

_____ (2006). The case for, and the experience with, regional financial cooperation. In *Regional Financial Cooperation*. José Antonio Ocampo, ed. Brookings Institution, Washington, DC, and Economic Commission for Latin America and the Caribbean, Santiago.

_____, and Juan Martin (2003). *Globalization and Development: A Latin American and Caribbean Perspective*. Stanford University Press, Stanford, CA, Economic Commission for Latin America and the Caribbean, Santiago, and World Bank, Washington, DC.

_____, and José Gabriel Palma (2005). Dealing with volatile external finances at source: the role of preventive capital account regulations. Initiative for Policy Dialogue, Columbia University, New York.

Organization for Economic Cooperation and Development/Development Assistance Committee (2004). *The DAC Journal: Development Co-operation Report 2004*. OECD, Paris: chapter 1.

_____ (2005). OECD calls for more aid, used more effectively, to bring safer, healthier lives. 18 January. OECD press release. Available from www.oecd.org/dac. See inset entitled "Final ODA data for 2003".

_____ (2005). Paris Declaration on Aid Effectiveness, updated August 3, 2005" at http://www.oecd.org/dataoecd/45/46/35230756.pdf).

_____ (2005). Aid rising sharply, according to latest OECD figures2005 (OECD 2005 at www.oecd.org/ dataoecd/0/41/35842562.pdf).

_____ (2006). Aid flows top USD 100 billion in 2005 http://www.oecd.org/document/40/0,2340,en_2649_33721_36418344_1_1_1_1,00.html

Ortiz, Guillermo (2004). Basel II and Latin American economics. Speech given at the Annual Meeting of the Association of Latin American Regulators (ASBA), Mexico City, July 2004.

Oxfam (2003). The IMF and the Millennium Goals: Failing to deliver for low income countries. Oxfam Briefing Paper No 54, September.

_____, and T. Conway (2004). *Assessing the Poverty Impact of the Doha Development Agenda*. Overseas Development Institute, London.

Pallage, Stephane, and Michael A. Robe (2001). Foreign aid and the business cycle. *Review of International Economics*, vol. 9, no. 4, pp. 641–672.

Palma, Gabriel (2002). The three routes to financial crises: the need for capital controls. In *International Capital Markets: Systems in Transition*. John Eatwell and Lance Taylor, eds. Oxford University Press, New York.

Park, Yung Chul (2006). Regional financial integration in East Asia: Challenges and prospects. In *Regional Financial Cooperation*. José Antonio Ocampo, ed. Brookings Institution, Washington, DC, and Economic Commission for Latin America and the Caribbean, Santiago.

Persaud, Avinash (2000). Sending the herd off the cliff edge: the disturbing interaction between herding and market-sensitive risk management practices. Institute of International Finance Competition in Honour of Jacques de Larosiere, First Prize Essay on Global Finance for 2000, Washington, DC.

_____ (2003). Liquidity black holes: Why modern financial regulation in developed countries is making short-term capital flows to developing countries even more volatile. In *From Capital Surges to Drought: Seeking Stability for Emergency Economies*, Robert Ffrench-Davis and Stephany Griffith-Jones, eds. UNU-WIDER Studies in Development Economics and Policy Series. Palgrave Macmillan, Basingstoke.

Polak, Jacques J., and Peter B. Clark (2005). A new perspective on SDR allocations, new rules for global finance. Available from http://www.new-rules.org/docs/polak.pdf (accessed 23 June 2005).

Prasad, Eswar, and others (2003). Effects of financial globalization on developing countries: some empirical evidence. International Monetary Fund, Washington, DC.

Rajaraman, Indira (2001). Capital account regimes in India and Malaysia. National Institute of Public Finance and Policy, New Delhi.

Rato, Rodrigo de (2004). The IMF at 60: evolving challenges, evolving role. Opening remarks at the conference on "Dollars, Debts and Deficits: 60 Years After Bretton Woods", Madrid, 14 June. Available at www.imf.org.

_____ (2005). Is the IMF's mandate still relevant?. *Global Agenda* (January).

Reddy, Y.V. (2001). Operationalizing capital account liberalization: the Indian experience. *Development Policy Review*, vol. 19, no. 1.

Reisen, H. (2003). Ratings since the Asian crisis. *From Capital Surges to Drought: Seeking Stability from Emerging Economies*. Ricardo Ffrench-Davis and Stephany Griffith-Jones, eds. Palgrave, Basingstoke.

Republic of South Africa Department of Foreign Affairs (2005). Cape Town Ministerial Communique, India-Brazil-South Africa (IBSA) Dialogue Forum. Press release. 13 March. Also available from http://www.dfa.gov.za/docs/2005/ibsa0311.htm.

Rodrik, Dani (2000). Comments on 'Trade, Growth, and Poverty' by D. Dollar and A. Kraay. Harvard University, Cambridge, MA, October.

_____ (2004). Getting institutions right. Processed, Harvard University Cambridge, MA.

_____, and Andrés Velasco (1999). Short-term capital flows. NBER Working Paper No. 7364, National Bureau of Economic Research, Cambridge, MA.

Rogoff, Kenneth, and Jeromin Zettelmeyer (2002). Bankruptcy procedures for sovereigns: a history of ideas, 1976-2001. *IMF Staff Papers*, vol. 49, no. 3, pp. 470-507.

Roubini, Nouriel (2001). Debt sustainability: how to assess whether a country is insolvent. New York University, Stern School of Business, New York. 20 December. Available from http://pages.stern.nyu.edu/~nroubini/papers/debtsustainability.pdf.

Roubini, Nouriel, and Brad Setser (2005). Will the Bretton Woods 2 regime unravel soon? The risk of a hard landing in 2005-2006. Paper prepared for the Symposium on "The Revived Bretton Woods System: A New Paradigm for Asian Development?", organized by the Federal Reserve Bank of San Francisco and the University of California, Berkeley, San Francisco, 4 February.

Sachs, Jeffrey D., and Andrew Warner (1995). Economic reform and the process of global integration. *Brookings Papers on Economic Activity*, no. 1. Washington, DC

Sagasti, Francisco, and Fernando Prada (2006). Regional Development Banks: A comparative perspective. In *Regional Financial Cooperation*. José Antonio Ocampo, ed. Brookings Institution, Washington, DC, and Economic Commission for Latin America and the Caribbean, Santiago.

Sagasti, Francisco, Keith Bezanson and Fernando Prada (2005a). *The Future of Development Financing: Challenges, Scenarios and Strategic Choices*. Palgrave Macmillan, Basingstoke (Forthcoming).

Schneider, Benu (2007). Clubbing in Paris: Is debt sustainability an illusion? In *Sovereign Debt Workouts*. Joseph Stiglitz and José Antonio Ocampo, eds. Initiative for Policy Dialogue, Columbia University, New York (forthcoming).

Shiller, Robert (2005). In favor of growth-linked bonds. *The Indian Express* 10 March.

Soros, George (2002). Special drawing rights for the provision of public goods on a global scale. Remarks delivered at the Roundtable on "New Proposals on Financing for Development", 20 February, Institute for International Economics, Washington, DC.

Spahn, B. (2002). On the feasibility of a tax on foreign exchange transactions. Report to the Federal Ministry for Economic Cooperation and Development, Bonn. February. Available from http://www.wiwi.uni-frankfurt.de/professoren/spahn/tobintax/ (accessed 23 June 2005).

Spiegel, Shari, and Randall Dodd (2004). Up from sin: a portfolio approach to salvation. A study for presentation to the XVIII G24 Technical Group Meeting, Palais des Nations, Geneva, 8 and 9 March.

Stallings, Barbara (1999). The World Bank at the Millennium. *Economic Journal*, vol. 109 (459), pp. F577-F597.

_____ (2000). Lessons from the global financial crisis. In *Global Financial Crises: Lessons from Recent Events*, J. R. Bisignano, William C. Hunter and George G. Kaufman, eds., pp. 89-107. Kluwer Academic, Boston.

Stallings, Barbara, and Wilson Peres (2000). *Growth, Employment and Equity: The Impact of the Economic Reforms in Latin America and the Caribbean*. Brookings Institution Press, Washington, DC, and ECLAC, Santiago.

Stiglitz, Joseph E. (1999). The World Bank at the Millennium. *Economic Journal*, vol. 109 (459), pp. F577-F594.

_____ (2001). Information and the Change in the Paradigm in Economics. Nobel Prize Lecture, Stockholm, December 8.

_____, José Antonio Ocampo, Shari Spiegel, Ricardo Ffrench-Davis and Deepak Nayyar (2006). *Stability with Growth: Macroeconomics for development*. Oxford University Press, New York.

Stoessinger, John, and associates (1964). *Financing the United Nations system*. The Brookings Institution, Washington, DC.

Subramanian, A. (2003). Financing of losses from preference erosion: note on issues raised by developing countries in the Doha Round. WT/TF/COH/14. 14 February, Geneva.

Summers, Lawrence H. (2004). The U.S. current account deficit and the global economy. Per Jacobson Lecture, Washington, DC.

Taylor, John (2004). New directions for the international financial institutions. Keynote address at the Conference "Global Economic Challenges for the IMF's New Chief", American Enterprise Institute, Washington, DC Available from www.treas.gov.

Technical Group on Innovative Financing Mechanisms Report (2004). Report of the Technical Group on Innovative Financial Mechanisms: Actions against Hunger and Poverty. September.

_____ (2004). Sub-regional financial institutions in Latin America and the Caribbean. Paper prepared for presentation at the Conference on Regional Financial Arrangements, United Nations, New York, 14 and 15 July.

Titelman, Daniel (2006), Subregional financial cooperation: the experiences of Latin America and the Caribbean. In *Regional Financial Cooperation*. José Antonio Ocampo, ed. Brookings Institution, Washington, DC, and Economic Commission for Latin America and the Caribbean, Santiago.

Triffin, Robert (1960). *Gold and the Dollar Crisis: The Future of Convertibility.* Garland, New York.

Underwood, John (1990). The sustainability of international debt. International Finance Division, World Bank, Washington, DC.

United Kingdom Treasury and the International Monetary Fund (2003). Strengthening the international financial system. In *Stability, Growth, and Poverty Reduction.* International Monetary Fund, Washington, DC: Chap. 3.

United Nations (1949). *National and International Measures for Full Employment.* Report by a Group of Experts appointed by the Secretary-General, United Nations, Department of Economic Affairs, December, Lake Success, New York. E/1584. Sales No. 1949.II.A.3.

_____ (1991). *Report of the Second United Nations Conference on the Least Developed Countries, Paris, 3-14 September 1990.* A/CONF.147/18, part one. United Nations, New York.

_____ (1999). *World Economic and Social Survey, 1999.* Sales No. E.99.II.C.1. United Nations, New York.

_____ (2000). *Millennium Declaration.* United Nations, New York.

_____ (2001a). Towards a new international financial architecture: report of the Task Force of the Executive Committee on Economic and Social Affairs of the United Nations. Available from http://www.un.org/esa/coordination/ecesa/ecesa-1.pdf.

_____ (2001b). Finding solutions to the debt problems of developing countries: report of the Executive Committee on Economic and Social Affairs of the United Nations, Sect. 3. Available from http://www.un.org/esa/coordination/ecesa/ecesa-2.pdf.

_____ (2001c). International financial architecture and development, including net transfer of resources between developing and developed countries: report of the Secretary-General. A/56/173, Sect. III.D.

_____ (2001d). Report of the High level Panel on Financing for Development (Zedillo Report). http://www.un.org/reports/financing/full_report.pdf.

_____ (2002a). *World Economic and Social Survey, 2002.* Sales No. E.02.II.C.1. United Nations, New York.

_____ (2002b). *Report of the International Conference on Financing for Development, Monterrey, Mexico, 18-22 March 2002.* Sales No. E.02.II.A.7.

_____ (2002c). International financial system and development: Report of the Secretary-General. A/57/151, Sect. III.E. 2 July, United Nations, New York.

_____ (2003a). *Report of the Committee for Development Policy on the fifth session (7-11 April 2003).* Official Records of the Economic and Social Council, 2003, Supplement No. 13 (E/2003/33). United Nations, New York.

_____ (2003b). *Report of the International Ministerial Conference of Landlocked and Transit Developing Countries and Donor Countries and International Financial and Development Institutions on Transit Transport Cooperation, Almaty, Kazakhstan, 28 and 29 August 2003.* A/CONF.202/3. United Nations, New York.

_____ (2003c). State of South-South Cooperation: report of the Secretary-General. A/58/319. United Nations, New York.

_____ (2004a). *World Economic and Social Survey 2004: International Migration*, Sales No. E.04.II.C.3. United Nations, New York.

_____ (2004b). *World Economic Situation and Prospects 2004*. Sales No. E.04.II.C.2. United Nations, New York.

_____ (2004c). A review of progress in the implementation of the Programme of Action for the Sustainable Development of Small Island Developing states: report of the Secretary-General. E/CN.17/2004/8. United Nations, New York.

_____ (2004d). Summary by the President of the Economic and Social Council of the special high-level meeting of the Council with the Bretton Woods institutions and the World Trade Organization (New York, 26 April 2004): addendum 2: summary of informal hearings of the business sector on financing for development (New York, 24 March 2004). A/59/92/Add.2–E/2004/73/Add.2. 1 June. United Nations, New York.

_____ (2005a). *World Economic Situation and Prospects 2005*. Sales No. E.05.II.C.2. United Nations, New York.

_____ (2005b). *In larger freedom: towards development, security and human rights for all: Report of the Secretary-General*, A/59/2005, United Nations, 21 March.

_____ (2005c) World Summit Outcome, A/60/1, United Nations, New York, 24 September.

United Nations Conference on Trade and Development (1974). External debt experience of developing countries: economic development following multilateral debt renegotiations in selected developing countries. TD/B/C.3/AC.8/9. 19 November. UNCTAD, Geneva.

_____ (1975). Present institutional arrangements for debt renegotiation: note by the UNCTAD secretariat. TD/B/C.3/AC.8/13. 13 February. UNCTAD, Geneva.

_____ (1978). Report of the Intergovernmental Group of Experts on the External Indebtedness of Developing Countries. TD/B/670 TD/AC.2/7. 28 July. UNCTAD, Geneva.

_____ (1986). *Trade and Development Report, 1986*. Sales No. E.86.II.D.5. UNCTAD, Geneva.

_____ (1998). *Trade and Development Report 1998: Financial Instability, Growth in Africa*. Sales No. E.98.II.D.6. UNCTAD, Geneva.

_____ (2000). *World Investment Report, 2000: Cross-border Mergers and Acquisitions and Development*. Sales No. E.00.II.D.20. UNCTAD, Geneva.

_____ (2001a). *Trade and Development Report 2001: Global Trends and Prospects, Financial Architecture*. Sales No. E.01.II.D.10. pp. 136 ff. UNCTAD, Geneva.

_____ (2001b). *World Investment Report, 2001: Promoting Linkages*. Sales No. E.01. II.D.12. UNCTAD, Geneva.

_____ (2003a). *Trade and Development Report, 2003: Capital Accumulation, Growth and Structural Change*. Sales No. E.03.II.D.7. UNCTAD, Geneva.

_____ (2003b). *World Investment Report, 2003: FDI Policies for Development: National and International Perspectives, 2003*. Sales No. E.03.II.D.8. UNCTAD, Geneva.

_____ (2003c). *Economic Development in Africa: Trade Performance and Commodity Dependence.* Sales No. E.03.II.D.34. UNCTAD, Geneva.

_____ (2004a). *World Investment Report, 2004: The Shift Towards Services.* Sales No. E.04. II.D.33. UNCTAD, Geneva.

_____ (2004b). *Economic Development In Africa: Debt Sustainability, Oasis or Mirage?* Sales No. E.04.II.D.37. UNCTAD/GDS/AFRICA/2004/1. UNCTAD, Geneva.

_____ (2005). Report of the Expert Meeting on the Impact of FDI on Development, Trade and Development Board, Commission on Investment, Technology and Related Financial Issues, 24–26 January. TD/B/COM.2/EM.16/3. UNCTAD, Geneva.

UN Millennium Project (2005). *Investing in Development A Practical Plan to Achieve the Millennium Development Goals.* Earthscan, London.

United States Department of the Treasury (2000). Response to the Report of the International Financial Institutions Advisory Commission. June 8. Washington, DC.

University of Sussex, Institute of Development Studies (2000). *A Foresight and Policy Study of the Multilateral Development Banks.* Falmer, Sussex.

Weller, Christian (2001). The supply of credit by multinational banks in developing and transition economies: determinants and effects. UN DESA Discussion Paper No. 16. ST/ESA/2001/DP.16, United Nations, New York.

Wellons, Philip A. (1977). *Borrowing by Developing Countries on the Euro-Currency Market.* Organization for Economic Cooperation and Development, Paris.

Wen, Jiabao (2003). Let's build on our past achievements and promote China-Africa friendly relations. Address at the opening ceremony of the Second Ministerial Conference of the China-Africa Cooperation Forum, Addis Ababa, 15 December. Available from: http://chinaembassy.ru/eng/wjdt/zyjh/t56252.htm.

White, William (2003). International financial crises: prevention, management and resolution. Speech at the conference on "Economic governance: the role of markets and the State", Berne, 20 March. Available from www.bis.org.

_____ (2004). Making macroprudential concerns operational. Speech presented at the Financial Stability Symposium organized by the Netherlands Bank, Amsterdam, 25 and 26 October. Available from www.bis.org/speeches.

Williamson, John (2003). Proposals for curbing the boom-bust cycle in the supply of capital to emerging markets. In *From Capital Surges to Drought: Seeking Stability for Emergency Economies,* Ricardo Ffrench-Davis and Stephany Griffith-Jones, eds. UNU-WIDER Studies in Development Economics and Policy Series. Basingstoke, United Kingdom: Palgrave Macmillan.

_____ (2004). The future of the global financial system. *Journal of Post-Keynesian Economics,* vol. 26, no. 4 (Summer).

Winters, L. Alan (2000). Trade and poverty: is there a connection? World Trade Organization, Geneva.

Working Group of the Capital Markets Consultative Group (2003). Foreign direct investment in emerging market countries: Report of the Working Group of the Capital Markets Consultative Group. International Monetary Fund, September, Washington, DC.

World Bank (1998). *Assessing Aid: What Works, What Doesn't and Why.* Oxford University Press, New York.

_____ (2001). Measuring IDA's effectiveness. Development Research Group, World Bank, Washington, DC.

_____ (2002b). *The Role and Effectiveness of Development Assistance: Lessons from World Bank Experience*. World Bank, Washington, DC.

_____ (2003). *Global Development Finance, 2003*. World Bank, Washington, DC.

_____ (2004a). *Global Development Finance, 2004*. World Bank, Washington, DC.

_____ (2004c). *Global Economic Prospects, 2005*. World Bank, Washington, DC.

_____ (2004d). *World Development Indicators, 2004*. World Bank, Washington, DC.

_____ (2004e). *The Poverty Reduction Strategy Initiative: An Independent Evaluation of the World Bank Support Through 2003*. World Bank, Washington, DC. Also available from http://worldbank.org/oed. {4}

_____ (2005a). *Global Development Finance, 2005*. World Bank, Washington, DC.

_____ (2005b). *Global Development Finance* Heavily Indebted Poor Countries (HIPC) Initiative Statistical Update, April, Washington, DC.

_____ (2005c). *Global Development Finance 2005: Mobilizing Finance and Managing Vulnerability: vol. I, Analysis and Statistical Appendix*. World Bank, Washington, DC.

_____ (2005d). *Global Monitoring Report 2005: Millennium Development Goals: From Consensus to Momentum*. World Bank, Washington, DC.

_____, Operations Evaluation Department (2001). *Annual Review of Development Effectiveness: From Strategy to Results*. World Bank, Washington, DC.

_____, and International Monetary Fund (2005). Aid effectiveness and financing modalities and moving forward: financing modalities toward the Millennium Development Goals. Development Committee papers, April, World Bank, Washington, DC.

World Economic Forum (2004). *The Global Competitiveness Report, 2004-2005*. World Economic Forum, Geneva.

Xiang Huaicheng (2002). Statement at the International Conference on Financing for Development. 21 March, Monterrey, Mexico.

Index